THE BLUE G[...]

Countries Austria
Belgium and L[...]
Channel Islands
China
Corsica
Crete
Cyprus
Czechoslovakia
Denmark
Egypt
England
France
France: Burgundy
Western Germany
Greece
Holland
Hungary
Ireland
Northern Italy
Southern Italy
Malta and Gozo
Morocco
Portugal
Scotland
Sicily
Spain
Switzerland
Turkey: the Aegean and Mediterranean Coasts
Wales
Yugoslavia

Cities Athens and Environs
Barcelona
Boston and Cambridge
Florence
Istanbul
Jerusalem
London
Moscow and Leningrad
New York
Oxford and Cambridge
Paris and Versailles
Rome and Environs
Venice

Themes Churches and Chapels of Northern England
Churches and Chapels of Southern England
Gardens of England
Literary Britain and Ireland
Museums and Galleries of London
Victorian Architecture in Britain

Fountain of the Three Graces, Plaça Reial

BLUE GUIDE

Barcelona

Michael Jacobs

Maps and plans by John Flower

A & C Black
London

WW Norton
New York

First edition 1992

Published by A & C Black (Publishers) Limited
35 Bedford Row, London WC1R 4JH

© A & C Black (Publishers) Limited 1992

ISBN 0–7136–3229–1

A CIP catalogue record for this book
is available from the British Library

Published in the United States of America by
WW Norton & Company, Incorporated
500 Fifth Avenue, New York NY 10110

Published simultaneously in Canada by
Penguin Books Canada Limited
2801 John Street, Markham, Ontario L3R 1B4

ISBN 0–393–30887–1

The publishers would like to thank Michael Jacobs and Ray Roberts for
their permission to use their photographs in this edition.

The publishers and the author have done their best to ensure the accuracy
of all the information in Blue Guide Barcelona; however, they can accept
no responsibility for any loss, injury or inconvenience sustained by any
traveller as a result of information or advice contained in the guide.

Please write in with your comments, suggestions and corrections. Writers
of the best letters will be awarded a free Blue Guide of their choice.

Michael Jacobs was born in Genova, Italy, in 1952. He studied at the
Courtauld Institute of Art in London, where he received a Ph.D. in 1982 for
his researches into 18C Italian art and architecture. A full-time author, he
has written numerous books on art and travel, including the Phaidon
Companion to Art and Artists in the British Isles (1980; with Malcolm
Warner), The Good and Simple Life: Artist Colonies in Europe and America
(1984), The Road to Santiago de Compostela (1991), guides to Provence
(1988) and Andalusia (1990), and Blue Guide Czechoslovakia. He is currently writing a travelogue covering the whole of Spain.

PREFACE

The history of Barcelona since the late Middle Ages has been one of continual conflict with the authorities from the Spanish capital of Madrid. Barcelona has survived all the repressive measures imposed upon the city from afar to become a place which enjoys a greater political power and cultural autonomy than perhaps any other of the 'second cities' of Europe. Some might even see a certain poetic justice in the fact that Barcelona today, whether rightly or wrongly, has also a more widespread appeal to tourists than does Madrid, a fact which partially accounts for this this being the first Spanish city to be the subject of an individual *Blue Guide*.

Barcelona's popularity as a tourist destination is a relatively recent phenomenon, the city having been largely spared the attentions of the thousands of travellers who poured in to Spain following the 'romantic' discovery of the country in the early 19C. To the 'romantic' traveller, who essentially came to Spain in search of the exotic, Barcelona was depressingly like the rest of Europe, the place being, in the words of the effusive Italian writer of the last century, Eduardo de Amicis, 'the least Spanish' of Spain's cities. The beginnings of a tourist interest in Barcelona are connected with the growing appreciation in the late 19C of Europe's Gothic heritage, and the realisation that Barcelona was special among the major European cities in preserving a remarkably extensive and intact medieval core. However, it was essentially as a modern city that Barcelona came to attract the attention of the world. The years of the city's dramatic industrial expansion, in between the World Exhibition of 1888 and the International Exhibition of 1929, saw Barcelona developing a repuation as being in the forefront of European culture, a place which absorbed the latest ideas from Paris while nurturing such distinctive talents of its own as Gaudí, Nonell, Casals, Miró, and the young Picasso. This image of Barcelona as a centre of modernity and the avant-garde has persisted throughout this century, and in the last years of Franco's regime, the theatrical productions of Nuria Espert and her company, the continuing presence of Miró, the international prestige of such outstanding younger artists as Tàpies, and the initiation of a design boom by such lively groups as Studio Per, led the outside world to think of Barcelona almost as the cultural conscience of Spain.

The death of Franco in 1975, and the subsequent rise of Madrid's progressive young generation known as the '*movida*', briefly shifted outside interest from Barcelona to Madrid, and encouraged fears that Barcelona would lose much of its former vitality. Barcelona today, however, remains as culturally alive as ever, with a theatrical and musical life unrivalled by that of Madrid, and a reputation as one of the leading world centres of fashion and design. The city's tourist appeal continues to grow, the place being thought of as having all the excitement of a capital city such as Paris, but with the added attraction of a magnificent situation by the shores of the Mediterranean. Other factors that have promoted the tourist growth of the city include the endless fascination with the art of Picasso, and the present status of Gaudí as perhaps the most popular of all western architects. Finally, and perhaps most important of all, an added glamour has been acquired in the course of Barcelona's architectural and urban transformation in preparation for the city's hosting of the Olympic Games in 1992.

In the build-up to 1992, a great many guide-books have appeared on Barcelona, though the present one—the first in the *Blue Guide* series—can claim to be the only one in English to have attempted a relatively full and up-to-date coverage of the city's artistic and architectural monuments, giving as much emphasis to the unfamiliar as to the familiar. In addition I have departed from normal *Blue Guide* practice in my inclusion of numerous shops, bars, restaurants and cafés, places that I believe to be as essential to an understanding of the culture of the city as any church or museum: the rigid division between sight-seeing and entertainment has always struck me as a vestige of Victorian puritanism. As a warning, I should add that the research for this book was carried out at a time when Barcelona was changing more rapidly than almost any other European city: intensive building activity was being carried out while whole districts of the city were being demolished or radically restored, the city's maritime façade , for instance, being almost entirely transformed within a mattter of only a couple of years. I have consulted carefully the main urban and architectural projects for 1992 and beyond, but feel it wise to voice a certain amount of scepticism about all that is promised for the Barcelona of the future. Such scepticism may be particularly relevent in the case of the many monuments and museums that are mentioned in the text as being scheduled for re-opening in 1992. Let us only hope that the situation will not be like the one as described in Eduardo Mendoza's satirical science fiction work, *No News of Gurb* (1990), the narrator of which visits a Museum of Modern Art towards the end of the millennium only to find a place still being transformed into a 15-storey cultural centre which should have been ready in 1992 but which had only been started in 1998.

This book has benefited greatly from the enormous amount of help and hospitality which I have received in Barcelona and elsewhere in Catalonia. Considerable assistance was provided by the Ajuntamient de Barcelona, the Colegi de Arquitectura de Catalonia, the Generalitat de Catalonia and the Patronat de Turisme de Barcelona; in particular I should like to thank Pere de Manuel, Bel Moretó, Mònica Colomer i Membrado and Josep Anton Rojas. Gemma Beltrán of the Estudio Mariscal kindly devoted a morning showing me every cartoon in which Cobi appeared, while the great Mariscal himself hovered silently in the background. Porters, security guards and museum curators, too numerous to list individually, were unfailingly generous in allowing me access to buildings and collections, the only difficulty which I encountered being at Bofill's recently completed INEFC building, the guards to which seem to believe that they are guarding a nuclear power station rather than a sports stadium. But above all I am indebted to my Barcelona friends, without whom my stays in the city would not have been either so enjoyable or productive. Andres Modollel, Pablo Capilla, and Stuart Goodsir, have all put me up in in their homes at some stage during the research for this book, and have all been willing assistants in my investigations of the city's bar and restaurant life. Lola Matalonga, a former actress of the Nuria Espert company and a resident for many years of the Barri Xinès, has regaled me with stories of the Bohemian Barcelona of old, as has her daughter, the equally talented actress, Maite Brik. I have also learnt a great deal about Barcelona and Catalonia from my conversations with Maria Ronan and Bignia Kuoni, both of whom have sustained me with their enthusiasm and companionship. The Parris family have been excellent hosts at Manlleu and the Pyrenees, while Tomás Echevarria has accompanied me on numerous walks throughout Barcelona, and given me an insight into another aspect of the city's life by introducing me to the Folch i Torres School at Hospitalet, where I was a regular guest at lunch, and where the predominantly Andalusian pupils put on a show of Sevillana dancing for my benefit.

Bob Sulatycki from London's Holland Park School supplemented my investigations into the Barcelona bars with researches of his own, and Jackie Rae kept up my spirits when I was writing this book in London and Galicia. Felipe Fernández-Armesto, an eminent and provocative Oxford historian, has greatly enhanced the book with his lively and thought-provoking historical introduction. The maps are by John Flower, while the thankless task of editing has been undertaken by Judy Tither and Gemma Davies, who have shown an exceptional amount of patience in dealing with my inconsistencies and barely legible handwriting, and in tracking me down at a time when I was nearly always on the move.

A Note on Orientation

Owing to Barcelona's diagonal, elongated shape, and the fact that its streets tend to run parallel or at right-angles to the sea, most maps of the city—including the ones in the present guide—are tilted so that the coastline runs along the bottom of the page. Accoringly, the compass references given in the text of this guide have been simplified so that north-west is referred to as true north, and so on.

A Note on Blue Guides

The Blue Guides series began in 1915 when Muirhead Guide-Books Limited published 'Blue Guide London and its Environs'. Finlay and James Muirhead already had extensive experience of guide-book publishing: before the First World War they had been the editors of the English editions of the German Baedekers, and by 1915 they had acquired the copyright of most of the famous 'Red' handbooks from John Murray.

An agreement made with the French publishing house Hachette et Cie in 1917 led to the translation of Muirhead's London Guide, which became the first 'Guide Bleu'—Hachette had previously published the blue-covered 'Guides Joanne'. Subsequently, Hachette's 'Guide Bleu Paris et ses Environs' was adapted and published in London by Muirhead. The collaboration between the two publishing houses continued until 1933.

In 1931 Ernest Benn took over the Blue Guides, appointing Russell Muirhead, Finlay Muirhead's son, editor in 1934. The Muirheads' connection with Blue Guides ended in 1963 when Stuart Rossiter, who had been working on the Guides since 1954, became house editor, revising and compiling several of the books himself.

The Blue Guides are now published by A & C Black, who acquired Ernest Benn in 1984, so continuing the tradition of guide-book publishing which began in 1826 with 'Black's Economical Tourist of Scotland'. The Blue Guide series continues to grow: there are now more than 40 titles in print with revised editions appearing regularly and many new Blue Guides in preparation.

'Blue Guides' is a registered trade mark.

CONTENTS

Preface 5
A Note on Orientation 7
A Note on Blue Guides 7
A History of Barcelona by Felipe Fernández-Armesto 9

PRACTICAL INFORMATION

Tourist Offices 23
Formalities and Currency 23
Getting to Barcelona 23
Transport in Barcelona 25
General Information 26
Food and Drink 31
Bars and Restaurants 37

BARCELONA

1. Ciutat Vella
    A. La Rambla 42
    B. The Barri Gòtic 55
    C. The Barris de Santa Anna, Sant Pere and Santa Maria del Mar 77
    D. The Raval 88
    E. Maritime Barcelona and the Cuitadella 95
    F. Plaça d'Espanya and Montjuïc 113

2. The Eixample 124

3. Greater Bracelona
    A. Pedralbes and Diagonal 142
    B. Gràcia and Tibidabo 145
    C. The Park Güell, Parc de la Creueta del Coll and Horta 149
    D. Poble Nou and North-eastern Barcelona 151

4. Excursions from Barcelona
    A. South of Barcelona 156
    B. West of Barcelona 159
    C. North of Barcelona 160

Useful Catalan Words 164

A Chronology of Medieval Rulers of Barcelona 166

Further Reading 167

Index 171

MAPS

Barcelona (Central) 40–41
Barcelona (Environs) 154–155
Barcelona (General) 140–141
Barcelona (Metro) 180
Barri Gòtic 56
Girona 161
Tarragona 158

A HISTORY OF BARCELONA

By **Felipe Fernández-Armesto**

On the ceiling of Barcelona's Llotja—an 18C Temple of Commerce—in a painting by Pere Pau i Montaner, a buxom figure of Prosperity clothes thankful Nakedness, while Poverty and Disaster are driven off with scourges. The image is typical of a tradition of civic propaganda, which can be traced back to the Middle Ages and which has generated, in our own day, the brash and ebullient figure of Cobi—merchandising symbol of the 1992 Olympiad. His cheeky smile, bouncy girth and epicene aspect all betray the opulence and resilience which are Barcelona's pride.

Yet poverty and disaster have never been effectively banished and an 'alternative' image of Barcelona has been nourished in the gutters and alleys. Jean Genet, picking the lice out of the trouser seams of his homosexual lovers in 1932, recorded memories of the city bespattered with every kind of bodily excretion. Picasso and Nonell painted brilliant portraits of sitters drawn from low life. The recurrence of disaster is documented in a long history, in overlapping phases, of plagues and social conflicts.

Out of the tension between these rival perceptions of the city—out of the efforts of the Barcelonese to re-mould Barcelona in their own image—extraordinary achievements have been wrought. In the Middle Ages, without a natural harbour, Barcelona became the centre of a great maritime empire. In modern times, without iron or coal, she led Spain's industrial revolution. Though her status as a national seat of government was extinguished in 1716, she has remained the capital and, in a sense, the embodiment—the 'head and hearth', as Catalans say—of Catalan culture. Today, by a fitful and fragile rise, she has become the centre of the biggest conurbation on the western Mediterranean seaboard.

Ancient and medieval Barcelona

Visible to an explorer at street level, Roman graves line a 2C street under the Plaça de la Vila de Madrid. Along the Carrer dels Arcs, the towers of the 4C gates are revealed, abutted by what may be the remains of an aqueduct. Astonishingly, in the middle of a modern megalopolis, the Roman walls can be followed, not only in the street plan but also above ground in stretches and patches. In the Carrer del Call a Roman tower can be visited inside a draper's shop; the vast pillars of a temple grace the Centre d'Excursionistes in the Carrer del Paradis; and Roman floors and foundations can be viewed underneath the palaces of the medieval count-kings and early-modern royal lieutenants. These abundant, exciting remains of a remote past could easily mislead the visitor into supposing for Roman Barcelona a grandeur it never really possessed.

Although the Roman colony fed well off its 'sea of oysters' and served 'rich men' with such civilised amenities as porticoed baths and a Forum with seven statues, it was always a 'small town' of up to 10 or 12 hectares, dwarfed by nearby Tarragona and Empùries. For Catalan historians, it used to be a point of honour to imagine antique greatness stretching back to the supposedly autochthonous forebears of modern Catalans. But, although the whole plain of Barcelona was well populated from neolithic times, and coins prove the existence of a pre-Roman urban civilisation, no evidence of continuous settlement of the central site of historic Barcelona, on Mont Tàber, has yet been found earlier than the 1C AD. Pre-Roman 'Barcino' (named on coins) may have been on the hill of Montjuïc, which the Romans inherited as a ritual centre. Finds from there include an impressive aedile's (magistrate's) seat, set ceremonially in the midst of the remains of a stone enclosure.

For half a millenium after the end of Roman rule, Barcelona's history remains sparsely documented. Of the occupiers of those years—the Visigoths, the Moors, the Franks—only the first seem to have esteemed the city highly. According to Jordanes, pity for the inhabitants of Hispania, smarting under the blows of less Romanised barbarians, moved Athawulf to seize Barcelona ' with his best men', leaving those 'less adept in arms' to occupy the interior. This suggests that Barcelona was thought particularly desirable, or particularly defensible, or both. Perhaps, as it was Visigothic practice to make the army a charge on conquered territory, Barcelona drew the 'best men' because it commanded the richest land. Narrators of the next century of Gothic history continue to associate Barcelona with politically important events: Athawulf's assassination and Amalaric's rise and murder, followed, in 540, by the meeting of a synod. The modest growth of the Visigothic period can be detected in excavations under the Palau Reial. Between the 4C and 6C, the *intervallum* between the Roman building line and the ramparts was filled with new constructions. At the same time, streets were narrowed by building extensions. A building of noble proportions appeared on part of the present palace site: the written sources with their catalogue of royal assassinations seem to confirm that Visigothic Barcelona was a sporadic courtly centre.

The city was still without long-range commerce and, for the Moors and Franks, seems to have been significant only as a frontier garrison or *ville-carrefour*. Barcelona's potential for greatness only began to be realised when she was conquered, late in the 9C, by a fledgling state of regional importance, with heartlands close by: its granary in the plain of Urgell, its defences in the mountains. The warrior paladins of protean Catalonia adopted Barcelona as their favourite place of residence; they endowed religious foundations which stimulated urban growth; they kept—and sometimes spent—their treasure there; and, as their state developed, they concentrated in Barcelona such permanent institutions—chancery, court and counting-house—as they created.

Of the man acclaimed as the founder of the House of the Counts of Barcelona little trace survives in the modern city: only the visitor brave enough to enter the dark alley of the Carrer d'Amargos, under straggling balcony-plants and dangling laundry, will find the painted ceramic plaque proclaiming—almost certainly wrongly—that this was the limit of the palace of Wilfred the Hairy (d. 898). But by the early 10C Barcelona was already, in a sense, the 'capital' of a sovereign principality, which would come to be known as the principality of Catalonia. In about 911, Count Wilfred II chose a house of religion outside the walls for his mausoleum. His neglected grave, marked by an inscription discovered among rubble, deserved better treatment: the sort of patronage he conferred turned the former hick-town into a medieval metropolis.

For the next 200 years, Barcelona's wealth continued to come from farming and war, her urban character from her courtly status. The first known boom happened in the late 10C. Most historians have assumed that this must have been the result of commercially-generated wealth; but it is at least as likely that the presence of the knights, the court and the growing colony of clergy were the sources of stimulation. The growth of the cathedral chapter is the first clue to general growth: there were six canonries in 974, 17 by 1005. The canons were growing in sophistication as well as numbers: retiring to houses of their own; acquiring a reputation for erudition; building up libraries worthy, in one instance, of attracting a reader as famous for his learning as the future pope, Gerbert of Aurillac. They were not the only people building, and the first new burghs began to grow up outside the walls. In 989 Barcelona was a target of sufficient prestige to attract a raid by al-Mansur, the wide-preying vizier of Cordova. The raid inspired traditional lamentations, with lists of buildings destroyed and victims martyred. But, except for Sant Pere de les Puelles (burned with all the nuns), real losses appear to have been slight. By encouraging re-building, al-Mansur may have stimulated the boom.

Moorish hegemony only briefly survived al-Mansur's death in 1002. The empire of Cordova, enfeebled by squabbles at the centre and eroded by usurpation at the edges, collapsed in the 1030s. Like much of the rest of Christian Spain, Barcelona enjoyed a bonanza on the proceeds of booty, tribute, ransom, payola and the wages of mercenaries. An illumination in Barcelona's *Liber Feudorum* shows Count Ramon Berenguer I counting out coins from a lapful of gold for the price of the counties of Carcassonne and Béziers. The sort of expansion his forebears could contemplate only by conquest, he could undertake by purchase. In Barcelona, by the 1070s, 95 per cent of transactions were made in gold. To judge from the pattern of the circulation of coinage, even the Valencia of El Cid had less Moorish gold to mint than Barcelona.

Some of this money was invested in a maritime vocation which for the next 500 years supplied the city's wealth and formed its character. In 1060, although Barcelona was already a 'great town', according to the fastidious al-Bakri, the Barcelonese were still applying to Moorish ports to hire their galleys. By 1080 the counts possessed a fleet of their own, though it may not have been based in Barcelona. Two charters of Ramon Berenguer III (1082–1131) mention what sounds like substantial seaborne trade. In 1104 he granted a tenth of dues paid on 'all goods that come in on any ship in all my honour'; in the following year Jews were granted a monopoly of the shipping home of ransomed Moorish slaves. That some at least of this trade was going through Barcelona is suggested by the terms of privileges Ramon Berenguer granted to Genoa and Pisa in 1116. Despite the deficiencies of her shoaly harbour, Barcelona was the point of departure of a fleet big enough to attempt the conquest of Mallorca—500 vessels strong, according to the poet who accompanied the expedition. International commerce continued to develop gradually and in 1160 Benjamin of Tudela reported vessels of 'Pisa, Genoa, Sicily, Greece, Alexandria and Asia' off the beach of Barcelona.

Most of the buildings of this period were replaced in later eras of even greater prosperity: only Sant Pau del Camp, Santa Llúcia and the Capella de Marcús remain. For a flavour of what Catalonia was like in the 11C and 12C the visitor to Barcelona has to go to the Museu de l'Art de Catalunya, where the collection of murals transferred from rural churches shows the high quality that Catalan money could buy, the search for classical and Byzantine models by the artists: the wolf of Sant Joan de Boi bares predatory teeth as he stares around in a classical pose; the Seraphim of the apse with their feathery, eyed wings recall Byzantine mosaics. In the streets, the explorer can match the map to documents that record the expansion of the 12C city. In 1160, Ramon Berenguer IV gave permission for a new public bath outside the city wall, where today the Carrer dels Banys Nous curls in the spectral shadow of lost ramparts: the profits of this enterprise were to be divided equally between the count and the Jewish investor.

Because of the winds and currents of the western Mediterranean, to become a great centre of long-range commerce, rivalling Genoa and Pisa, Barcelona needed to solve her problem of access to the Balearic islands. An illumination in Barcelona university library shows a leading merchant of the city, entertaining the count-king 'and the greater part of the nobles of Catalonia' in November or December 1228, and persuading them of the merits of conquering the islands. In his extraordinary *Book of Deeds*, Jaume I (1213–76) identified his own motives for launching the conquest as essentially chivalric: there was 'more honour' in conquering a single kingdom 'in the midst of the sea, where God has been pleased to put it' than three on dry land. To chivalric and crusading satisfactions, the nobles who took part added substantial territorial rewards. The Barcelonese, however, and the other merchant-communities of the Catalan and Provençal worlds, needed little inducement. Their participation is adequately explained by commercial motives: the anxiety to break the entrenched position of Moorish traders and their privileged partners from Genoa and Pisa.

Like so many imperial adventures, Barcelona's marked the apogee of her achievement and sowed the seeds of her decline. The marks of both are everywhere in the old city today, in the form of great churches begun in the 13C or 14C; in vast ritual and even industrial spaces that survive from that time; in building works slowed or halted in the 15C; and in decayed aristocratic streets of the late Middle Ages. The new walls of the reign of Jaume I enclosed an area ten times as big as those they replaced. The cathedral is the dominant monument of the 13C: the cloister portal, transitional in feel, with its carving of harpies and wild men dragging a half-naked, pudge-faced warrior, contrasts with the elegant High Gothic of the interior. The early 14C, when the profits of empire were perhaps at their height, was a time of frenzied building. The Capella de Santa Agata, in the Palau Reial, was built by Jaume II (d. 1327). The first stone of the church of El Pi was laid in 1322, that of Santa Maria del Mar, renowned for its glazing, in 1329. Not even the Black Death—which killed half of the city council and four of the five chief magistrates—could dent the city's confidence or interrupt the building boom. Never was the city so spectacularly embellished as in the reign of Pere III (1336–87); he built the vaulted halls—more reminiscent of Italy than Spain—of the Saló del Cent in the town hall and the Saló de Tinell, with its martial wall-paintings, in the palace. He reconstructed the shipyards on a larger scale, where galleys from the Mediterranean war-effort had been built since the reign of Pere II (1276–85): the eight great bays can still be visited, on the frontier of the Raval and the port, housing the Maritime Museum. Of Pere's vastly extended walls, a fragment can still be seen near the foot of the Paral·lel. Private builders were also active. An example of late medieval 'urbanisation', the Carrer de Montcada, was driven through the old town in a broad, straight line and was promptly colonised by the aristocracy: the modern visitor, seeking the street for the sake of the Picasso Museum, runs the risk of being more impressed by the medieval architecture of the palaces in which it is housed.

The trading empire which paid for all this was essentially a western Mediterranean affair. The deeds of Catalans in the east—of mercenaries in

Thrace and Athens, of merchants in Alexandria and Constantinople—are justly renowned. But they happened in the wings of the main theatre. The conquests of Mallorca (1229), Ibiza (1235), Sicily (1282), Sardinia (1324) and the series of treaties from 1271 which gave the count-kings something like a protectorate over a number of Maghribi ports: these were the landmarks of an empire of grain and gold, silver and salt.

As the empire grew, its costs came to exceed its benefits. Mallorca proved a thankless daughter, sustaining a turbulent political relationship with the count-kings and using Catalan savoir-faire to set up shipping, arms and textile industries to rival Barcelona's own. The ambition to control the western Mediterranean sea-lanes caused wars with Genoa which were wasteful because Barcelona never had sufficient resources to exploit her victories. Above all, Sardinia was Barcelona's 'Spanish ulcer'. The city seems largely to have borne the costs of conquest and defence by herself, with little support from the count-kings' other realms. Sardinian resistance lasted, intermittently, for a hundred years, and exhausted the over-committed conquerors. The empire which made a metropolis of Barcelona also sucked the rural life-blood of Catalonia: as the centre of gravity of the count-kings' realms moved towards the city, the balance of population shifted. By the eve of the Black Death, Barcelona contained twenty per cent of the population of Catalonia.

The countryside no longer had the means to keep the armies supplied with men or, perhaps, the city with food. In 1330 Barcelona experienced her first serious famine. Never was a city more obviously the victim of its own success. Barcelona evinced the classic symptoms of the monster: corpulence induced by over-feeding, tentacles stretched to uncontrollable lengths. Yet resolute civic spirit remained etched into the faces of the élite depicted, for instance, in Lluís Dalmau's *La Verge dels Consellers*, painted in 1443 to project a magnificent image of the city magistracy in the intimate company of heavenly protectors.

Like the similar problem of the 'decline of Spain' in the 17C, that of the decline of Catalonia in the 15C has to be treated cautiously. Though it appears with hindsight that by the end of the century the centre of gravity of power in the Iberian peninsula had shifted forever towards Castile, Catalonian experience seems too mottled with intermediate shades to justify the use of a sweeping term like 'decline' except in a relative sense. Especially in the late 15C, the neighbouring kingdoms of France and Castile were developing the means to mobilise unprecedented strength. Barcelona's 15C was at best an 'era of difficulties'—progressive exhaustion and something close to ultimate prostration, redeemed only by the mental resilience of an indomitably optimistic ruling class. The city's predicament was compounded of social violence, demographic stagnation and economic constraint. In the century after 1360, not a decade went by without a recurrence of plague, sometimes accompanied by famine; from 1426, the yield of the customs and wool tax plummeted and did not recover until the next century. Hearth-counts suggest a modest increase of population until the cataclysmic civil war of the 1460s: that of 1500, showing 5765 hearths, probably represents the lowest tally since the Black Death. Protracted insecurity caused social tension. The first uncontrollable outburst was the pogrom of 1391, when the authorities were powerless to protect the Jews from massacre. In 1436 and 1437 popular agitations were effectively suppressed, but by the mid-century the failures of the city's natural rulers had attracted the sympathy of the city governor for a movement to democratise the municipal institutions or—at least—to enlarge the élite. The name of the incumbent party, the *Biga*, probably signifies a large beam used in the construction of a building; that of the challengers, the *Busca*, a piece of tinder or bunch of kindling. The names evoke the natures of the parties: the solidity of the establishment; the incendiary menace of its opponents.

Their conflict in the 1450s did not in the long run unseat the traditional patriciate, but left it enfeebled and embittered against the Count-king Joan II (c 1458–79). His unpopularity grew as he tried to exploit Catalonia in what was felt to be a private attempt to meddle in Castile; he exacerbated his relations with his subjects by attempting to exclude his son and one of his daughters from succession to the throne; and by appealing to popular elements in the towns and to the peasants in the country he alienated the urban patricians and rural aristocrats alike. No part of Catalonia entered the rebellion of 1462 more wholeheartedly than Barcelona; none suffered so much from the long conflict and disastrous defeat. The insurgents' cause, never very promising, became desperate as each of the pretenders they put up to challenge the king died or dropped out in turn. The siege that finally ended resistance in 1473, followed by punitive measures, left Barcelona devastated. 'Today no trade at all is practised in this city', the *consellers* wrote. 'Not a bolt of cloth is seen. The workers are unemployed and the men of property are deprived of their rents and goods... And of all our troubles, the worst is this: for we see our city turning into something no bigger than a village on the road to Vic.'

The city in modern history

No visitor to Barcelona can fail to be struck by the relative dearth of great buildings of the Renaissance and baroque. There are examples of grandeur: the Palau de la Generalitat hides its medieval core behind a Renaissance façade; and examples of charm: the Casa de l'Arcidiacà in the Carrer de Santa Llúcia was decorated by a snobbish connoisseur, who was Archdeacon in the early 16C, as a setting for his antiquities and heraldic vanities. But most of what survives in the city from the 16C and 17C reflects private efforts, rather than public wealth, and a chequered history of slow recovery until 1640, when began the terrible era of war and unrest in which more was destroyed than built and which lasted until 1715.

Sixteenth-century Barcelona kept sufficiently closely in touch with fashion to earn praise from almost every visitor who left an account. With the unremitting confidence that has characterised them in every age, the city fathers poured money into the creation of an artificial port in an attempt to recover lost trade: the task would remain incomplete for 300 years, but was never abandoned. Private patrons like the Fiveller family could build splendid new palaces—theirs still stands in the Plaça de Sant Josep Oriol. The Carrer Ample (a straight gash across the view of the town by Philip II's official topographical artist, Anton van Wyngaerde) was opened as a gesture to Renaissance town planning, although it seems to have attracted few of the hoped-for noble residents. At the beginning of the century, a Florentine diplomat commended the city for beauty while lamenting the decline of its commerce; by the end, a measure of recovery can be detected in the terms of praise from Lope de Vega, the most renowned poet and playwright of the day: 'Just as a splendid façade enhances the value of a building, so great Barcelona stands at the entrance to Spain, like a portico framing a famous threshold.'

Barcelona's decline had coincided with the progressive loss of the courtly status which, before the rise of the city's commercial importance, had been the foundation of her fortune. After the extinction of the House of Barcelona in 1412, she had been ruled by a series of kings whose main interests were in Castile or Naples and who spent ever less time in Barcelona. For a while from 1479, and continuously from 1516, her counts were also kings of Castile and were mainly concerned with the affairs of that larger and fiscally more productive country. Yet the Barcelonese patriciate never lost their sense of ruling the capital of a sovereign principality—or even a quasi-polis, a city with the potential, at least, to be a city-state like Genoa or Venice. From inside the Spanish monarchy, Barcelona affected the status of a foreign power and her representatives swaggered like the emissaries of foreign potentates. When, for instance, a new viceroy of Catalonia was appointed in 1622, the congratulations of Barcelona were tendered by an ambassador, attended by 200 carriages, in what was rumoured to be the most magnificent procession ever seen in the streets of Madrid. Twenty years earlier, the city's representative at court was honoured with so much pomp that 'even the leading nobles of this court,' he reported, 'say that neither the nuncio of his Holiness himself, nor the envoy of the Emperor has ever been given such a reception... and the Castilians are all amazed that an ambassador who is a vassal of the king should be received with so much honour.' A similar war of protocol was carried on inside the city, where the leading magistrates demanded the right to remain hatted in the king's presence and disputed seats of honour in church with the viceroy's wife.

This was more than play-acting. The 'privileges' (*privilegis*) and 'liberties' (*furs*) which meant so much to Barcelona were never systematically codified and are difficult to define. The Castilian models, and the different nuances of Castilian thinking, which could not be translated into Catalan, tended to mislead policy-makers in Madrid into misapprehensions about the sort of traditions they had to deal with in relations with Barcelona. In Castile, civic liberties normally consisted in a charter granted by the king: they were a negotiable commodity, revered but not made sacred. Barcelona's identity, however, was bound up with the juridical status of the Principality of Catalonia as a distinct and equal partner in the Crown of Aragon and, separately, in the Spanish monarchy. She had liberties not granted by the prince as an act of grace, but governed by the *constitucions*—the statutes irrevocable except by the representative parliamentary assembly (the *corts*), which limited royal authority in the principality. The most important *constitucions* guaranteed fiscal exemptions. During the early 17C, when the Spanish monarchy was tottering from the inevitable effects of immoderate greatness, the growing need of money and manpower made the Catalans apprehensive of their immunities. At a time when to be 'a very good Catalan' was to be 'jealous of the country's privileges', the implicit constitutional conflict was bound to be noticed in Barcelona, where all the institutions of the statehood of Catalonia, inherited from the Middle Ages, were concentrated, and where a large body of professional lawyers more or less lived by watching the *constitucions*. The costs of the Thirty Years' War, and direct hostilities with France from 1635, brought the demands of the monarchy to a peak and the differences with the principality to a head. When Catalonia rose in revolt in 1640, Barcelona was the centre and sustainer of the rebellion.

Like the roughly contemporary rebellion in England, Catalonia's was reluctantly espoused. An anonymous but representative diarist in Barcelona blamed the king's bad counsel for 'the greatest sorrow this principality of Catalonia has suffered... May God and most holy Mary be pleased to return us to the grace of our father and lord, Philip.' But, like the English war, the Catalans' juggernaut rolled out of control. The élite of Barcelona had to share power with popular elements; Catalonia enfeoffed herself to Louis XIII of France; and 16 years of war devastated her land, depopulated her towns and despoiled her wealth. The siege of Barcelona in 1652 was one of the most desperate episodes of the war; it ended only when the citizens were 'reduced to eating grass'. Yet the king's commander, Don Juan José of Austria, was architect of a restoration which left the status quo unimpaired.

The very success of this policy raised the danger of another round of similar conflict. In the second half of the century, Barcelona had little respite. Civic-minded optimists like Narcis Feliu de la Penya had hardly begun to revive the 'Catalan Phoenix' before the French wars of the 1680s and 1690s exposed her lands to more campaigns and the city to another siege. Barcelona had still not reconstructed her stake in stability when the War of the Spanish Succession plunged the entire monarchy into crisis. The Bourbon claimant, Philip V, arrived in 1702, scattering rewards and promises with a lavish hand; but he was suspected of an arbitrary disposition and absolutist plans—an impression confirmed by his failure to invite the chief magistrates to cover their heads in his presence. An insensitive viceroy, Francisco Fernández de Velasco, blundered into other infringements of the *constitucions*.

Despite the naturally peaceful inclinations of a mercantile élite, many of the leading members of Barcelonese society were willing to respond to Velasco's indelicate rule with violence. Many of them were the sons of fathers who had fought against Madrid in the 1640s and 1650s. They owed an obligation of honour to memories dating from those years. Psychologically inclined to fight, they were also ideologically equipped. It was an almost unquestioned assumption that Catalonia was a sovereign state with a right, in principle, to secede from a monarchy which was thought to be federative. Catalans' reading of their own history represented theirs as a contractual monarchy, in which the contract between people and prince, once broken, could be repudiated. By the end of the war, when Barcelona was fighting on alone, the inhabitants were inclined to blame the English for inveigling them into the fight with promises: the trick was performed, almost equally, with implicit threats. On 20 June 1705, when representatives of 'the most Illustrious, Famous and Renowned Principality of Catalonia' signed a treaty with England in Genoa, the guns of English ships could be heard in Catalonian waters. Catalans came to see the episode as a typical instance of Albion's habit of acquiring by bribery or intimidation an ally whom she would later abandon. From their point of view, the sixth clause of the treaty was the most important, by which England guaranteed that 'now and in the future the Principality of Catalonia shall keep all the graces, privileges, laws and customs which severally and in common her people have enjoyed and do enjoy'.

In Barcelona, it seems, appetite for war *vient en mangeant*, and the Barcelonese, after their shy start, would become the most committed opponents of Philip V. They joined the allied cause in a calculating spirit but clung on when it was hopeless and all the other allies had withdrawn. They dared beyond hope, endured beyond reason and reaped the usual reward of that sort of heroism: defeat. The precedent of 1652 was fatally misleading: it encouraged the Barcelonese to believe that their liberties could be ventured again and that a hopeless resistance would save them. The final siege lasted from August 1713 until November 1714. The rule of visionary priests and populist fanatics throve on short rations. The 'repression' denounced by Catalan historians after Philip's victory was really rather mild: clerics and generals were its only individually targeted victims. But the *constitucions* were abolished; Barcelona was reduced to the rank of a provincial city in a unitary state and subjected to the indignity of a permanent garrison—an army of occupation overlooking the city from the new citadel. In this once grim symbol of oppression the present visitor can enjoy the delights of the zoo and the park.

Defeat turned the energies of the citizens to a mood of *enrichissez-vous*. Though the city was prostrate and revival slow, the 18C as a whole was an era of forward-looking prosperity in which sustained economic growth began, thanks to new activities such as direct trade with the Americas and the beginnings of industrialisation based on American cotton. Some of the palaces and villas of the Bourbon collaborators can still be seen: the finest of them, the Palau de Comillas, houses the Generalitat bookshop in the Rambla; around the corner, the palace of the Comte de Fonallar enhances the grandeur of the expensive shops in the Carrer de Portaferrissa; a metro ride into the suburbs can be rewarded with the sight of the Can Carabass between the Carrer de Llobregós and the Carrer de Peris Mencheta. The ensemble which has most to say about Barcelona's 18C is the Barceloneta district, the first industrial suburb, begun in 1753 to house a population then beginning to burst out of a city diminished by the destructions and demolitions of the era of war. The tight, neat grid of its streets, the contrast with the traditional cityscape of Barcelona, make it one of the earliest surviving examples of 'enlightened' town planning in Europe. It was an attempt to put into reality the vision with which Pere Pau i Montaner decorated the ceiling of the Llotja—the headquarters of the merchant community—where crowned Prosperity clothes Nakedness, while Industry and Commerce urge the sourging of Poverty and Disaster.

In the 'lost world' of pre-industrial Barcelona, manufacturing was a mainstay of the economy; but it was confined to the intimate society of the workshop and the master's home, regulated not by the impersonal 'market' but by the collective morals of powerful guilds. A visitor to the Museu d'Història de la Ciutat can see the sort of images which dominated the mental world of the guilds: their art reflected professional pride and devotion to the patron saints. The book of privileges of the shoemakers is decorated with a huge but elegant gilt-bronze slipper with tapering toe; the silversmiths' pattern books record, in meticulous detail, the masters' copyright to thousands of intricate designs. The market-gardeners' book of privileges, begun in 1453, is flanked by busts of their otherwise obscure patrons, Saints Abdó and Senen, and the gaudily painted coffer in which their relics were preserved. Everywhere the images of saints are reminders that the guilds doubled as devotional confraternities. Evidence of their prestige and wealth can be found around the city today: the shoemakers' palatial hall, for instance, in the Plaça de Sant Felip Neri, decorated with the lion of St Mark, who converted the first Christian shoemaker; the graves of the masters in the cathedral cloister, bearing the same emblem; the sumptuous premises of the silk weavers' guild in the Via Laietana. The beginnings of the conversion of Barcelona's economy to an industrial basis can be traced in the decline of the guilds. Eighteenth-century immigrants to Barcelona—most of them from communities in southern France, where languages similar to Catalan were spoken—'preferred factory life to subjection under the oligarchy of guild-masters'. The bridle-makers had 108 members in 1729, 47 in 1808 and 27 in 1814; the decline occurred during a period when the population of the city trebled and was at its most acute at a time of war and high demand for harnesses. In the textile industry, which was directly affected by reorganisation into factories, the decline was even more spectacular. By 1825, the cloth-dressers had only three members left, who had neither studios nor workshops and were too old to work.

In the last quarter of the 18C a number of economic indicators seem to have accelerated. The rate of increase in wages between 1780 and 1797, for instance, was double that of Madrid. Manufacturers' profits, which had already doubled between 1720 and 1775, more than kept pace. When Joseph Townsend visited in 1786, he was particularly impressed by the Bernis factory, which employed 350 operatives making woollen cloth for America; the following year, Arthur Young could hear 'the noise of business' everywhere. The Napoleonic war and its aftermath interrupted progress. Amid post-war unemployment, after a terrible yellow fever epidemic in 1821, the city council of Barcelona lost its habitual optimism and publicly doubted whether the city would ever recover. In fact, though recovery was socially painful, it was complete: in 1836, the first steamship rolled off the slipway of Barceloneta; in 1848 Spain's first railway linked Barcelona to Mataró.

Working-class degradation and unrest accompanied economic change. The pattern of life in Barcelona in the mid 19C was of fitful mass violence and intermittent plague. The horrific symptoms induced by the poisonous atmosphere of the mills were described by Jaume Salarich, a philanthropic physician, in 1850, and confirmed from personal experience by the literate worker, Ramon Simó. Ildefons Cerdà surveyed the working-class way of life in the 1850s and found that a diet of bread and potatoes, enhanced with the odd sardine, was all an average family could afford. Most observers blamed the cholera epidemic of 1854, which claimed nearly 6000 lives on overcrowding in insanitary conditions. Disorder incubated with disease and riots were a regular feature of the long, hot summer. With increasing frequency these took on revolutionary proportions. The rioters' targets gradually changed: there had been disturbances in the 18C—in 1766, 1773 and 1789, when the targets had been grain speculators and the military service quotas. The insurgents of 1835 also attacked the steam-power factories, the representatives of the government and the houses of religion; the disturbances of 1840–42 culminated in a political revolution by a coalition of the disaffected whose only rallying-point was the call for protective tariffs: it was suppressed by a memorable bombardment. In 1854 a long series of strikes and Luddite outrages began, only to be deflected into political channels by the fall of a 'progressive' ministry in Madrid. The barricades of Barcelona had to be reconquered bloodily, in the worst scenes the city had witnessed since 1714. A conservative observer noted with satisfaction: 'The rebels were massacred as they were captured... The spectacle was magnificent.'

The authorities' conviction that the bourgeoisie would soon recover from this shock proved justified. The confidence of the burgeoning city was displayed in the competition, held in 1859, for a design for enlargement (*eixample*) of the city beyond the walls. The public exhibition attracted huge crowds. Antoni Rovira i Trias submitted a popular plan, sympathetically integrating the old town; Ildefons Cerdà's proposal looked more rigidly 'modern'. He made only minimal use of nodal piazze and surrounded the old town with a grid of boulevards and public gardens. Political controversy, caused by the Madrid government's determination to impose Cerdà's solution, delayed work while the case grew desperately urgent: in 1863, for instance, the rate of growth of the population of Barcelona was 27.42 per cent—three times the national Spanish average. The Spanish revolution of 1868, which swept the Bourbons from the throne, temporarily abated the differences between Barcelona and Madrid and in 1869 the laying out of the Eixample proceeded along the lines of the Cerdà plan. Despite the delayed start and the slow initial growth, Barcelona's boom in the late 19C was so rapid that the expectations of the plan were exceeded. In-filling robbed it of its best feature, the expansive parks and garden squares. The sudden grafting of a criss-cross of 19C branches onto the trunk of an ancient town created the view from Montjuïc—the image which defines the city's character, despite the subsequent (even greater) growth to this day.

The era of the Eixample was accompanied by relative social peace. The political energies of the Barcelonese were deflected into Catalanism—the movement for the recognition of Catalonia's distinctive institutions and the conservation of her language and cultural heritage. Bourgeois life moved out of the cafés onto pavement terraces and out of the house into the gas-lit streets that dazzled Hans Christian Andersen when he visited in 1862. The industrialisation of Barcelona swallowed up huge amounts of capital, scattered among too many under-funded firms. The 'gambler's synagogue'—the unofficial Bourse, where 'everybody played and won'—opened in 1858. Slack money and new money created a market for art and architecture that impressed Barcelona with the showy, experimental look that has characterised Barcelonese style ever since.

The symbol of this era of self-assurance was the 'Universal' Exhibition of 1888. The idea originated with a Galician entrepreneur who had seen the Paris and Vienna expositions; the opportunistic Rius i Taulat took it up when he became mayor in 1885. When he summoned the world to Barcelona on 13 June 1887, everything had still to be extemporised. Not only did the citizens build on time the exhibition ground that sarcasts had deemed impossible, but also planted the Plaça de Colon with palms and drove the Rambla de Catalunya and the Paral- lel through suburbs where they had previously been thwarted. The Hotel Internacional was built in only 60 days and its five floors proved unequal to the demand. The exhibition opened ten days late, drew exhibitors from 20 countries and attracted nearly 2¼ million visitors. The young Puig i Cadafalch was inspired with a vision of a 'great Barcelona' which animated his later work as an architect and politician. The idea of Barcelona as a model of 'go-ahead hard work' entered popular fiction.

Rapid growth rarely happens painlessly. In 1860, Barcelona had less than 200,000 inhabitants. By 1897, when the city limits were redrawn to incorporate the towns of the immediate hinterland, the official figure was 383,908. By 1930, the conurbation contained well over a million people. Social conflict could hardly be avoided. When the rail link was completed, young French anarchists took the Barcelona Express and were frightened by the prostitutes on arrival: this was the character of the revolutionary anarchism that became the most potent force of Barcelona's political underworld: naïf and puritanical. In the 1890s, Barcelona was the 'city of bombs'; explosions detonated in the opera house, at a Corpus Christi procession and on a royal visit. In the early 1900s, while terrorism collapsed, the workers' movement was infused by anarchism: the general strike of

1901–02 was Bakuninite in inspiration. The Setmana Tràgica of 1909, when a strangely self-disciplined mob systematically destroyed 70 buildings of religious orders while sparing other targets, was attributed to anarcho-syndicalism; the movement's spokesman, Francesc Ferrer, was executed for presumed complicity after a trial which shocked the world.

Some of these tensions were reflected in the work of the modernist artists who gathered in the Quatre Gats café, (today expensively restored in the Carrer de Montesio). The most representative figure was Ramon Casas, whose father had made a fortune in the Indies and who, on his mother's side, was the heir to a textiles mill. His inheritance thus combined two typical sources of the wealth of Barcelona in his day. His best works were problematical genre-scenes, but his most memorable canvases, perhaps, were those in which the social commentary was most overt. *Barcelona 1902* is an extraordinarily dynamic composition, in which a mounted civil guard is about to trample a sprawling, dramatically foreshortened worker in the foreground, while the crowd is cleared by the cavalry from a space which seems to grow before the onlooker's eyes. Casas' most famous work was *Garrote Vil* of 1893, recording the public execution of a 19-year-old who had cut the throats of his victim and accomplice for a gold watch. Some aspects seem ironic: the clergy are a corpulent contingent, under an enormous crucifix; the penitents' black conical caps prod towards the centre of the canvas like pitchfork prongs. The public loved the engaging horror more than they feared the social import; horror-paintings in Barcelona were always popular and frequently connected with the traditions of public scourging—common until the early 19C—and public execution, which continued until 1908.

From 1901 to the First World War, anarchism and anarcho-syndicalism, though conspicuous, did not command genuine mass allegiance. The political loyalty of the working class lay with the Andalusian demagogue, Alejandro Lerroux and his patriotic 'Republican Fraternities'. He was not above recourse to violence: in election campaigns he was escorted by intimidatingly grown-up 'schoolboys' and, in anticipation of rigged defeat, carried a pistol with two shots 'one for the returning officer and the other for myself'. Still, under his influence, bombing raids were succeeded by 'republican picnics' and a workers' press 'which sold like blessed bread' supplanted terrorism as a means of publicity.

The industrialist Gual Villalbí remembered the First World War as a time when it 'rained orders' in the factories and the streets were strewn with 'flowers of evil'—spies, deserters and refugees. It was a frivolous time—the Teatre Principal was enlarged with an American Bar and a casino—and a time of suspense, lived under the threat of an end to the boom. Cotton exports, which doubled during the war, plunged to little more than half their pre-war levels in the early 1920s. Wartime full employment, followed by post-war lay-offs, created ideal conditions for unions to breed. The anarchist C.N.T. had 15,000 members in Catalonia in 1915, and 73,860 in July 1918, 54,572 of them in the Barcelona branches. Conflictive strikes were at their height in 1919 and 1920, when 7.76 per cent and 8.4 per cent respectively of the working year were lost: the figure had never been more than 2 per cent before 1916.

Workers' issues, however, lost political prominence under the 'iron surgery' of General Primo de Rivera's dictatorship from 1923 to 1931, when the most urgent cause seemed that of Catalanism, ham-fistedly repressed. The unions generally held aloof from Catalanist politics, partly because many of their members were immigrants from other parts of Spain and partly because, as the workers' leader, Salvador Seguí, said: 'A problem of independence or autonomy doesn't exist in Catalonia because we, the workers from there, don't want any such problem and don't feel it!' Under a detested centralist regime, however, Catalanism was an issue which could unite all classes and during the transition to a republic in 1931–32 Catalan autonomy was cheered in the Plaça de Sant Jaume by workers and bourgeois, natives and immigrants alike.

That alliance was broken by the experience of the civil war. The anarchist revolution of 1936 made an enemy of anyone who wore a tie in the street. When Franco's troops marched in with the slogan 'Spain has arrived', a collaborationist bourgeoisie came out of the woodwork. Catalan culture went deeper underground than under Primo de Rivera. Josep Viladomat's monumental allegory, La República, found an ignominious refuge among the packing-cases of the municipal storehouse. The big threat to Barcelona's identity under Franco came, however, not from repression but from economic growth. Three-quarters of a million immigrants, mostly from southern Spain, came to the city between 1950 and 1970. The case of the immigrant from Badajoz who in 1950 sold his house for 7000 pesetas to buy a cave in Sabadell for 3000, shows the scale of the opportunities which attracted them, and of the degradation they underwent. It was easy for Francosim to 'buy' these people with job security and modest economic rewards, hard for Catalanism to win them with the blandishments of an alien tongue, an inhospitable culture and a mandarin creed. Yet when the exiled Catalan leader, Josep Taradellas, appeared after Franco's death on the balcony of the Generalitat in the Plaça de Sant Jaume, he found the immigrants willing to vote for autonomy. His cry, *'Ja sóc aquil!'* (Here I am at last!) contrasted with the 'Spain has arrived' of the Francoists. A survey found that many *soi-disant* Andalusians also considered themselves Catalans: but the main reason for favouring autonomy was rejection of Francoism, not Catalanist sentiment. The dictatorship's other legacy was a proletariat with drawn fangs. Communists took the lead in organising a clandestine union movement from 1963: by the 1970s it was strong enough to attempt political strikes. But, as it grew in numbers, it became ideologically diluted. The union elections of 1975 put apolitical leaders in control of most branches. 'Responsible' unionism has been dominant ever since.

The Spanish constitution of 1978, which restored to Barcelona the autonomous government of the four provinces of the historic Principality of Catalonia, has boosted demand and morale alike. Creative tension between the left-wing city government and right-wing Catalan government has stimulated the flow of official funds into urban renewal and cultural programmes. Spanish membership of the EEC, with the prospect of the development of a genuine regional economy around the western Mediterranean seaboard, has enhanced Barcelonese confidence in the future by promising to free the city from the traditional economic role of maker and purveyor of goods to a protected Spanish market. The choice of Barcelona as the site of the 1992 Olympiad has brought to bonanza to the construction industry and embourgeoisement to neglected inner-city areas. Still the Barcelonese remain dissatisfied. The policy of 'coffee all round'—granting comparable levels of autonomy to all Spain's historic communities—has wounded Catalonia's sense of her own uniqueness. Barcelona's upstart rival, Madrid, whose rule the Barcelonese endured while convinced of their economic and artistic superiority, has caught up in terms of achievement as well as presumption and Barcelonese anxiety to cultivate a non-Spanish sense of identity—as Catalans, 'Mediterraneans' or Europeans—seems as strong as ever. To remain the 'head and hearth' of Catalonia. Barcelona has to Catalanise the huge numbers of Spanish-speaking immigrant workers who have filled the outlying districts in the last half-century. Civic art patronage in recent years has taken on an increasingly desperate air, detectable in the bizarre post- moderist 'sculpture park' that stands outside Sants railway station or the oppressive cement monoliths that adorn the Plaça de la Palmera.

Thus Barcelona's achievements continue to incubate in frustration and, as they confront the challenges and opportunities of 1992 and after, the Barcelonese merit as much as ever the characterisation of a Castilian humanist, 500 years ago: 'I now behold her citizens, triumphant despite their dearth of natural resources, and her people possessed of all worldly prosperity, thanks to their efforts alone'.

PRACTICAL INFORMATION

Tourist Offices

General information, including how to get to Barcelona, suggestions for accommodation and how to travel around may be obtained from the Spanish Tourist Office, 57 St. James's St, London SW1A 1LD, tel. 071-499 0901. In the US: 665 5th Ave., New York, NY 10022, tel. 212-759 8822; Water Tower Place, Suite 915 E 845 North Michigan Ave., Chicago, Ill 60611; tel 312-944 0216. 8383 Wilshire Blvd, Suite 960, Beverly Hills, CA 90211, tel. 213-658 7188. 1221 Brickell Ave. 33131 Miami, Fl., tel. 305-358 1992. In Canada: 102 Bloor St W. 14th Floor, Toronto, Ontario M5S 1M8, tel. 416-961 3131.

Formalities and Currency

Passports and Visas

Passports are necessary for all British and American travellers to Spain. British passports, valid for ten years, are issued by the Passport Office, Clive House, Petty France, London SW1 and from provincial offices. British Visitors' Passports (valid for one year) are available from post offices in the UK.

Visas are **only** required for visits of over 90 days; these may be obtained from the Spanish Consulate, 20 Draycott Place, London SW3, tel. 071-581 5921. in the US: Spanish Embassy, 2700 15th St., NW, Washington, DC 20009, tel. 202-265 0190.

Money

The monetary unit is the peseta. There are bank notes of 10,000, 5000, 1000 and 500 pesetas and coins of 500, 200, 100, 50, 25, 10, 5 and 1 pesetas.

Insurance

You are strongly recommended to take out private travel insurance (available from banks and travel agents) which will cover the cost of cash and valuables lost or stolen as well as personal health care. (See also Medical Assistance, p 28.)

Getting to Barcelona

By Air

Iberia Airlines, 130 Regent St, London W1R 5RG, tel. 071-437 5622 and British Airways, tel. 081-897 4000 operate regular scheduled flights to Barcelona. Cheaper services are available on charter flights, though certain restrictions may be imposed. Details of these flights can be found in the small ads of Sunday newspapers and magazines such as Time Out.

The Barcelona International Airport of El Part is situated 12km to the south of the city, and has daily services to London (1hr. 5min.), Manchester (1hr. 25min.), and New York (7hrs. 40min.); there is also a shuttle-stop service to Madrid (55 min.), with flights leaving every 15 minutes on working days. The main terminal, which features a large mural by Miró, has been remodelled and extended for 1992 by the leading post-Modernist architect Ricardo Bofill.

The fastest connection between the airport and the city is the train service to the Central-Sants and Plaça de Catalunya stations, an 18-minute journey; trains leave every 30 minutes, and run from 06.12 to 22.42. The bus service, which has both a day and night-time service, also terminates in the Plaça de Catalunya.

By Train

Travelling to Barcelona by train from London will mean having to change trains and stations in Paris, and, on some services, at the Spanish border. The fastest route is to take the Barcelona Talgo Eurocity train from Paris. The 'Catalàn-Talgo' Eurocity Train runs from Barcelona to Geneva (14 hours), passing through Perpignan, Narbonne, Montpelier, Nîmes, Avignon and Grenoble; the journey from Barcelona to Paris (11 hours) is undertaken by the Barcelona Talgo Eurocity Train, while the 'Pau Casals' Eurocity Train runs directly both to Zurich (13 hours) and to Milan (13 hours). For details of rail travel offered by British Rail Continental Ltd, contact the Ticket and Information Office, PO Box 29, Victoria Station London SW1V 1JX, tel. 071-834 2345. Couchette and sleeper reservations in France should be made through French Railways, 179 Piccadilly, London W1, tel. 071-409 3518.

The main international train services arrive at present at the Estació Central-Sants and Passeig de Gràcia Stations, though these will be shortly be complemented by the Estació de França, which has been closed for many years for modernisation.

By Bus

There are regular bus services from London to Barcelona. Buses leave from Victoria Coach Station and the journey time is about 26 hours. For more information on servies and times contact Eurolines, 52 Grosvenor Gardens, Victoria, London SW1, tel. 071-730 0202 (credit card reservations 071-730 8235) or your local National Express agent.

By Car

The only direct ferry service from the UK to Spain is that operated by Brittany Ferries, Millbay Docks, Plymouth, Devon PL1 3EW, tel. 0752-221321, from Plymouth to Santander which takes about 24 hours. The longer and more expensive alternative route is the cross-Channel ferry to France.

You will need an international drivers' licence (contact the AA or RAC or any automobile club in the USA) and a Green Card. The speed limit is 100km per hour on national highways and 120km per hour on motorways. The wearing of seatbelts is compulsory. There are no petrol concessions or coupons for tourists in Spain. For car hire contact the government-owned company ATESA.

Those coming to Barcelona by car are strongly recommended to leave their vehicle as soon as possible in one of the city's growing number of underground car parks, and from there visit the city on foot or by public transport; you should also avoid arriving in the city on a Sunday evening, as the traffic jams of returning week-enders lead to an almost total congestion of Barcelona's approach roads. Street parking is difficult in the centre of the city, and often means obtaining a special ticket at machines that are not always immediately visible from where you park your car; a sign with the word *Grua* means that your car is likely to be removed by crane, a hazard involving great expense and much time wasted at the police station. Cars with a foreign or at least non-Barcelona licence plate should ideally not be left on a quiet street at night, and in any case luggage should always be removed beforehand from the boot.

By Boat

Regular international boat services are limited to a weekly departure to Livorno and Sicily from 2 March to 16 September; for further information contact Alimar (International Maritime Station) at 412 33 21. In the summer months there are also daily departures by boat to the Balearic Islands and Valencia, though these are often booked up a long time in advance.

Transport in Barcelona

It goes without saying that by far the best way of getting to know Barcelona is on foot, and this is perfectly possible in the Ciutat Vella or Old Town, where the distances are relatively small; once you enter the Eixample, however, walking can become tiring, not least because of the monotony of the regular grid plan. Public transport in Barcelona is both very cheap and—as with most aspects of this city's life—exceptionally efficient, the main problems being caused by the heavy traffic and the traditional lack of communications between the outlying former townships (to go from one suburb to a neighbouring one it is often quicker to return to the centre of Barcelona).

The metro is the fastest and most practical transport system within the centre of the city, with four lines, and stations near most places of tourist interest. One of its drawbacks is that the hot and stuffy corridors that lead to the platforms are often depressingly long, and you are likely to be in an overheated state when you enter the freezingly air-conditioned carriages. Another disadvantage is that though the metro functions from 05.00am. onwards, it closes down on weekdays as early as 23.00; on Fridays, Saturdays and the eves of public holidays, its hours are extended slightly, but only to 01.00. In contrast, many of the principal bus routes run throughout the night. A third transport system is the commuter trains known as the Ferrocarrils de la Generalitat de Catalunya, which have their terminals in the Plaças d'Espanya and de Catalunya, and are often indistinguishable from the metro trains; they serve not only such nearby districts as Gràcia and Sarrià, but also faraway places such as Terrassa and Montserrat.

Tickets for individual journeys by metro, commuter train or bus can be bought at the stations or on the buses, but it is far cheaper and more convenient to buy a card valid for ten trips, which is best obtained either at the metro or commuter train stations. A T-2 card is valid for both metro and commuter trains, while for a minimum additional price you can purchase a T-1 card, which can be used as well on the buses and the *Tramvia Blau* (Blue Tram; see p. 146). In addition there are passes valid for 1, 3 or 5 days which allow unlimited travel around the city by bus and metro, but for these you will need a photograph. For visitors a remarkably cheap and useful service is provided by the so-called *Bus Turistic* (No. 100), which was recently instituted by Barcelona's Patronat de Turisme but has up till now been used more by the inhabitants of the city than by tourists. This bus, which operates from 22 June to 15 September, runs every half an hour from 09.00 to 21.30, and makes 16 stops, which take in not only all the major sights in the centre of the city, but also such outlying attractions as the Park Güell and the Monastery of Pedralbes, and even the little known Parc de la Creueta del Coll. Your ticket—which is valid for either a day or half a day, and is purchased on the bus—allows you to alight wherever you want, and continue your journey with a later bus; furthermore you will be able to travel free on the *tramvia blau*, the Tibidabo funicular and the Montjuïc cable-car and receive discounts on the tickets for the Poble Espanyol, the Zoo, the Golondrinas and the guided tours of the Barri Gòtic. Two of the most generally convenient points for catching the bus are the Plaça de Catalunya (outside the El Corte Inglés department store), and the Plaça de Sant Jaume.

There are regular bus services to all parts of the city between 06.30 and 22.00, with a night buses operating between 22.00 and 04.00. Bus stops and buses are colour-coded according to the direction of the route. Bus maps are obtainable from the Patronat de Tourisme and offices at Sants Estació, Plaça de Catalunya and Plaça de la Universitat.

Taxis are easily recognisable by their yellow and black colouring, and remain exceptionally cheap, despite the minimum charge in Barcelona of 225 pesetas (pts); a green light on the roof, and the sign *Libre* or *Lliure* (Free) indicate that they are not occupied. Though they can usually be flagged down in the street without too many problems, it is often best to go to a taxi rank or *Parada de Taxis*. The most difficult times to find a taxi are on Friday and Saturday nights, when it is advisable to ring for one; in such cases you can arrange to meet at a given place, your particular taxi being recognised by a given number. The main taxi companies are: Barna Taxi, 355 77 55; Taxi Radio Móvil, 358 11 11; Tele Taxi, 392 22 22; Radio Taxi, 490 22 22; As. Radio Taxi Miramar, 433 10 20; Coop. Radio Taxi Metropoli-tana de Barcelona, 300 38 11; and Taxi Mens, 397 81 11. A special credit card or 'Taxi Card' for paying fares has recently been issued by the Metropolitan Transportation Department; for information about this you should ring 412 20 00. Tipping usually involves leaving the small coins from your change, and rarely exceeds 50 pesetas.

General Information

Accommodation

With major exceptions such as the Hotel Ramada Renaissance (see p 44), Barcelona's luxury hotels are mainly to be found in the commercial areas of the Eixample or even further afield, one of the most famous of them all, the Hotel Principesa Sofia (see p. 144) being located near Pedralbes. The city's hotel capacity has been greatly increased to accommodate visitors to the Olympic Games, but moderately priced hotels remain in relatively short supply, and tend to be fully booked up during the spring and autumn trade fairs. The starring sytem of these hotels is often baffling, and a three star rating does not necessarily mean greater comfort than a one star one. Many of these hotels are little better than the cheaper establishments such as the *Hostales, Casas de Huéspedes* and *Fondas*, which are marked respectively by the signs HsT, CH and F. These cheaper establishments, which at their most basic might offer a bare room with an iron bed, a washbasin and a crucifix, tend to be friendlier and more intimate than the hotels, and certainly have far greater character. Whatever your needs, the best place to go and look for somewhere to stay is around La Rambla, where there is plentiful accommodation in all categories; the cheaper places here will amost always have rooms available, particularly if you start your search for a room in the late morning. More cautious travellers who have not arranged for accommodation beforehand can make bookings (for hotels only) from hotel booking agencies situated at the airport and main railway stations (a small charge is made). Lists of hotels in Barcelona can be consulted at Spanish Tourist offices; see p 23. The Patronat de Turisme will provide information on the agencies that help with finding rooms in private houses, a form of accommodation which has mushroomed with the Olympic Games in mind. General information on hotels can be had from the Barcelona Hotel Association (47 Via Laietana, tel. 301 62 40; fax 301 42 92). If you have any complaints about the hotel you choose, you can register them in the *Libro de reclamaciones*, which every boarding and catering establishment in Spain is obliged by law to keep.

The nearest camp site to Barcelona is Camping Barcino, at Esplugues, 2km from the centre (50 Carrer Laurà Miró, tel. 378 85 01). For further information on camping contact the Barcelona Camp Site Association, (Gran Via C.C., 608, 3, A, tel. 419 59 55).

Information about youth hostels is available from Catalonia Young Tourists Office, Gravina 1 (08001), tel. 302 06 82, fax 412 50 26.

Museums and Churches

The opening hours of Barcelona's museums are more generous than those of most other Spanish cities, and you can generally count on museums being open Tuesdays–Saturdays, 09.00–13.00/14.00 and 16.00/16.30–19.00; furthermore many of the more popular museums such as the Museu d'Art Modern and the Museu Picasso are open without a break up to as late as 20.00 or 21.00. Almost all museums are closed on Mondays, Sunday and holiday afternoons. An admission charge is usually made to foreigners, though students and pensioners are sometimes allowed in at half price. Admission is often free to Spaniards, young children and official residents in Spain (eg. those with a work permit); this same concession is applying increasingly in Spain to members of Common Market countries, but in such cases a passport is essential and entrance is often restricted to certain times (the author has also had to prove on certain occasions that Great Britain belongs to the Common Market!).

Entrance to churches is more problematical, and is often possible only immediately before and after services, which are usually held either very early in the morning or in the evening. The time-wasting recourse of hunting down the priest to open up the church for you meets with relatively little success in Barcelona, perhaps owing to unfortunate experiences with anarchists during the Civil War. The major ecclesiastical monuments—most notably the Cathedral, Santa Maria del Mar, Santa Maria del Pi, the

Sagrada Família and the Monestir de Pedralbes—have set opening hours comparable to those of the museums (though Santa Maria del Mar closes as inexplicably early as 12.00).

Shopping and Banking Hours

Shopping hours are usually 09.00–13.00/13.30, and 16.30–20.00, though the major stores in the centre often stay open all day; most of the stores have sales lasting from the second week of January to the end of February, and during the months of July and August. The city's three main drugstores are: Drugstore, 71 Passeig de Gràcia (open 24 hours a day, every day of the week); Drugstore David, 19–21 Carrer de Tuset (open every day 09.00–05.00); Vip's, 7 Rambla de Catalunya (Sunday to Thursday, 09.00–02.00); Fridays, Saturdays and the eves of public holidays, 09.00–03.00).

The normal banking hours are Monday–Friday 08.30–14.00; most banks are also open on Saturday mornings 08.30–12.00/13.00, though not in July and August. The banks at the airport and Estació Central-Sants railway station are open thoughout the day up to 22.00 and 23.00 respectively, and also on Sundays and holidays; the Banco Bilbao Vizcaya (tel. 490 26 95), is also open daily, 08.15–22.00.

Telephones and Postal Services

Pay phones in bars and public booths take 5, 25 and 100 peseta (pts) coins; a minimum of 15 pts is required for local calls and 50 pts for calls outside the province; certain bars have metre-connected phones, though these are more expensive than the pay phones. All the public booths give the relevant international operator service number for those wishing to make collect calls to their home country. The main telephone exchange in the centre of the city is the Telefónica in the Carrer Fontanella, facing the Plaça de Catalunya (open Monday–Saturday, 08.00–21.00); fax facilities are also available here.

The main Post Office is at the Plaça d'Antoni López, s/n (see p. 100), and is open Monday–Saturday, 08.00–21.00; stamps (*timbres postales* in Catalan) are available at all tobacconists.

Medical Assistance

British travellers, covered by the British National Insurance Scheme, may obtain free medical assistance from the Spanish Health Service. The Barcelona Medical Center Association (437 Avinguda Diagonal, 3a, tel. 414 06 43) provides up-to-date information about the modern medical services offered by the city, and also helps those from any part of the world who wish to come to Barcelona for medical or surgical treatment.

Crime

As with most large modern cities today, drug-related crime is on the increase in Barcelona, though the most dangerous areas are the outlying suburban districts that few tourists are likely to visit. The enormous red-light district which extends on either side of the lower end of La Rambla has an evil reputation, but, as with banditry in Spain in the 19C, this reputation has become integral to the romantic fascination of the district. The district is now well policed at all times of day, and you are unlikely to experience any problems here if you respect such obvious precautious as not wandering off on your own into some of its darker alleys at night, carrying expensive camera equipment or being dressed too ostentatiously. The Barcelona Municipal Police (*Guardia Urbana*), in collaboration with the Barcelona *Patronat de Turisme*, now offers an assistance and counselling service for anyone who has suffered any accident or criminal act during their stay in the city. This service, known as 'Tourist Attention', is situated at 43 La Rambla (tel. 301 90 60) and is open 24 hours a day; it provides facilities for reporting a crime, legal advice, translation services, information about receiving temporary identification papers and help with contacting members of your family.

Public Holidays

The main public holidays are 1 January, Good Friday, Easter Monday, 1 May, Pentecost, 24 June (St. John's Day; fireworks and bonfires are lit the night before throughout the city), 15 August, 11 September (Catalan National Day; Catalan flags are hung from many of the houses), 24 September (the Mercè Holiday, a local holiday preceding a week of festivities), 12 October (The Feast of the Spanish-speaking nations), 1 November (All Saints' Day), 6 December (Constitution Day), 25 December and 26 December. The festival of St. George (Sant Jordi), on 23 April, when it is customary to exchange a book and a rose as a sign of love and friendship (see p. 69), is not a public holiday, and all shops and museums are open that day.

Climate

Barcelona enjoys a mild Mediterranean climate, with average temperatures of 10°C (50°F) during its coldest month (January), and 25°C (78°F) during July and August; owing to its position by the sea, Barcelona never experiences the oppressive heat of Madrid or Seville, though atmospheric pollution combined with humidity make for unpleasant conditions at the very height of summer.

Tourist Information Offices

Barcelona Estació Central-Sants, Plaça Països Catalans, s/n, tel. 490 91 71 (08.00–20.00); Palau de Congresos, Avinguda Maria Cristina, s/n, tel. 423 31 01, ext. 8356 (open during main trade fair events, 10.00–19.00/20.00); Ajuntament de Barcelona, Plaça de Sant Jaume, tel. 302 42 00 (open 24 June–30 September Monday–Friday, 09.00–20.00, Saturday 08.30–14.30); 'Palau de la Virreina' Information Service, tel. 301 77 75, ext. 243 (open 24 June–30 September Monday–Saturday, 09.30–21.00; Sunday 10.00–14.00); 658 Gran Via de les Corts Catalanes, tel. 301 74 43 (Monday–Friday 09.00–19.00, Saturday 09.00–14.00); Barcelona Airport, International Arrivals Vestibule, tel. 325 58 29 (Monday–Saturday 09.30–20.00, Sunday 09.30–15.00).

During the summer months there also exists the so-called 'Red Jackets' Street Information Service, comprising pairs of young information officers—easily recognisable by their red and white uniforms and badges marked 'i'—parading the Rambla, the Passeig de Gràcia and the streets of the Barri Gòtic.

Consulates

Australia: 98 Gran Via Carles III, tel. 330 94 96. Canada: 125 Via Augusta, tel. 209 06 34. France, 11 Passeig de Gràcia, tel. 317 81 50; Germany, 111 Passeig de Gràcia, tel. 415 36 96; Great Britain, 477 Avinguda Diagonal, tel. 419 90 44; Italy, 270 Carrer de Mallorca, tel. 215 16 54; United States, 33 Via Laietana, tel. 319 95 50.

Language

The Spanish and Catalan languages have equal status in Barcelona, but though everyone who speaks Catalan is fluent also in Spanish, the opposite is not true: owing to the large immigrant population from other parts of Spain, and the fact that many of the city's older inhabitants were brought up at a time when the Catalan language was officially prohibited, the city's fluent Catalan speakers account for little more than 50 per cent of the population. None the less all street names and signs are now solely in Catalan, as are most information panels in museums, exhibition catalogues, restaurant menus and so on; in some cases you are more likely to find a Catalan text translated into English than into Spanish, and there are certain Catalan nationalists who have even argued that Catalan authors who do not write in Catalan, such as Juan Goytisolo and Eduardo Mendoza, have no right to receive sponsorship from the Catalan Government. Not even the most fervent of these nationalists will take offence if a foreigner addresses them in Spanish, but on the other hand if you belong to that tiny minority of visitors to Catalonia who have bothered to learn some Catalan, you will find yourself welcomed into the Catalan community in a way which few others will experience. Anyone who is planning an extended stay in Barcelona would be well advised to try to learn Catalan as well as Spanish; intensive and other courses in the Catalan language are organised by the University of Barcelona (for further information you could ring 318 42 66 or 318 99 26).

The Catalan language is spoken not only throughout Catalonia, but also (with variations) in the Valencian provinces of Valencia, Castelló and Alacant (Alicante), the Balearic Islands, a narrow strip of eastern Aragon, the Republic of Andorra and the town of Alguer (Alghero) in Sardinia; altogether it has more speakers than have Albanian, Danish, Finnish, Gaelic, Lithuanian and Norwegian. It is a member of the Romance family of languages, and anyone with a basic command of Spanish will have few problems at least in understanding the gist of a Catalan text; an additional knowledge of French or Italian will also greatly help, as many Catalan words or phrases are closer to these two languages than they are to Spanish, for instance *si us plau* (please) or *menjar* (eat). The main difficulties come with the pronunciation, which is complex compared to Spanish, and affected by more accents (thus whereas in Spanish the sole accents are the acute and the tilde, in Catalan the accents are the acute, grave, umlaut and the cedilla). Among the more idiosyncatic features of the pronunciation are that the *h* is always silent; *j* is pronounced like the French *j* or *g* (and not as an *h* as in Spanish); *ny* is the equivalent of the Spanish tilde, ~, even at the end of a word; *ll* without a dot has a strong consonantal y sound as in the English *lli*; *ig* at the end of a syllable is like the English *tch*; *gü* is pronounced *gw* and x sounds like the English *sh*. For example, to use names that you will come across again and again on a trip to Barcelona, Joan Maragall (the great Catalan poet) = *Jhone Maraga-ye*, Puig i Cadafalch (the Moderniste architect) = *Putch ee Kadalfak*, and Güell (Gaudí's patron) = *Gwé-ye*.

Anyone who wishes to learn more about the Catalan language should read Alan Yates' scholarly and very thorough study of the language in the *Teach Yourself Books* series (London, 1975). Listed at the end of the book are some of the words that you will encounter as a tourist (the days of the week, numbers and the more common Christian names are included at the end of the list, while food names will be found at the end of the introductory essay, Food and Drink; see pp. 35–37).

Food and Drink

The Catalan love of food is exemplified in the character of Pepe Carvalho, the protagonist of a popular series of detective novels by the leading Catalan writer of today, Vázquez Montalbán. Carvalho is a passionate cook and gourmet whose obsession with what he eats is unaffected by crises in both his professional and personal life, his obsession being such that Montalbán was able recently to bring out a book dedicated solely to *The Recipes of Pepe Carvalho* (Barcelona,1989). It is with a heavy heart that this fat and balding hedonist is forced on one occasion to leave his home town of Barcelona and go off on an assignment to Madrid, a place which, in his own words, 'has given no more than a stew, an omelette and a dish of tripe to the gastronomic culture of our country'. Most Madrilenians would rightly take offence at Carvalho's assessment of their gastronomy, though few of them would retaliate with an attack on Catalan food, which in certain Spanish circles is regarded as the Catalans' main saving grace.

The virtues of Catalan food were outlined as far back as the 14C, in an encyclopaedic manual of learning written by a Franciscan monk, Francesc Eiximenis, from the Catalan town of Girona. Eiximenis, who came from a wealthy mercantile family, was a man of broad international outlook who had travelled widely throughout Europe, including Paris, Cologne, Oxford and Rome. Such a background lent an added authority to the section of his manual which was entitled 'Why the Catalans eat more finely and in a better way than other nations' (*Com catalans menjen plus graciosament ab millor manere que altres nacions*). Among the reasons that he gave were that the Catalans avoid excess and superfluity, that they accompany their food with wines rather than beers or sweet brews, that their diet is a regular and balanced one which takes into account both the nutritional and dietary elements of the food, and that in their table manners and cutting of meat they show a respect for hygiene not generally found elsewhere.

Further reflections on Catalan food are to be found in another 14C treatise, the *Libre de Sent Soví*, but the first Catalan cookery book was not to appear until the end of the following century. This work, the *Llibre de Coch*, was written by Robert de Nola, a cook who was claimed to have worked in the service of Ferdinand I of Aragon. Translated shortly afterwards into Castilian, the book was perhaps the most influential of its kind in 16C Spain. Certain of its recipes might not be entirely to present-day tastes, such as the one for roast cat (*menjar de gat rostit*), which involves roasting the animal in oil, garlic and herbs and serving it in slices with more garlic; Catalan refinement and hygienic concerns were in this case reflected in the delicate detail of removing the cat's brains beforehand, these being considered prejudicial to human sanity. Many of the principles of modern Catalan cookery were outlined in the book, but the basic repertory of so-called traditional Catalan dishes does not seem to have been established until the late 19C, at a time of growing Catalan nationalism. The two leading cookery writers of this period were Ignasi Domènech Puigcercós—the author of some 30 books on the subject—and Ferrán Agulló, a lawyer and journalist who was born in Girona in 1863. Agulló's most important work was the *Llibre de la cuina catalana* (The Book of Catalan Food), the introduction to which begins with the words: 'Catalonia, just as it has its own language, constitution, customs, history and political ideals, has its own cuisine. There are regions, nations, peoples, who have their own gastronomic specialities, but not a cuisine. Catalonia has this, and it has something more: it has an extraordinary capacity to assimilate the specialities of other cusines such as that of France or Italy; it appropriates these specialities and modifies them in accordance with its own tastes and traditions'.

To this ability to assimilate should be added the exceptional natural resources of Catalonia, a region which can be divided into three main gastronomic areas, one reliant on the exceptional variety of seafood from the Mediterannean, another on the cattle farming and rich vegetable produce of the densely agricultural hinterland, and a third on the abundance of game in the mountains. Within each of these areas there exists a wealth of local variations in the cuisine, particularly in the agricultural parts of the interior. The dishes that Barcelona itself has contributed to this rich gastronomic culture have been much debated, but what is certain is that it has acted as a melting-pot to all the many strands of the regional cuisine, bringing together the culinary traditions of the maritime, agricultural and mountainous areas of Catalonia, as well as those of the many peoples who have settled in the city from other parts of Spain and Europe.

From the Romantic period onwards, tourists have tended to denigrate the food of Spain generally, and there is certainly an irony in the fact that this very tourism, particularly in the coastal resorts, has been a major contributory factor to the decline of traditional Catalan cuisine. Vázquez Montalbán, in a polemical book on Catalan food written in 1979, expressed his worry that the food of his region was becoming so blandly international in character that soon all that would be left of Catalonia's gastronomic traditions would be a piece of soggy toast rubbed with oil and tomato and spread with a layer of ham as thin and tasteless as clingfilm. Fortunately the decline in the local gastronomy has recently been halted, thanks to a combination of resurgent regional pride and the beneficial influence of *nouvelle cuisine*, the principles of which were ideally suited to Catalan food, which has traditionally been characterised by a meticulous care in its preparation, an insistance on freshness of produce, a preference for quality over quantity and a love of unusual combinations. None the less the ubiquitous *pa amb tomaquet* or bread rubbed with oil and tomato—which is not only a dish in its own right when served with ham, but is also an accompaniment to most other dishes—has become as integral to the gastronomic image of Catalonia, as pasta has to that of Italy, or dumplings to that of Czechoslovakia.

Agulló, and most other cookery writers from the 19C onwards, have defined the true essence of Catalan food as lying in the four sauces known as the *sofregit*, the *picada*, the *samfaina* and the *allioli*. In contrast to other parts of Spain, both fish and meat in Catalonia are rarely presented simply in a fried, boiled, baked, grilled or roasted state, but with an accompanying sauce. The two most important ones are the *sofregit* (which means literally 'a fry-up') and the *picada* (literally 'chopped-up'). The first one is prepared— preferably in a terracotta casserole or *cassola de fang*— by slowly frying an onion in oil or lard, and then adding a chopped and peeled tomato;

garlic and parsley are usually added to the resulting mixture, which should have the consistency of jam. The *picada* is a more complex sauce and one which varies slightly according to the dishes with which it is used, the one essential element being the mortar in which all the ingredients are pounded together. The most usual ingredients are garlic, saffron, pine nuts, almonds, biscuits, fried or toasted breadcrumbs, and fish, chicken or other livers (which can be put in either raw or cooked). Dry or sweet wine, or even anis, is frequently used to make the mixture more liquid, and honey, sugar and grated chocolate are often added as sweeteners, the love of mixing sweet and sour ingredients being very strong in Catalonia. *Samfaina* is the Catalan equivalent of the French *ratatouille*, and is made with onions, tomatoes, red or green peppers and, occasionally, pumkin. *Allioli*, which is common to several Mediterranean regions, including Provence, Greece, North Africa and southern Italy, is a paste made by pounding garlic in a mortar and slowly amalgamating olive oil; other ingredients, such as cheese, can be added to create a thicker mixture, the most common addition being egg yolk, which produces a garlic mayonnaise. The exact origins of *allioli* are not known, though a comparable sauce is mentioned in the *Llibre de Sent-Soví.*

A typical Catalan meal is likely to begin with a salad, a vegetable dish or a soup. One of the most common salads is the *escalivada*, which in its most basic form comprises skinned and roasted peppers and aubergines cut into strips and dressed with oil, salt and vinegar; this should not be confused with an *esqueixada* (with which it is sometimes served), which is a salad of shredded salt cod. The vegetable dishes include cabbage (*col*) with *allioli*, spinach with currants and pine nuts (*espinac amb panses i pinyons*), and numerous stews made with beans (*mongetes*), broad beans (*faves*) or chickpeas (*cigrons*), into which are usually incorporated pieces of the ubiquitous Catalan pork sausage known as the *botifarra*. Two of the finest soup dishes are the *sopas* of *rape* (monkfish) and *sepas* (ceps), both of which feature a *picada* of saffron, garlic and toasted almonds.

The main fish or meat dishes, though usually prepared or served with a sauce, are rarely accompanied by vegetables other than potatoes. A popular fish dish which is claimed to be of Barcelona origin is dried salt cod (*bacalla*) with *samfaina*; other traditional ways of preparing this type of cod are *a la llauna* (with paprika, garlic, parsley and white wine) and with honey (*mel*). Almost certainly originating from the fish restaurants of the Barcelona district of Barceloneta is the *zarzuela*, a name borrowed from a Spanish form of operetta but applied in culinary usage to the Catalan equivalent of the Provençal *bouillabaisse*; the mixture of seafood used, which usually includes mussels, monkfish, crayfish and squid, is cooked in a *sofregit* to which saffron and chopped garlic and parsley are added. Owing to its relatively recent origin this is a dish which has horrified traditionalists, including the leading Catalan writer Josep Pla, who not only complained of its 'horrible name' of theatrical origin, but also opined that it comprised a ratio of one good fish to every six fishes of the 'vilest quality'. Pla was unimpressed by all mixtures of seafood, and reserved his strongest criticism for the *parrillada*, a culinary fashion of even more recent origin than the *zarzuela*; described by Pla as a dry version of the latter, this mixture of grilled or deep-fried seafood can indeed have a desiccated, archaeological character when served in some of the cheaper restaurants of Barceloneta. A better bet is the *suquet*, a seafood stew originating in the Costa Brava, and prepared in both a *sofregit* and *picada*.

The variety of meat, game and poultry dishes is very great in Catalunya, poultry in particular being more commonly and interestingly served than it is in other parts of Spain; as with the fish dishes, most of these dishes gain their distinction from the use of the *soffrito*, *picada*, *samfraina* and *allioli* sauces. Among the exotics are duck cooked with pears (*anec amb peras*), rabbit with chestnuts and ceps (*conill amb castanyas i setas*) and stuffed turkey (*gall dindi farcit a la Catalana*); the latter, a Christmas dish, features a stuffing of ham, sausages, plums, apricots, currants, pine nuts, chestnuts, wine and cinnamon.

Meat, game and poultry are sometimes prepared together with seafood, an excellent if rare and very expensive example of such a combination being lobster with chicken (*llagost amb poll*). A Barcelona invention of the 1950s was the *mar i muntanya* (literally 'sea and mountain'), which, as its name suggests, brings together a veritable excess of ingredients, including snails, cuttlefish, trotters, sausages, rabbit, mussels, chicken, tomatoes, onions, almonds, pinenuts, chocolates and hazelnuts. In the debased form in which this dish is usually served today, this rich mixture has been pared down to a chicken and prawn ragout.

The most famous of all Catalan dishes, and a meal in itself, is the *escudella i carn d'olla*, which is a variant of the Castilian *cocido* and the Andalusian *puchero*. This is a stew made with potatoes, cabbage, chickpeas, chicken and a variety of meats, including the *botifarra* sausage. The broth is served as a first course, usually today with noodles, but traditionally with pasta cut into alphabet shapes, an addition which inspired Miguel de Unamuno to write that the Catalans were 'such lovers of culture that they even eat the letters of the alphabet'. The vegetables and meats are piled up separately on a large plate.

Rice and pasta dishes are very common in Catalonia, the former being an import from the neighbouring region of Valencia. The Catalan equivalent of the *paella* is the *arròs a la Catalana*, but a more traditional rice dish is the *arroseixat*, in which saffron-flavoured rice is prepared with potatoes, onions and fish; the delicious *arròs negre* or 'black rice' is rice cooked in the ink of cuttlefish. Pasta dishes, though of distant Italian origin, have become one of the great Catalan specialities, in particular cannelloni, which are known in Catalan as *canalons*. An unappetising version of cannelloni is usually found in the cheaper restaurants, but this is traditionally a festive dish, prepared with the remains of roast or stewed meats; the pasta is usually filled with a sauce made of onions, pork, veal, chicken livers and chicken breasts, and covered with a bechamel flavoured with nutmeg. The other main pasta dishes are macaroni (*maccaròns*) and noodles (*fideus*), the former being combined with a thick sauce made of tomatoes, bechamel and pieces of ham, sausage or bacon. The classic Catalan way of preparing noodles is *a la cazuela*, a dish unlike any Italian one, comprising noodles incorporated into a stew of pork ribs, *botifarra* sausages, tomatoes and wine.

The sweet tooth of the Catalans is evident more in their use of sugar, honey and chocolate in savoury dishes than it is in the range of their desserts. The usual restaurant stand-by is the *crema catalana*, a cream custard with a caramelised crust as in the French crème brulée; as in other parts of Spain, many of the more elaborate desserts and pastries are only to be found around Easter and Christmas. An institution peculiar to Catalonia where you can eat pastries, cakes and *bunyuelos* (a type of doughnut) are the milk-bars known as *granjas*.

Eiximenis' statement that the Catalans accompany their food with wine rather than beer still holds true today, and Catalonia is one of the most important wine-producing regions in Spain. The four official denominations are Alella, Penedès, Tarragona and Priorato. The Alella wines come from the district of Girona, the white ones being particularly renowned (a well-known mark is Perelada). The Penedès district extends to the south of Barcelona, and produces the most famous of Catalonia's wines. The whites here tend also to be much finer than the reds, but the great speciality of the district are the champagne-like wines known as *cavas*, the capital of which is the town of Sant Sadurní d'Anoia, in the northern half of the district. The local wine-growers failed in their attempts to label the *cavas* as 'champagne', but the dryer of these wines can be a good and cheaper substitute for champagne, despite the opinion of the *Larousse Gastronomique* that they are *'franchement détestables pour nos palais français'*. The quality of the *cavas* is very variable, and the best are by no means the Freixenet and Codorniu, which are at present being widely promoted in the rest of Spain and Europe. South of the Penedès district lies the wine-growing district of Tarragona, and further south still is the Priorato. Both these districts specialise in full-bodied reds, and are also renowed for their sweet dessert wines or *mostos*.

A Glossary of Food and Drink in Catalan

albercoc, apricot
albergínies, aubergine
allioli, garlic and olive oil dressing, sometimes an egg mayonnaise
amanida, salad
ametller, almonds
ànec, duck
anyell, lamb
arròs, rice
avellana, hazelnut
bacallà, salt cod
bledes, Swiss chard
bolets, mushrooms
botifarra, pork sausage
bou, beef
bullit, boiled
cabrit, kid
caça, game
calamar, squid
calçotada, grilled green onions with spicy sauce
canalons, cannalloni
cargols, snails
carn, meat
castanya, chestnut
ceba, onion
cervell, brains
cervesa, beer
cérvol, venison
cigales, crayfish
cigrons, chickpeas
ciureny, cepes

cogombre, cucumber
col, cabbage
colom, pigeon
conill, rabbit
costella, cutlet
cranc de mar, crab
crema catalana, vanilla custard with caramelised crust
escalivada, peeled and roasted aubergines, peppers and onions, usually served as a salad
escudella de payes, bean and cabbage stew
escudella i carn d'olla, meat and vegetable stew, the broth of which is served as a first course
esqueixada, shredded salt cod served cold with dressing
faisa, pheasant
faves, broad beans
fideus, noodels
formatge, cheese
galldindi, turkey
gelat, ice cream
llagost, lobster
llagosti, large prawn
llegum, legume
llenguado, sole
llenties, lentils
llimona, lemon
llimonada, lemonade
llobarro, sea bass
llobina, haddock
lluc, hake
mariscos, shellfish
mongetes, white beans
muscó, mussel
nata, whipped cream
oca, goose
oli, oil
orada, gilt-head
ostra, oyster
pa, bread
pao, duck
peix, fish
petxina, clam
pintada, guinea-fowl
pinyol, pinenut
poll, chicken
postres, dessert
rap, monkfish
refresc, soft drink
remolatxa, beetroot
samfaina, a type of ratatouille (see p32)
sarsuelam or *zarzuela*, mixed seafood (see p 33)
suquet, seafood stew
te, tea
tomàquet, tomatoes
truita, trout

vedella, veal
verduras, vegetables
vi, wine
vi blanc, white wine
vi dolc, sweet wine
vi negre, red wine
vi rosat, rosée wine
xai, lamb
xocolata, chocolate

Bars and Restaurants

Not only does Catalonia have its own distinctive cuisine, but also eating and drinking habits that are very different from those of the rest of the peninsula. The most immediately apparent difference is in the eating hours, which are much earlier than in other parts of Spain, and comparable to those of Europe generally. Furthermore the Spanish love of *tapas* or bar snacks, often as a substitute for a meal, is not characteristic of Catalonia, where the tradition is to have two proper meals a day, at around 13.30 and 21.00; the anarchic approach towards food, which is typical above all of Andalusia, is not generally popular among the Catalans. Barcelona, being a city with such a large immigrant population, naturally offers a wider range of eating and drinking possibilities than some of the smaller Catalan towns, and those who wish to follow the Spanish tradition of *salir de tapas* (go out on a 'tapa-bar' crawl) will have no difficulties in finding the appropriate places, the largest concentration of such bars being around the Carrer de la Mercè. But, eating out in Barcelona means essentially going to a restaurant, and the city's prosperity since the 19C has ensured that this is one of the great restaurant centres of Spain, with the whole range of international and regional Spanish cuisine represented. The earliest of the grand Barcelona restaurants were establishments of wholly French leanings, and carried such pretentious names as 'Le Grand Restaurant de France', 'Chez Martin' or 'La Maison Dorée'. Only in comparatively recent times have the more important restaurants discovered the virtues of Catalonia's own cuisine, and overcome to a certain extent their bias towards French food. Even so a French-style elegance characterises the decoration of even some of the more moderately priced of Barcelona's restaurants, and you will rarely find here the homely wooden beam interiors so typical of Castile. Smart fashionable surroundings tend to be regarded here as having the same importance as the actual food, and in recent years Barcelona's restaurants have been struck by the city's all-consuming obsession with 'Design', an obsession which has a particular relevance to the story of the city's bars.

The bars and nightlife of Barcelona have become as integral to the romantic tourist image of the city as have the buildings of Gaudí. The nightlife here is in fact not as exciting as is sometimes thought, and is distinctly more sedate than that of Madrid or other Spanish towns, owing to the earlier hours of this city, and the exceptionally organised way in which the city's inhabitants tend to arrange their lives. The bars themselves, however, have a quality which is is very special to Barcelona and deserve to form part of any cultural tour of the city. The unusual ones can be divided into two radically opposed categories, one of which will appeal to those with both a romantic fascination with the squalour of port life, and a yearning for the Barcelona of old. Founded mainly in the early years of the century, these bars have often retained the rococo mirroring, gilt panelling and marble tables that were characteristic of the restaurants of this period, the main inspiration in this case being the bars of Marseilles' harbour. Their situation in the red-light district which extends on either side of La Rambla has resulted in a particular type of clientele comprising prostitutes, drug-addicts, criminals, budding writers and, increasingly, foreigners searching for the 'real Barcelona'. Jean Genet was one of the many writers enamoured of the nightlife of the notorious Barri Xinès, as was Juan Goytisolo, who as a young man from a cultured middle-class background was struck down by *l'amour de boue* (literally the love of mud). The main place of pilgrimage today for those seeking out the squalid, old-fashioned bar is the *Bar Marsella*, which is possibly one of the few surviving places in Europe where you can openly drink absinthe.

Those interested in the Barcelona of today, the city of fashion and *yuppís*, will have to visit instead the so-called 'Designer-Bars', a type of bar which originated in Barcelona and is more prevalent here than in any other Spanish city. These are for the most part bars *'de copas'*, places that cater for the Spanish love of following an evening meal with a *copa* or strong drink, which usually takes the form of a whisky, a gin and tonic or a rum and coca-cola. Despite the generally loud music, and discotheque element of many of these places, these bars attract a wide clientele, and are by no means restricted to the young, smart and beautiful; none the less they exude all the wealth and obsession with fashion characteristic of present-day Barcelona. Whatever your taste in bars, the designer-bars are of indisputable architectural interest, representing as they do some of Barcelona's most important and entertaining developments in interior design in recent years. The phenomenon of the designer-bar—whereby the character of an establishment is dictated largely by its avant-garde design—had its origins in Barcelona in the late 1970s, one of the pioneering early bars of this type being *Zig-Zag*, which was designed by Alicia Nuñez and and Guillem Bonet in 1980. This same team was responsible five years later for the creation in 1985 of *Otto Zutz*, one of the first of the designer-bars to achieve a truly widespread popularity. This, and contemporary bars such as *Sí Sí Sí* and *Universal,* were characterised by the sparsity of their design, the latter having the character of some futuristic prison. A new phase in bar design was initiated in 1986 by Eduardo Samsó's *Nick Havanna*, which went in for extravagant, varied and humorous effects, effects that were pursued to an even greater degree in the near contemporary *Velvet* and *Network*, which were inspired respectively by the films *Blue Velvet* and *Blade Runner*. Both bars were the work of Alfredo Arribas who, together with the designer Mariscal, went on to create the two leading designer-bars of the moment, *Gambrinus* and *Torres de Ávila*. A feature of all the designer-bars since the time of *Network*, has been the importance given to the washrooms, which have been turned into such strange and luxurious places that they attract large crowds of admirers, and consolidate the popularity of a particular bar: not even as you go about your ablutions in Barcelona can you escape from the notion of design. The absurdity of the whole phenomenon of the designer-bar was admirably expressed in Eduardo Mendoza's witty and satirical novel, *No News of Gurb* (1990), which is set in a Barcelona of the near future, and deals with an extra-terrestial's search for the elusive and similarly extra-terrestial Gurb. The search takes the protagonist through all of the city's fashionable bars, and details are given of whether or not a place has received, or was a finalist for, the prestigious award for design presented by the Federacion de Architectos y Diseñadores (FAD). Eventually, at 04.21, after a succession of designer-bars which has included a bar in Poble Nou which has won the 'FAD award for the renovation of urban spaces', the protagonist throws up in the Plaça Urquinaona, and then in the Plaça de Catalonia, and again on the pedestrian crossing at the corner of Muntaner and Aragón, and finally in the taxi which takes him home after his nocturnal ordeal through a designer hell.

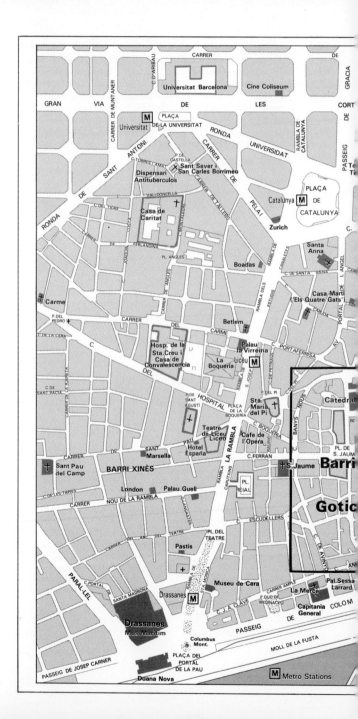

M Metro Stations

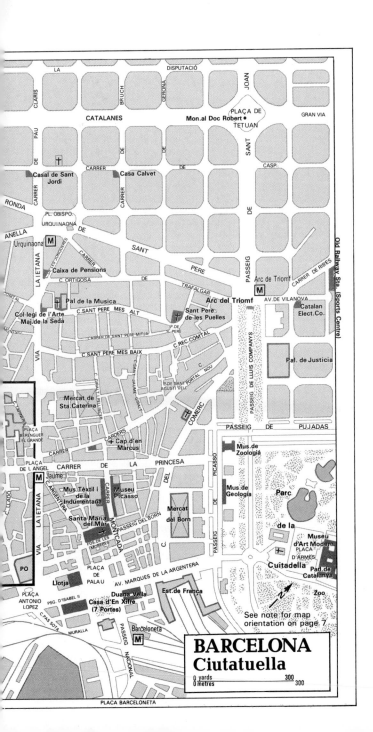

BARCELONA
Ciutatuella

0 yards   300
0 metres   300

1   Ciutat Vella (Old Town)

A.   La Rambla

Almost immediately on arriving at Barcelona, visitors will find themselves being drawn into **LA RAMBLA**, the main artery of the old town, and one of the most famous thoroughfares in the world. Though compressed between a picturesque variety of buildings, it derives its essential character from its central pedestrian area, which is shaded by rows of plane trees, and crowded by kiosks, stalls, buskers and a fascinating cross-section of the city's motley population. Its upper end serves as a funnel into which are sucked the crowds from the vast Plaça de Catalunya (see p. 124), eventually depositing those who survive its whole course, about 1.5km further down, near the entrance to the old port. In the last stages of its gradual descent, the crowds thin out, and the overall character of La Rambla becomes decidedly seedier, so that this same thoroughfare which attracts the grander elements of Barcelona society ends by disgorging a sinister assortment of drunks, drug-addicts and other social outcasts. So much unfolds in the course of La Rambla's journey towards the sea that writers such as Manuel Vázquez Montalbán have been tempted to see in this thoroughfare 'a metaphor of Life', the sea being the oblivion where all destinies are united.

The origins of La Rambla are in a seasonal torrent which was used as a road in the dry season; the actual name is from the Arabic word *raml*, which means sand. The torrent, converted after 1366 into a covered sewer, lay some distance to the west of the walls that contained the Roman settlement of Barcino. However, with the extension of Barcelona during the reign of the 13C ruler Jaume I, the torrent was lined with walls on its eastern side, and came to represent the western boundary of the city. These walls were to remain intact right up to the beginning of the 18C, despite the construction in the 14C of a new line of walls to the west, embracing the district known as the Raval. Beginning with the building in 1553 of a Jesuit monastery, a large number of monastic institutions grew up on the western side of La Rambla, directly facing the 13C walls. The first stage in the demolition of these walls was undertaken in 1704, after which La Rambla was slowly transformed into a proper street, acquiring palaces and a central row of trees. By 1781, when the earliest street lamps were put up, the thoroughfare had become a popular promenade, complete with seats for hire. The fame of La Rambla spread widely, and by 1845 the French writer Théophile Gautier was describing the place as one of the city's main attractions. George Sand, accompanied by Chopin, came here in 1838, and—as with so many later visitors to the city—was fascinated by the life on La Rambla. 'Isolated from the rest of Spain by banditry and civil war,' she wrote, 'the brilliant youth (of the city) stroll under the sun along La Rambla, a long avenue lined by trees and buildings, just like our boulevards. The women, beautiful, graceful and coquettish, are concerned by the arrangement of their mantilla shawls, and by the play of their fans; the men, occupied with their cigars, are smiling, speaking, casting oblique looks at the ladies, talking about Italian operas, and giving the impression of being largely uninterested in anything that happens outside the city'.

In terms of its future look and character, the most significant development to have taken place in La Rambla in the 19C resulted from the suppression in 1835 of Spain's monastic institutions, the closure of which was to lead here to the creation of squares, tall residential blocks and such important buildings as the Teatre Liceu, Spain's most impressive opera house. Another development occurred with the popularisation of cast iron after 1860, and the subsequent construction in the middle of the promenade of flower stalls, urinals, newspaper kiosks and other such structures that form today such a major component of La Rambla.

Various other Catalan cities such as Girona attempted to emulate La Rambla, though no other city in Spain, and particularly not Madrid, can boast a promenade which offers to the stroller so great a variety of diversions, from bird cages to fortune-tellers. Writers on Barcelona have usually devoted a great deal of space to the listing of these diversions, foreigners loving in particular to point out the wealth of books and foreign newspapers to be bought at the kiosks, believing this to be indicative of the traditional cosmopolitanism and cultural sophistication of the Catalans. Tourists tend also to assume that the human spectacle to be observed here is a virtual 24-hour affair, though in fact life on La Rambla is relatively quiet after about one o'clock in the morning, a time when the streets of other Spanish cities are experiencing their greatest nocturnal animation.

La Rambla is often referred to as Las Ramblas, and indeed is broken down unofficially into five distinct sections, the northernmost of which is LA RAMBLA DE CANALETES. The ancient spring of 'Les Canaletes', which gave rise to the saying 'to drink the waters of Canaletes' (meaning to live in Barcelona), survives in the form of a cast-iron fountain of the turn of the century, the waters of which are traditionally drunk by foreigners who hope to return to the city. The surrounding late 19C and early 20C buildings include at No. 129 an elegantly stuccoed structure of c 1850, housing on its ground floor the 'Musical Emporium', which has a fine glass portal of 1917, engraved with a Moderniste design. There are various bars and cafés here, none of which is as large as the cavernous *Zurich*, which stands on the south-eastern corner of the Plaça de Catalunya, directly facing the entrance to La Rambla. Originally the bar of a railway station, *Zurich* was founded in 1920 by a Catalan who had lived in Switzerland. The establishment was at one time popular with writers, and in its heyday international chess championships were held here, some of the contestants even taking part by telephone from Latin America; today the place is mainly frequented by young, leather-jacketed foreigners, who sit at the outside tables, contemplating La Rambla as if from a balcony. Among the older drinking establishments on La Rambla de Caneletes itself were the *Baviera* (at No. 127) and the *Caneletas* (at No. 135), which have been turned respectively into the *Cervecería* and *Burger King*; despite brash modern conversion, these two places of 1920s origin have retained elements of their original decoration, including in the case of the latter, a colonnade supporting a gilded upper gallery. Rather more sophisticated is *Boadas*, on the corner of La Rambla with the Carrer dels Tallers; founded in 1933, though recently reformed, this is one of the city's better known cocktail bars, much favoured by those returning from the Teatre Liceu, and renowned in particular for its daquiris.

On the other side of La Rambla is the entrance to the CARRER DE LA CANUDA, where, at No. 6, you will find the palace built in 1796 for Josep Francesc Ferrer de Llupià, baron of Sabassona. This austere neo-classical building, which has retained inside several of its ceiling paintings by the leading late 18C painter Francesc Pla ('el Vigatà'), was extended and remodelled in 1907 after becoming the seat of the important cultural institution known as the *Ateneu Barcelonès*. Founded in 1836 as the 'Ateneu Català', this institution played a central role in the history of the Catalan revival, acquiring especial notoriety after an inaugural speech given provocatively in Catalan by Àngel Guimerà in 1895. The painter Antoni Tàpies, in his autobiography, *Memòria Personal* (1977), recalls how as a young boy he saw little of his father, who spent much of his time attending meetings and discussions at the Ateneu. His family home at the time was at 39 Carrer de la Canuda, where Tàpies was born on 13 December 1923.

Returning to La Rambla and continuing to head south you will enter the RAMBLA DELS ESTUDIS, so-called because of the University building which once blocked off its northern end. The University, founded by Martí I in 1402, was closed down by Philip V at the beginning of the 18C, following a history of anti-Castillian activity, including having supported the Revolt of the Reapers in 1647. The actual building—the first stone of which had been laid by Charles V in 1536—was turned into a military barracks, but this was demolished in 1843. In the absence of the University a more appropriate name for this stretch of La Rambla is the popular one of 'La Rambla dels Ocells' ('of the birds'), a reference both to the numerous sparrows that haunt the plane trees, and to the bird market which is always held here. This market, with its rows of cages containing a wide variety of exotic birds, fascinated the young Picasso who, newly arrived in the city, was regularly brought here by his father.

Bird market in La Rambla dels Estudis

Most of the Rambla dels Estudis is now taken over by turn-of-the-century buildings, many of them housing hotels, and the inevitable bars and cafés. One of these cafés, the *Café Moka* (at No. 26), though radically modernised, is the same establishment mentioned by George Orwell in *Homage to Catalonia* as the scene of a shoot-out involving the various rival groups comprising the Republican forces, such as the anarchists, the communists, POUM and the guards of the *Generalitat*. The western side of the street is dominated by the former Hotel Manila, which was dramatically remodelled in 1988 and transformed into the luxurious and fashionable *Hotel Ramada Renaissance*; a favourite place for the rich and famous, its guests have included Bruce Springsteen and Michael Jackson, as well as many of the stars who have appeared at the nearby Liceu such as Pavarotti and Plácido Domingo. Formerly the whole western side of the Rambla dels Estudis was taken over by a Jesuit College and Convent, but these institutions were destroyed shortly after the expulsion of the Jesuits from Spain in 1767. All that remains of this vast complex is the former Jesuit *Església de Betlem (Church of Bethlehem), at the corner of La Rambla and the Carrer del Carme.

Dating back to 1553, the church was burnt down in 1671 and rebuilt after 1680 to a plan attributed to Josep Juli; the construction work, supervised at first by the Jesuit priests Tort and Diego de Lacarre, was completed by 1732. The building, which combines a simple plan with exuberant decorative touches, is of interest today above all for its well preserved exterior. Its long side façade, overlooking La Rambla, has a heavy, austere character, relieved only by two elaborate portals sculpted by Francesc Santacruz with representations of John the Baptist and the child Jesus. The magnificent main façade, on the CARRER DEL CARME, was completed in 1690, and is crowned by an undulating pediment adorned with finials. Its richly modelled frontispiece comprises a main portal flanked both by Solomonic columns (a characteristic feature of the Catalan baroque) and by dynamic statues of Sant Ignacio and Sant Francisco de Borja, attributed to Andreu Sala. Above the portal is a relief of the Nativity by Francesc Santacruz, who was also responsible for the statue of Sant Francis Xavier to be found in the elaborate corner niche on the side of the façade bordering with the CARRER DEL XUCLÁ. The dark, single-aisled interior was once the most sumptuously decorated of all of Barcelona's churches, with marble marquetry and a wealth of gilded and polychromed fittings, including—in the gallery—lattice-work screens that marked the area of the church reserved for the aristocracy; none of this remains, the building having been gutted during the Civil War.

On the other side of La Rambla to the church is the elegant *Palau Moja (at No. 118), a classical French-inspired structure built in 1774–89 to the designs of Josep Mas i d'Ordal; the exterior had neo-classical painted decorations by by Josep Flaugier and Francesc Pla, but these were destroyed in a recent series of mysterious fires. At the end of the 19C the building came into the hands of the Marquis of Comillas, whose guests here included Alfonso XII and the poet Jacint Verdaguer; while under the Marquis's patronage, Verdaguer wrote his celebrated epic, *Atlàntida*, which shows how Columbus' discovery of America restored the cosmic order upset by the disappearance of Atlantis. The building has now been extensively restored and adapted for use by the Cultural Department of the Generalitat de Catalunya, but has retained inside a number of Pla's original fresco decorations, most notably the splendid cycle of allegories and mythological scenes that cover the walls and ceiling of the two-storeyed *Grand Salon. The main entrance to the building is on the attractive pedestrian street of the CARRER DE LA PORTAFERRISSA, which leads towards the Cathedral (see p. 60), and features a number of tall and dignified 18C and early 19C palaces. Today, the shops here are given over mainly to clothes, but early this century included one of the most influential of Barcelona's private art galleries. Known as the Dalmau Gallery, it was run by Josep Dalmau, whom Miró once described as 'a sort of genial fool who managed to exploit artists and look after them at the same time'. A favourite meeting-place for artists and critics, the gallery introduced Barcelona to some of the leading figures of the French and foreign avant-garde; of particular importance was an exhibition of Cubist art, held here between 20 April and 10 May 1912.

South of the Carreres del Carme and de la Portaferrissa begins the most beautiful stretch of La Rambla, a stretch known sometimes as 'de Sant

Josep' but more usually as 'de les Flors' ('of the flowers'). Markets have been held here since the 13C, but with the construction of the market of Sant Josep in 1836 (see below), most of the stalls were cleared from the street, leaving only the young women who sold flowers.

The flower stalls, which share the street today with kiosks selling books and news-papers, provide La Rambla with a constant colourful spectacle which, to many of the city's visitors and inhabitants, has represented the essence of Barcelona's beauty. 'A week without seeing the Rambla of the Flowers', sighed the writer Eugenio d'Ors, prevented once by a strike from coming here. The attraction of the area lay as much with the women who sold the flowers as with the flowers themselves, as is suggested by the silly lyrics of a popular Barcelona song of the 1940s: 'How lovely is Bar-celona,/pearl of the Mediterranean,/how lovely it is to stroll,/and watch the women,/on the Rambla de las Flores'. The painter Ramon Casas was one of the many to have fallen in love with one of the street's legendary 'flower girls', the girl in question becoming first his favourite model and later his wife. The English travel-writer H.V. Morton—who claimed that a summer evening spent on La Rambla was one of the highpoints of a tour he made of Spain in 1954—was also delighted by these women, and was prompted to reflect on how much London had been impoverished when it had cleared its own flower girls from Piccadilly Circus at the end of the 19C.

On the eastern side of the RAMBLA DE LES FLORS is a fine group of 18C houses at Nos 114, 112 and 110, the latter containing traces of sgraffito decoration. Opposite them, at No. 105, is the grandest palace on the whole Rambla, the **Palau de la Virreina**.

The palace was built in 1772–78 as a retirement home for Manuel Amat i Junyet, who had made a fortune while viceroy of Peru, where he had achieved notoriety for an affair with an actress called Perricholi. He died shortly after moving into the palace, for which reason the place is known after his young widow, who had originally been betrothed to his nephew. The story goes that the former Viceroy, seeing this woman dressed up for her intended wedding to the nephew, said to her that he would have married her himself if he had not been so old; to this she is said to have replied that the walls and cloisters of the convent where she had been staying were older still and very much to her taste.

Manuel Amat i Junyet had a great knowledge of architecture, and it seems likely that he had a hand in the design of his palace, which was carried out under the supervision of the architect Josep Ausich i Mir and the sculptor Carles Grau. The powerful main façade, set back slightly from the street, comprises a rusticated basement supporting an upper level articulated by giant pilasters, the whole crowned by a parapet with finials; lacking the classical French elegance of the nearby Palau Moja (see above), it has a characteristically Spanish top-heaviness, with elaborate detailing set against otherwise austere expanses of heavy masonry. Behind the entrance vestibule you come to a patio impressively decorated with Corinthian columns and military trophies; a double-ramp staircase, with exquisite ironwork railings, leads to a series of rooms containing fragments of the original decoration, including painted rococo allegories in the former dining-room. Appropriated at one time by the Museum of Decorative Arts and the Cambó Collection, the place is now used for temporary art exhibi-tions; an excellent modern bookshop off the vestibule sells numerous art books and other publications issued by Barcelona's enterprising Town Hall.

Immediately below the palace was the convent of Sant Josep, the demoli-tion of which in 1836 led to the creation by Francesc Daniel Molina of an arcaded market square inspired by the work of John Nash. The arcades remain but have been almost entirely hidden by an exuberant ironwork structure of c 1870 covering one of Barcelona's largest and most animated markets, *La Boquería*. A good way to appreciate the bustling life of this place is to have a drink at the bar of the tiny kiosk inside known as *Pinocho*, a favourite place of the designer Mariscal. This bar is also mentioned in Raul Nuñez's comic novel *Sinatra* (1984; translated into English as *The Lonely Hearts Club*), which is set around La Rambla: 'It was just a little bar, with three or four stools, set into one wall of the market. It was enjoyable sitting there, drinking something and letting luck take care of the rest'.

Continuing down La Rambla, you will reach almost immediately, at No. 83 (at the corner of the Carrer de Petxina) an early 19C building housing on the ground floor a Moderniste shop of jewel-like beauty. Known as the *Antiga Casa Figueres*, this shop dates back to 1820, but owes its present appearance to a remodelling carried out in 1902 to a design by Antoni Ros Güell. Güell, who worked mainly as a landscape painter and stage designer, assembled a remarkably varied team of artists and craftsmen to carry out the decoration of this shop, which features metalwork by Vila i Domènech, mosaics by Merogliano, paintings by Boix, sculptures by Lambert Escaler and Bernadors and stained-glass windows by Granell Rigalt, the latter giving to the interior a magical, multi-coloured glow; dominating the exterior is a corner frieze by Escaler representing an allegory of a wheat harvest. The shop has recently been restored following its transformation into a high-class confectioners. Further down the street, at No. 77, is a fantastical Gothic structure of 1911, built originally as a pharmacy, the entrance to which was under a large Gothic arch with a keystone portraying the attributes of Esculapius.

Just along from here is the main focal point of La Rambla, the PLAÇA DE LA BOQUERÍA, which marks the site of the medieval gate of Santa Eulàlia. In medieval times this gate was a favourite meeting-place for countryfolk and other visitors to the city, who attracted in their wake jugglers and professional gamesters; the bodies of executed criminals were also hung here as a warning to those among the city's newcomers who were contemplating crime themselves. Today the numerous tourists who gather here gape instead at the pavement decoration by Joan Miró, who was born in the nearby Passatge del Crèdit (see p. 73). Another landmark of the present-day square is the recently restored *Casa Bruno Quadros, on its eastern side, at No. 82 La Rambla. Now occupied by a bank, this former shop was decorated in 1883–85 in a neo-oriental style, complete with a famous Chinese dragon which supports both a lantern and an umbrella.

Immediately below the Plaça de la Boquería begins the RAMBLA DE LOS CAPUTXINS, where strollers are concentrated not simply in the central area, but also in the now broad pavements on either side of the thoroughfare, where you will find various open-air bars and cafés. The first building to your right, despite its deceptively modest façade, is one of the most important of Barcelona's institutions, the **Teatre de Liceu**.

In 1844 the Barcelona operatic society with the tortuous name of 'Liceo Filarmónico Dramático Barcelonés de S.M. la Reina Doña Isabel II', applied for permission to build a theatre on the site of a Trinitarian convent which had been dissolved in 1835. Superstitious misgivings about building a place of entertainment on the site of a holy institution were voiced at the time, and were to be vindicated in the light of the building's subsequent troubled history. Work on the theatre was none the less begun the following year, the architect chosen, Miquel Garriga i Roca, basing his designs on La Scala in Milan, which it was almost to equal in size, becoming the second largest opera house in Europe, with a seating capacity of 4000. The building, inaugurated in 1847, was almost entirely destroyed by fire in 1861, but was rebuilt in the space of one year by Garriga's former collaborator, Oriol Mestres. There were to be several remodellings in later years, most notably by Pere Falqués, who in 1884 provided the theatre with its present neo-baroque seating. After 1882 the place became one of the main centres in Europe for the production of Wagner's operas, the Barcelona public being among this composer's greatest enthusiasts. The most notorious event in the theatre's history, however, occurred in 1893, and superseded in dramatic power anything which has been officially put on here.

In September of that year the anarchist Paulino Pallás, on the point of being shot for his failed assassination attempt on the Captain General of Cataluña, Martínez Campos, swore that his death would soon be avenged by his anarchist colleagues. That revenge came one month later, on 7 October, and was directed at the Teatre Liceu, a symbol of bourgeois decadence. Half-way through the second act of Rossini's *William Tell*, the anarchist Santiago Salvador threw two bombs from the fifth-floor balcony of the theatre. The number 13 proved for once to be unlucky, for the bombs landed on the 13th row of the stalls, killing 20 people outright and wounding at least 50 others. Only one of the bombs had actually gone off, the other having been prevented from doing so by landing in the lap of a dead woman: it is now one of the more macabre exhibits in Barcelona's Museu d'Història de la Ciutat. Salvador was not caught until several weeks later, by which time most anarchists had distanced themselves from him, refusing to provide this obvious psychopath with any more bombs. When in prison awaiting execution he told the journalist Tomás Caballé y Clos how 'magnificent' the whole occasion had been in the theatre, and how much satisfaction he had received from witnessing the panic and confusion among the bourgeoisie; he also boasted of his enormous strength, for it had been no mean feat to throw a bomb as far as the 13th row. On 21 November 1893, a large crowd came to see him being garotted in the courtyard of the old prison on the Carrer d'Amalia. Excited by this audience, he shouted 'Long live anarchism!', and had begun singing an anarchist song while the metal around his neck tightened and silenced his voice for ever.

The Teatre Liceu, with its associations with wealth and the establishment, has continued to provoke the wrath of left-wing fanatics, and in 1977, shortly after the death of Franco, a group of militants stood outside the doors of the theatre to taunt and jeer at the well-dressed members of the public; as Vázquez Montalbán pointed out, these same people were unaware that one of the leading trade unionists of this time, José Luis López Bulla, was himself a fanatic of the opera, knowing several works completely by heart, and believing, like Trotsky, that opera is the heritage not just of the middle classes but of humanity in general.

Needless to say, as with so many of Barcelona's cultural institutions, the Liceu is at present being completely overhauled in preparation for 1992, and a large modern extension is being built to house new service areas. The architect in charge is Ignasi de Solà- Morales.

Oriol Mestrès' fussy, classical-style entrance façade of the Liceu is a singularly undramatic work, scarcely enhanced by the addition in 1898 of a glass and ironwork canopy by Salvador Viñals. Nothing will prepare you for the shock of entering the superb auditorium, with its spectacular oval sweep, its tiered design of gilded neo-baroque balconies, and its enormous panelled ceiling with representations of scenes from works by Aristophanes, Shakespeare, Schiller and Lope de Vega. The adjoining halls feature sumptuous illusionistic and Pompeian decorations, but particularly impressive are the Moderniste paintings carried out by Alexandre de Riquer and Ramon Casas in the rooms belonging to the private club known as the Cercle del Liceu.

Across La Rambla from the Liceu is the *Cafè de l'Òpera*, an establishment founded in 1929 and one of the few places from this period to have remained unchanged in its decoration. Its small and constantly packed interior is panelled, mirrored, gilded and decorated with cheerful linear designs in a pseudo-classical style. Built initially to serve the Liceu, and still experiencing a great rush of clients during the intervals at that theatre, the place later developed a slightly Bohemian character and came to be filled in the 1970s with many of the more disreputable-looking types from the nearby Barri Xinès (see p. 92). Today the café is particularly popular with foreign tourists with a nostalgia for traditional café life. Another survival of old Barcelona is the *Hotel Oriente*, which is situated just below the Liceu, at Nos 45–47. The *Hotel*, with its elegant pale yellow façade, and ground-floor Ionic arcade, was opened in 1845 on the site of the 17C Franciscan College of St. Bonaventura; one of those who stayed here during its heyday was Hans Christian Andersen. The public spaces of the hotel, with their gilded columns and grand 19C character, include obvious remodellings of the cloister and refectory of Pere Serra i Bosch's Franciscan College of 1652. Adjoining the hotel, at No. 43, is the former theological *College of Sant Angelo, dating back to 1593 and rebuilt in 1786–90; occupied until 1985 by the Guardia Civil, the building retains its elegantly simple cloister and single-aisled neo-classical chapel.

Facing the *Hotel Oriente* are three arches marking the entrance to the **PLAÇA REIAL**, a large traffic-free square built on the site of the Capuchin monastery after which this stretch of La Rambla is known. Designed in 1848 by Francesc Daniel Molina, its architecture was inspired by the formal public squares of Napoleonic France. The arcading which surrounds the whole square supports an elegant stucco frontage articulated by a giant order of pilasters, the tall attic level above being crowned by a white balustrade. Tall palm trees, placed at regular intervals in the stone pavement, give the square a certain look of Nice, and the French character of the place is reinforced by the central Fountain of the Three Graces, which is a standard late 19C model provided by the Parisian firm of Duresne. Unmistakably Catalan, however, are the splendid Moderniste lamp posts on either side of the fountain: designed by Gaudí in 1878, they are this architect's first known works.

Benches and numerous café tables make the square a popular place for tourists, though its appeal is less widespread among the inhabitants of Barcelona, who largely come here either to sit outside at the cafés on summer nights or else to attend the regular Sunday stamp market held under the square's arcades. From the late 1960s onwards, the square came to attract hippies and other Bohemians, and it was here, during the period of the avant-garde comic magazine Rollo Enmascarado (the early 1970s), that the designer Mariscal and the painter Miquel Barceló shared a house. Tramps, alcoholics and drug-addicts, rollicking on the benches in the square's centre followed suit, and, despite the recent restoration of the place and the constant presence of tourists, continue to give the square today a tense and seedy character. Traditionally the Plaça Reial had been the haunt of boot-blacks, who until comparatively recently had a group of stands under the square's northern arcade. Boot-blacks had been working here from the 1840s onwards, the earliest and most famous one being Fructuòs Canonge, one of the more popular Barcelona personalities during the reign of Isabel II. As well as cleaning shoes, Canonge was an organiser of carnival festivities and a magician with such a reputation for supernatural powers that he came to be known as the 'Spanish Merlin'. Though the Plaça Reial no longer has its Canonge, a strong magical aura pertains to the so-called *Museu Pedagógico de Ciencias Naturales, a bizarre shop and taxidermist establishment situated at No. 8, on the square's eastern side.

This unusual 'Natural History Museum' was founded in 1889 by Lluis i Pujol, a man who began his career studying for the church, but later devoted himself to taxidermy and natural history. He gave his shop—originally situated on the Carrer de Rauric—the title of 'museum' to emphasise his strong scientific interests. These interests led him to publish in 1921 his *Manual of Taxidermy*, the first Spanish treatise on the subject, and a work which can still be bought in the shop. Such was the success of his establishment that he was soon able to transfer its premises to the Plaça Reial, then a much more fashionable address than it is today; installed at first at No. 10, it has been at No. 8 since 1926. A number of celebrities have been fascinated by this place, one of them being the painter Joan Miró, who also had a great love for the Plaça Reial itself, claiming to have been influenced in his work by the shapes created both by the water splashing from the Fountain of the Three Graces, and by the branches of the palm trees. He regularly visited the shop during the many years that he lived at the nearby Pasatge del Crèdit, but, being a very shy person, never asked for anything, and merely contented himself by staring at the exotic show cases. Salvador Dalí, in contrast, had no such inhibitions and, shortly after the Civil War, went into the shop to demand 200,000 ants. From then onwards Dalí used to pay at least two visits a year here, making several other exotic requests from its owners, who stuffed for him a lion, a tiger, and even a large rhinoceros. Dalí insisted that the rhinoceros should be carried out on wheels into the Plaça Reial so that he could have himself photographed seated on top of it. On another occasion Dalí asked the shop-owners to make him a walking stick with a handle incorporating two live snakes, but as this proved impossible, he had to allow two stuffed snakes to be used instead.

Another client was Ava Gardner, who came here once with the bull-fighter Mario Cabré and requested the owners to stuff the head of a bull which he had dedicated to her in a fight.

The shop, which is run today by the grandchildren of its founder, has recently undergone a face lift, but still retains a musty old-fashioned character; its interior is packed with natural curiosities, the most macabre of which are the rather battered-looking stuffed birds, gorillas and other animals that fill the attractive old display cases. Taxidermy is still carried out in an upstairs studio, the most requested animal for stuffing apparently being foxes. However, in the more ecologically-minded climate of today, the fashion for taxidermy is no longer what it used to be, and the shop is now forced to make a living largely by the selling of rare minerals and sea shells; the owners plan to use the basement for scientific exhibitions and lectures.

Before returning to La Rambla, you should proceed to the north-eastern corner of the square, off which leads the tiny dark alley known as the Carrer del Vidre. Here, at No. 1, you will find a fascinating survival from the mid 19C, a herbalist known officially as the *Antigua Herboristería Ballart*. Its tiny shopfront comprises panes of glass set in a neo-classical framework but with Gothic detailing; the grubby and virtually unchanged interior was originally painted a clear blue, but has acquired over the years a mildewy green hue. Presiding over the mysteriously lit interior is a marble fountain crowned by a bust of the naturalist Linnaeus, whose features have frequently been mistaken for those of Charles III, thus giving rise to the shop's popular name of 'L'Herbolario del Rei'.

Back on La Rambla you will find immediately to your right the entrance to the sombre and grimy CARRER NOU DE LA RAMBLA, which leads into a part of Barcelona traditionally famed for drugs and prostitutes. The latter district will be explored more fully in Rte 1D, but for the moment you should make a short detour up the street if only to see, at Nos 3–5, the superlative **PALAU GÜELL**, one of the most important of Gaudí's earlier works, and the only one of his Barcelona houses with an interior open to the public.

Built in 1885–89 as the extension of the Rambla town house of the industrialist Eusebi Güell, the Palau Güell coincided in its construction with the intense and exciting years of architectural activity leading up to the Barcelona World Fair of 1888. Eusebi Güell, whom Gaudí had first met in 1878, is reputed to have said that he liked the building less and less the more it went up, to which the architect replied that he himself liked it more and more; if this is true, then Güell was almost certainly being flippant, for he was to remain the most faithful of Gaudí's patrons. The family fortune had been initiated by Eusebi's father Joan Güell i Ferrer, who had spent his early years in Cuba. With the vast amount of money which he had made there, Joan was later able to establish his own business in Barcelona, and managed between 1836 and 1860 to revolutionise in turn the local textile and metallurgical industries; he later developed an interest in agriculture and was able to take advantage of the phylloxera epidemic in France to build up Catalan viticulture. The finances and social position of the family were further improved by Eusebi, who married the daughter of another self-made man (the future Marquis of Comillas), and acquired for himself the titles of count, viscount and baron. Eusebi, a major voice in Catalan politics, was also someone who exploited an interest in culture to further his aristocratic image. His palace on the Carrer Nou de la Rambla—which was joined by a gallery to the main family home on La Rambla itself—was intended not only as a guest annexe, but also as a place for social gatherings, private concerts and other cultural functions.

The Palau Güell, neglected even during Eusebi's lifetime in favour of the family's estate on the outskirts of Barcelona (see p. 142), was later to be donated to the city by Eusebi's descendants. During and after the Civil War the building served as a police barracks and prison, and in its basement numerous political prisoners and delinquents were detained and tortured. Since 1954 the palace has housed a *Centre of Theatre Studies, with a museum devoted to the history of the Catalan theatre. With its atmosphere which is at the same time sinister, mysterious and exotic, the palace provided in 1977 the perfect setting for one of the key scenes in Antonioni's atmospheric thriller, *The Passenger*: in this scene the protagonist, played by Jack Nicholson, first sets eyes on Marie Schneider, with whom he subsequently embarks on an affair which begins in glamour and ends sordidly, and enigmatically.

Occupying a dark and cramped site, the white stone façade of the palace, now a dirty grey, has a forbidding look, and the use of colour—such an important feature of Gaudí's later work—has been limited to the ceramic decoration on the picturesquely-shaped chimneys, which are virtually hidden from the street. The most exciting feature of the exterior are the two large entrance arches of parabolic shape, a geometrical form much loved by Gaudí, and one which clearly illustrated his expressive and highly personal interpretation of the Gothic style. Also of interest is the portal's elaborate and rather aggressive ironwork, in which the initials of Eusebi Güell can clearly be made out, as can a medieval-inspired heraldic motif which reinforces the fortress-like nature of the façade. The interior features a number of old posters, portraits and other theatrical mementoes belonging to the Museu de les Arts de l'Espectacle, but these are entirely subservient to the gloomy evocativeness of the setting.

From the moment you enter the darkened vestibule, you will find yourself in a world in which a suggestive use of light and space has taken over from rational, symmetrical planning, and the experience is in itself a highly theatrical one. A central ramp winds down to the bare brick basement, which was originally used for horses and carriages, but became for a short time after the Civil War a much feared place of detention: until quite recently there had survived a wall covered all over with graffiti scrawled by detainees of that period. The interconnected main-floor rooms, where the public life of the palace would take place, has dark wooden surfaces, Moorish-style screens, medieval-inspired coffering and exquisitely wrought ironwork highlighted in gilding. The central feature is a towering salon, surrounded by screened galleries, and extending up three floors to a dome pierced by holes as in a Moorish bath; around the lower level are some rather gloomy murals on the theme of Charity. The rooms above the main floor were used as bedrooms, while at the very top of the house are the unornamented servants' quarters.

Directly in front of the Palau Güell is the Eden Cinema (at No. 12), which in the early years of this century was the notorious night club known as the *Eden Concert*. Specialising in French-style cabaret, it acquired a reputation no more salubrious than that of the famous 19C *café-cantante* which it replaced, the Café de la Alegría. The Catalan writer Josep Maria de Sagarra recalled in his memoirs that the Eden Concert was the only place which you were banned from mentioning in polite society, and that if you wished to refer to someone of certain standing who had gone down in the world you need only to have said that 'he had been seen in the Eden' or was 'frequenting the Eden'. One of its habitués was Picasso who, on returning from Paris to Barcelona in January 1902, hired a studio next door (at No. 10), which he shared with the sculptor Àngel Fernández de Soto and the painter Ramon Rocarol; the seedy low-life of the surroundings were a great influence on the development of his Blue Period.

Those interested in the Bohemian Barcelona of old might like to visit two nearby bars before returning to La Rambla. One of these, at No. 34 Nou de la Rambla, is the tiny *Bar London*, with an unmodernised interior of 1910; favoured by young musicians during the Franco era, this place attracts today numerous ageing hippies and intellectuals, who mingle with a younger crowd made up largely of foreigners. The other bar, situated on the narrow lane immediately behind the Palau Güell (the Carrer de Lancaster), is the *Bodega Bohemia*, which in the 1960s and 1970s was especially popular with those working in the theatre, and was the scene of much alternative cabaret; it has the memorable slogan, *'Donde nacen los artistas'* ('where artists are born').

Continuing down La Rambla you will pass to your left (at No. 40), the *Hotel les Quatre Nacions*, which was built in 1849 and enjoyed the reputation for many years as the city's most important hotel. The building overlooks to the south the PLAÇA DEL TEATRE, where you will find to your right the Teatre Principal, which stands on a site of a wooden theatre dating back to 1579. The present uninspired classical structure is of the early 19C, and is used at present for rehearsals by the Liceu. The *Lyon d'Or*, an unremarkable snack-bar adjoining the theatre, has its origins in a famous café of c 1900 which in turn had replaced the *Café de les Delicies*, a favourite meeting-place for the Catalan intellectuals associated with the revival in 1859 of the poetry traditionally known as the Jocs Florals; members of this group included Víctor Balaguer, Bofarull and Francesc Camprodon. Below the theatre is the arc marking the entrance to the narrow and sordid CARRER DEL ARC DEL TEATRE, where you will find immediately to your right the modest bar kiosk called *Cazalla*, which was founded in 1900 by an Andalusian, and has become a well-known Rambla institution; immediately beyond this could be found until recently *La Japonesa*, a shop specialising in 'rubber goods' and treatments for venereal diseases. Facing the theatre on the other side of the square is a delightful monument of 1900 commemorating a man regarded as 'the founder of the Catalan theatre', Frederic Soler ('Serafí Pitarra'; 1839–95). Designed by the architect Pere Falqués Urpí, and sculpted by Agustí Querol Subirats, this work in marble and dark stone represents a wonderful compromise between a Moderniste and neo-baroque style: Pitarra is shown seated nonchalantly on top of a huge volute which rises up like a wave on the point of breaking.

The decrepit look of the last stretch of La Rambla is explained by the presence of red-light districts on either side of the thoroughfare; to the west lies the heart of the so-called 'Barri Xinès', while to the east extends a similarly notorious district which has yet to receive a nickname (see Rte 2). One of the streets through the latter district is the CARRER DELS ESCUDELLERS, the entrance to which is on the Plaça del Teatre. This is a dark and narrow street with a particularly unsalubrious reputation, but you will only need to walk a few metres down it to find—at No. 8—a magnificent

The Carrer dels Escudellers Blancs, one of the more infamous streets red-light district east of La Rambla (see also p. 74)

Moderniste bar of 1902, the unappealingly named *Grill Room*. Its founder was Flaminio Mezzalama, who created in that same year, and with the same designer—Ricard de Campmany—the celebrated *Café Torino*, one of the most fashionable Barcelona cafés of the turn of the century. The *Café Torino*, which was situated on the Passeig de Gràcia, no longer survives, but a good idea of its decoration can be had from the *Grill Room*, which has been virtually unchanged over the years: the exterior comprises a flamboyant frontage in wood and stained glass, while the interior has a painted panelled ceiling, metalwork lamps and a dazzling series of ceramic wall tiles.

The stretch of La Rambla which runs below the Plaça del Teatre is known as the Rambla de Santa Mònica, its decayed character of today belying its aristocratic past. Ironically, this was once the smartest section of the whole Rambla, and the first to be dignified with the name of 'paseo' or 'prome-nade'. In the 18C aristocrats used to parade here in their carriages, and this was also one of the most exclusive residential districts in the city. On the northern side of the street a number of 18C houses have survived, including at Nos 16, 14, 12 and 10, the last of these being one of the first buildings to have been put up following the initial stage in the demolition of the medieval defensive walls. By far the most impressive of the remaining 18C palaces here is the *Casa March de Reus (at No. 8), which was built in 1775–80 by Joan Soler i Faneca, and has an elegantly simple façade, with rustication in shallow relief and a frontispiece articulated by giant Ionic pilasters; acquired in 1892 by the Bank of Spain, the building belongs now to the *Generalitat*. Next to this, but entered from the Passatge de la Banca, is a stately building erected in 1867 as the headquarters of the Compañía General de Crédito al Comercio. It houses today the *Museu de Cera or Waxwork Museum, certainly the best in Spain and well worth a visit for the architecture alone, which retains much of its original character, complete with a striking grand staircase and a patio glazed with stained glass. The idea of a waxworks museum in Barcelona was initially that of Nicomedes Méndez, an executioner who had been responsible for the garotting of a number of famous anarchists and murderers, including Salvador Santiago of Liceu fame. Méndez, noting the enthusiastic audiences who had at-tended each of his executions, had originally planned to create a pavilion filled with wax representations of Barcelona's most notorious criminals. In the end he was not to receive authorisation for this, and the museum which was eventually created concentrated on foreign criminals, its directors preferring to show the people of Barcelona in a positive light. The present, recently revamped museum includes a combination of world-famous, Spanish and Catalan personalities, one of the most recent of whom is Mariscal's horrible Olympics mascot, 'Cobi'. Among the tableaux are the infirmary of a bull-ring, a typical Catalan rural interior, a gypsy cave and a room in the Liceu, the latter being enhanced by the recorded voices of the famous opera stars who have sung there. Of particular interest to children are the science fiction tableaux called 'Space Capsule' and 'War of the Galaxies', the inevitable Chamber of Horrors (with spiders' webs, bats and monsters), and the so-called 'Fiction Journey', which is advertised as a journey by 'underwater craft' to a 'Submarine tunnel' and 'Ship-wrecked Galleon'.

Situated in a tall turn-of-the-century building on the western side of the Rambla de Santa Mònica is the *Jazz-Colón*, a tacky discothèque which was an important and progressive centre of rock music in the 1960s and 1970s, when the place was frequented by students and intellectuals; originally the building had housed the studios of the photographer Antonio Napoleón Fernández, and it was here, in 1897, that Barcelona's first cinema was installed. Nearby, at No. 4 of the adjoining Santa Mònica, is the infamous *Pastís*, a small, dark and musty survival of the 1940s, when Franch-style bars were still the fashion; its evocative decoration of old bottles and pictures continues to acquire further layers of dust and grease, while the ever more creaking sounds of Edith Piaf, Maurice Chevalier and other French classics are still played on its gramophone. At the end of La Rambla is the oldest surviving structure on the whole thoroughfare, the former *Convent of Santa Mònica, of which only the severe cloister and church tower remain. Dating back to 1626, and founded by the Discalced Augustinians, this convent was taken over in the late 19C by the 'Circ Barcelonès', a theatre which hosted in 1870 Spain's first Workers' Congress; today the building is used for temporary exhibitions. Below the former convent the Rambla widens into the Plaça Portal de la Pau, which is dominated by its monument to Columbus (see pp. 95–96).

B. The Barri Gòtic

The surviving medieval quarter of Barcelona is enormously extensive, and the term Barri Gòtic or 'Gothic Quarter'—which was not coined until 1927—refers only to a small part of it enclosed within the boundaries of the Roman city. Roman *Barcino*, as with the Iberian settlement which preceded it, grew up on the gentle elevation known as Mons Táber, its highest point being marked by the Temple of Augustus, a few columns of which have survived behind the medieval cathedral. Up to the time of Jaume I (1213–76), Barcelona did not extend beyond the Roman city, an oval-shaped area bordered to the west by the present Carrers Banys Nous and Carrer d'Avinyó, and to the north by the surviving stretch of walls extending—with long interruptions—between the Plaça Nova and the Carrer Correu Vell. This has always been the administrative heart of Barcelona, and it also became in the Middle Ages very much of a showpiece, its streets lined with elegant palaces that reflected the great wealth which poured into the city from the 13C to 14C. Wandering today around what was formerly known as the Barri de la Catedral or de la Seu, you have sometimes the feeling of being less in a real city than in some medieval mock-up, the whole seeming almost too well preserved, with every corner of this dark but tidy maze of streets being prettified by noble and picturesque masonry.

An appropriate and convenient place for beginning a tour of the Barri Gòtic is the PLAÇA DE L'ÀNGEL, which stands on the site of the Roman city's northern gate, a short distance away from the principal remains of Roman Barcelona. The site, lapped probably by the sea in ancient times, became from at least the 10C onwards the scene of one of Barcelona's liveliest markets, specialising in cereal products after the 12C. Known at one time as the Plaça del Blat or 'Wheat Square', the place acquired its present name after one of the various legends connected with Barcelona's patron saint, Santa Eulàlia.

In 878 the remains of the saint were discovered in the old church of Santa María del Mar. Subsequently they were transferred in a solemn procession from the church to the cathedral, but when they reached the city's northern gate they became so heavy that no-one was able to carry them any further. Finally, an angel appeared pointing an accusing finger to one of the cathedral's canons, who had to confess that he had

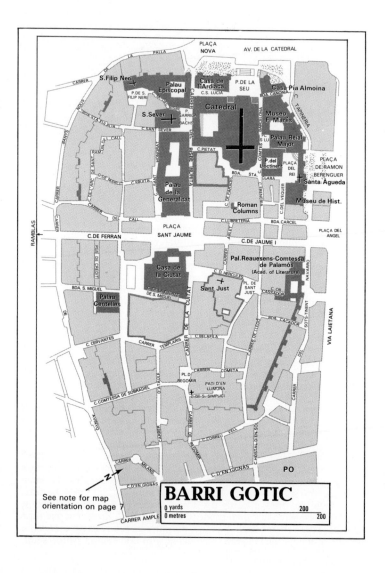

PLAÇA NOVA

AV. DE LA CATEDRAL

LA PALLA

CARRER

S.Filip Neri

P.DE S. FILIP NERI

Palau Episcopal

Casa de l'Ardiaca

C.S. LUCIA

P.DE LA SEU

Casa Pia Almoina

BDA. CANONJA

C. TAPINERIA

BDA STA EULALIA

BANYS

S.Sever

CARRER P. DE BACHS

C. SANT SEVER

Catedral

Museo F. Marés

C. SANT HONORAT

C.PIETAT

Palau Reial Major

C. DEL CALL

C. DE MARLET

C.ERUITA

C. BISBE IRURITA

BDA. STA. CLARA

P.del Lloctinent

PLAÇA DE RAMON BERENGUER

CARRER RAM.

Palau de la Generalitat

PLAÇA DEL REI

Santa Agueda

CARRER DEL CALL

C. DE ZARZANA

Roman Columns

C. DEL VEGUER

Museu de Hist.

CARRER

CARRER

C. LLIBRETERIA

BDA.CARCEL

PLAÇA SANT JAUME

PLAÇA DEL ANGEL

RAMBLAS

C. DE FERRAN

C.DE JAUME I

PTGE. DE CRÉDIT

Casa de la Ciutat

Pal.Reauesens-Comtessa de Palamós (Acad. of Literatura)

C. D. HERCULES

Sant Just

PL. DE SANT JUST

NAVARRO

BDA. S. MIGUEL

C. DE LA FUENTE DE S. MIGUEL

OB. CASSADOR

Palau Centelles

CARRER DE LA CIUTAT

BDA. CAÇADOR

C. CERVANTES

CARRER TEMPLARIS

C. BELAFILA

CARRER DE LLEDO

VIA LAIETANA

SOTS-TINENT

C. COMTESSA DE SOBRADIEL

PL.D REGOMIR

CARRER COMETA

CARRER

PATI D'EN LLIMONA

C. DE S. SIMPLICI

CARRER DE REGOMIR

C.EN GIGNAS

C. CORREU VELL

C.HOSTAL D'EN SOL

C.D'EN GIGNAS

PO

CARRER MILANS

See note for map orientation on page 7

CARRER AMPLE

BARRI GOTIC

0 yards 200
0 metres 200

removed one of the saint's toes; the toe was put back in its rightful position, and the procession was able to continue. To commemorate this event, the statue of an angel was erected above the gate, and in 1616 this was replaced by a bronze figure surmounting an obelisk; the obelisk was pulled down by the revolutionary town council of 1823, but a copy of the statue survives in a niche on the building at Nos 2–3 (the original is in the Museu d' Historia de la Ciutat).

The construction after 1908 of the Via Laietana (see p. 80), which cut a great swathe through Barcelona's old quarter, radically changed the character of the Plaça de l'Àngel, turning it into what is now a noisy junction. However, to the south and north of the square, and parallel with the busy Via Laietana, there have survived two long and impressive stretches of Barcelona's defensive walls. The stretch to the south is to be found on the CARRER DEL SOTS-TINENT NAVARRO (a street known unofficially as the Carrer de las Murallas Romanes), while that to the north rises above a narrow group of gardens stretching all the way to the Plaça Nova. By far the most impressive view of the walls is from the **PLAÇA DE RAMÓN BERENGUER**, a verdant square immediately above the Plaça de l'Àngel; this verdant square, planned in 1922, features cypresses and a central equestrian bronze of Ramón Berenguer III, a work executed by Josep Llimona in Rome in 1888. The tall and picturesquely uneven walls that loom up behind the statue reflect a complex constructional history dating back to the 4C AD, when the walls were first erected. The Roman walls, built of huge blocks of stone to a height of 9 metres and a width of 3.56 metres, were given an especial elegance by supporting a cornice; large fragments of this cornice have survived, as have many of the tall, cube-shaped watch-towers that were built at regular intervals above this. The walls remained untouched until the extension of the city in the 13C, after which Jaume I gave permission for houses to be built against them. The towers overlooking what is now the Plaça Ramón Berenguer were joined together and made to buttress the chapel of Santa Àgueda and other structures on the Plaça del Rei (see below). The arches on the lower level of the walls mark the site of the various medieval buildings that were attached to either side of the walls and thus helped to preserve the Roman masonry. Studied in 1837 by the classical scholar Mestres y Bernardet, the walls were restored in the second quarter of the 20C, red brick being used to replace the sections where the original masonry had disappeared.

West of the Plaça de l'Àngel runs the straight Carrer de Jaume I, which, together with its continuation, the Carrer de Ferran, divides the former Roman city in two; designed in 1820–23, and constructed in 1849–53, it is lined mainly with late 19C buildings. Parallel to the north, and also running in between the Plaça de l'Àngel and de Sant Jaume, is the narrower and older CARRER DE LA LLIBRETERIA , where at No. 16 is the charming *Mesón del Café*, an establishment dating back to 1909, and with a façade in the form of a tiny white house which seems to be taken directly from a fairy tale; within the cosy and always crowded interior, you can enjoy what is reputedly the best coffee in Barcelona, a particular speciality being coffee with whipped cream. Also of interest in the same street (at No. 7) is the *Cerrería Paulino Subirà*, a candle shop founded in 1761; one of the oldest shops in Barcelona, this has a beautiful interior of 1843 featuring columns, an upper gallery and a double-ramp staircase of great lightness and elegance.

Walking from the Carrer de la Llibreteria up the short CARRER DEL VEGUER, you enter the tourist heart of Barcelona, passing to your right (at No. 4) the *Casa Clariana Padellàs, a Gothic merchants' palace of 1497–

1515 with a simple main façade supporting a small upper gallery; originally situated in the Carrer de Mercaders, this building was reconstructed in its present position in 1930–31, following the creation of the Via Laietana. The palace houses the recently rearranged *Museu d'Historia de la Ciutat, which contains numerous maps, diagrams, models and photographs relating to the history of the city. Among its more interesting objects are a 14C volume listing the privileges of the city (the so-called Llibre Verd), and a clock of 1575 said to be the largest of its kind in the world (it was designed for the cathedral by the Flemish clockmaker Simon Nicolau).

From the top of the museum a wonderful view can be had of the Plaça del Rei, which lies immediately to the north. Within the museum are also steps leading down to a large **underground complex** built below the Plaça del Rei and displaying the results of excavations begun in 1931 and continued and completed in 1960–61. A fascinating section of the Roman city has been uncovered, comprising streets, columns, baths, the foundations of houses and shops, and huge urns used for the storage of wheat, wine and oil; in Visigothic times this area was built over and used as a burial ground, of which a large model can be seen. Beyond the excavations you enter two barrel-vaulted rooms forming part of the basement of the Palau Reial Maior (see below), and further still is an excavated passage directly underneath the Carrer dels Comtes; here you will find the remains of both a Visigothic palace and a 4C Christian basilica. A final attraction of the museum is that it gives access to the apse of the Capella de Santa Àgueda (see below), thus providing you with a close-up view of the magnificent altarpiece by Jaume Huguet (see below). The main body of this chapel can be entered from the Plaça del Rei, but is separated from the apse by a glass screen.

An abstract sculpture by the modern artist Eduardo Chillida marks the entrance to the remarkable architectural ensemble constituting the **PLAÇA DEL REI**, a tourist-filled square more like a stage set than a real urban space. Though formerly the courtyard of the royal palace, this served also for 300 years as a straw, hay and flour market, and even as a place where locksmiths exhibited their wares until their expulsion in 1387. In 1403 Martí I planned to have the square enlarged to the same size as the Born (see p. 87), but in the 16C the place was reduced to its present proportions by the construction on its southern side of the Palau del Lloctinent. The eastern side of the square is taken up by the *Capella de Santa Àgueda (Chapel of St. Agatha). This former palace chapel, built during the reign of Jaume II, was begun in 1302 under the direction of Bertran Riquer and completed by Pere d'Olivera in 1411; as with the Sainte Chapelle in Paris, this was a reliquary chapel, housing in this case the stone tablet on which the severed breasts of Santa Àgueda had been placed. Used as a workshop in the 19C, the building was later converted into an archaeological museum, and now is a venue for temporary exhibitions. The exterior is dominated at its northern end by a tall octagonal tower built over one of the defensive towers of the Roman walls.

The entrance to the building is from the top of the elegant rounded flight of steps which occupies the north-eastern corner of the square. The very theatrical nature of this great sweep of steps might perhaps account for the tradition that it was at the top of this staircase that Ferdinand and Isabella greeted Columbus on his return from America in June 1493; what is certain is that a peasant by name of Canyamàs made here an attempt in 1492 to cut Ferdinand's throat. The tall and narrow single-aisled chapel features Gothic arches supporting a polychromed wooden ceiling; within the apse are the coats of arms of Jaume II and his wife Blanca of Anjou. The highpoint of the chapel is undoubtedly the **retable** above the High Altar, one of the most outstanding paintings to be found in any of the city's churches. It was commissioned from Jaume Huguet in 1465 by Pere, Constable of Portugal, who was briefly king of the Catalans during the war against Joan II. A very decorative work in the International Gothic tradition, with extensive gold highlighting, the retable comprises a central scene of the Adoration of the Magi, flanked by scenes of the Annunciation, Nativity, Resurrection, Ascension, Pentecost and Assumption of the Virgin.

Adjacent to the chapel, at the northern end of the Plaça del Rei, is the main façade of the **Palau Reial Major**. The seat first of the Counts and then the Kings of Catalonia, this palace dates back at least to the end of the 10C, and possibly occupies the site of what had been the city's centre of political power in Roman and Visigothic times. The present structure dates essentially from the late 14C onwards, but incorporates masonry and other elements from earlier periods, for instance the elegant triple openings on the main façade, which are from the time of Pere II the Great (1276–85). The buttressing of this façade, as well as the upper row of rose windows, date from the reign of Pere III the Ceremonious (1336–87), and resulted from the creation behind this wall of the ceremonial hall known as the Saló del Tinell, which was commissioned from Guillem Carbonell in 1359. Rising above the side of this façade is the *Mirador del Rei Martí, which is in many ways the most distinctive feature of the whole square. Built by Antoni Carbonell in 1555, this is a tall rectangular tower comprising five superimposed galleries, the arches of which are sprung from Doric pilasters. The geometrical simplicity of this tower gives it an almost modern character, recalling the arcaded fantasies of the Italian painter De Chirico, or even the fascist structures put up by Mussolini.

The same flight of steps which leads up to the entrance to the Capella of Santa Àgueda will also take you to the Romanesque door which leads to the ante-room of the **Saló del Tinell**. The latter hall, completed in 1370, has been put to a variety of uses in the past, even serving between 1372 and 1377 as the seat of the Catalan Parliament; in 1479 the curious funeral rites of Joan II were celebrated here, the king's embalmed body being placed on a lavish catafalque in the centre. The destruction in 1715 of the Ribera district of Barcelona to make way for the Ciutadella (see Rte 1E) led to the demolition of a Clarissine Convent, whose nuns were subsequently offered the hall and adjoining Reial Audiència (see below) as compensation. Transformed by the nuns into a baroque church, the hall was later considered to have been lost for ever. Investigations carried out in 1934 revealed that the structure had survived almost intact underneath the baroque overlay; subsequently purchased and restored by the municipality, the hall serves today for temporary exhibitions. Of vast dimensions, the hall comprises enormous rounded arches supporting a timber roof. Against the inner north wall has been placed a recently discovered fresco of c 1300 representing a military procession headed by a king and bishop.

On the southern side of the Plaça del Rei is the *Palau del Lloctinent, which was built by Antoni Carbonell in 1549–57 as a residence for the viceroy of Catalonia; since 1836 it has housed the Archives of the Crown of Catalonia. The building is entered from the Carrer dels Comtes, which is reached by heading down from the square along the narrow Bajada de Santa Clara, and taking the first turning to the right. The entrance, at No. 2, leads to a fine Renaissance patio, with a tall upper arcade supported by the large basket arches so typical of Catalan architecture. An ancient vine runs up one of the patio's corners, while, off the left-hand side is a staircase vaulted with a magnificently elaborate wooden ceiling.

Continuing west up the CARRER DELS COMTES, you will come immediately to your left to the tiny Plaça de Sant Iu, where you will find the entrance to the former Bishop's Palace of the early 13C. Acquired by Jaume II (1291–1327) as an extension of the royal palace, this building was used in 1487 by the notorious tribunal of the Inquisition. In 1542 it became the seat of the Reial Audiència (Royal Law Courts), and in 1544–45 was extended and remodelled by Antoni Carbonell. Clarissine nuns occupied the complex from 1715 up to their expulsion in 1936, after which it was thoroughly restored; shortly afterwards it was adapted to house the **Museu Frederic Marés**, which was officially inaugurated in 1948. Marés (1893–1991), a wealthy sculptor who had studied at the Llotja and in the workshop of Eusebi Arnau, was a passionate collector, scholar and traveller.

His collections—displayed mainly in a series of gloomy stone rooms—are particularly rich in Spanish sculptures from ancient times up to the Renaissance. Iberian objects (including a group of bronzes from Jaén province) and an impressive series of 13C polychromed crucifixions are to be found on the ground floor, while in the basement are a number of medieval tombs and architectural fragments, most notably a splendid Romanesque portal from the Huesca village of Anzano. On the first floor is a superb polychromed relief of the Adoration of the Shepherds by Juan de Oviedo (1565–1625), originating from the Andalusian town of Cazalla de la Sierra; also here is a scattering of 15C paintings, including a heavily gilded and embossed Calvary Group by Jaume Huguet. The second and third floors are taken over by by what is known as the *Museu Sentimental, which contains the more ephemeral objects amassed by Marés, and date mainly from the 18C and 19C. Of greater historical than artistic interest, this section of the museum charms largely by its dazzling variety of objects, including cribs, scissors, pipes, ceramics, photographs, toy soldiers and so on; there is even the much-travelled, label-encrusted suitcase which Marés had used to assemble much of this loot.

The Carrer dels Comtes is flanked on its southern side by the cathedral, and, as you head back down the street and turn right into the Bajada de Santa Clara, you will skirt the building's apse. Before visiting the cathedral you should turn left into the dark alley of the CARRER DEL PARADÍS, where, at No. 10, you will find a much restored medieval palace occupied today by the Centre Excursionista de Catalunya, a mountaineering organisation which was founded in 1876, and was responsible for introducing skiing to Catalonia. However, the reason most people come here has nothing to do with either skiing or mountaineering, for you will find within the building's small glazed courtyard four tall Corinthian columns which originally formed part of a Roman Temple situated at the highest point of the Mons Táber. At one time this temple was popularly thought to have housed the tomb of Hercules, the mythical founder of Barcelona, but is believed today by most scholars to have been dedicated to Augustus. Originally dominating the forum of Roman Barcino, the structure later stood in the middle of the garden which gave the street its name of Paradise. The 18C scholar Antonio Ponz described the temple at length in Volume XIV of his Journey through Spain (1788), and hoped that the surrounding late medieval walls would be pulled down so that the monument could enjoy once again the prominent position worthy of its importance.

The tawny-gold mass of the **Catedral** today dominates the Barri Gòtic, its tall octagonal towers and openwork spires pushing their way high above the narrow surrounding streets and alleys that congest this area.

The origins of the cathedral go back to a three-aisled palaeochristian basilica of the 4C or 5C, the foundations of which can be seen in the basement of the Museu d'Historia de la Ciutat. Destroyed by the Moorish leader Al-Mansur in 985, this was replaced in 1046–58 by a Romanesque structure commissioned by Ramón Berenguer the Old. The present cathedral was begun in 1298, during the bishopric of Bernat Pelegrí and the reign of Jaume II. The unknown first architect was succeeded in 1317 by the Mallorcan Jaume Fabre, who remained in charge of the works until his death in 1339, bringing to completion the apse, ambulatory and crossing. From 1358–88 the construction of the building was taken over by Bernat Roca or Roquer, who laid out most of the nave, and initiated the construction of the cloister. Arnau Bargués, who was director of works after 1397, planned the magnificent chapter house, which was built in 1405–15. The choir, in the middle of the nave, was completed c 1460, after which the fabric of the cathedral was little altered until the 19C. In 1820 a modern solution was proposed for the cathedral's unfinished west façade, but Richard Ford was reporting over twenty years later that nothing had still been done to this façade despite the fact that 'the rich chapter have for three centuries received a fee on every marriage for this very purpose of completing it…' Financed by the banker Manuel Girona, Josep Oriol Mestres finally built the west façade in 1887–90, basing his design very closely on one which had been drawn up in 1408 by the French architect Charles Galtes (who is known in Catalan as Carlí); leading the team of sculptors working on the façade was Agapit Vallmitjana i Barbay.

Work on the cathedral was begun, unusually, at the south transept, the oldest feature of the exterior being the Romanesque portal overlooking the Plaça de Sant Iu. The portal, carved in marble and Montjuïc stone, is flanked by panels with inscriptions recording the commencement of work in 1298; above these are carvings of a man with a griffin and a man battling with a lion, while in the tympanum itself is a figure believed to be of Sant Iu (Ivo).The finest statuary on the exterior is the wooden relief contained within the tympanum of the Portal del Pietat, which leads into the cloister on the southern side of the building: attributed to the German artist Michael Lochner, this angular and expressive late 15C work represents the Pietà, the diminutive figure at Christ's feet being Canon Berenguer Vila. Among the most striking architectural features of the exterior are the two octagonal towers—dating from the 1380s—which rise above the transepts. The late 19C west façade is in a style more indebted to Northern European architecture than to the Catalan Gothic, not only because of the soaring proportions, but also because of the elaborate and intricate overall decoration, which is in sharp contrast to the ornamental restraint characteristic of most medieval Catalan exteriors. Three openwork spires punctuate the skyline of this façade, the enormously tall central one being reminiscent of those of Ulm and Freiburg.

The three-aisled interior, with its blind triforium and tiny rose windows in the clerestory, is spacious and atmospheric; large bosses decorate the Gothic cross-vaults, while a colonnade of tall piers forms a particularly elegant ambulatory. Rose Macaulay, in *Fabled Shore* (1949), described the cathedral as a 'triumph of Catalan Gothic magnificence', but added that 'it is outside my scope and power to emulate the guide-books in their persevering, detailed and admirable accounts of church interiors'. She was perhaps right in skimping on the detail, for the initial impact of the interior is more memorable than most of the individual features and furnishings. Thanks to its having been constantly guarded by the Generalitat during the Civil War, the interior is one of the few in Barcelona to have escaped the attentions of the anarchists, but you cannot help thinking that the destruction of of the 17C and 18C altarpieces that decorate many of the dark chapels of the nave and ambulatory would not have been such a great artistic loss. By far the most impressive of the chapels is the one at the western end of the south aisle. Covered with an elaborate star-shaped vault richly adorned with bosses, this was originally the *chapter house built in 1407 by Arnau Bargués. Following the canonisation in 1676 of the 12C Bishop of Barcelona, Ollegarius, this was transformed into a memorial chapel to the saint, and the partition walls that once made the place accessible only from the cloister were pulled down. Later the chapel was dedicated to the Christ of Lepanto in honour of its carved image of the Crucifixion, which is said to have been carried by Don John of Austria in the Battle of Lepanto, where it was placed on the prow of his flagship *La Real*. Directly opposite the chapel, in the first bay of the north aisle, is the *baptistery, where a plaque records the baptism of the six American natives brought back by Columbus from the New World in 1493; the stained glass above, representing Christ and Mary Magdalene, was executed by Gil Fontamet to designs by the great Cordovan artist Bartolomé Bermejo.

The central enclosed **choir**, which was begun after 1390, features some of the most impressive sculptural work to be found in the cathedral. The original stalls were the upper ones, which were completed by Pere ça Anglada in 1399; the elaborate canopies, with rich plateresque decoration, were added in the late 15C by Michael Lochner and Johann Friedrich. A further addition were the coats of arms painted on the stalls by Juan de Borgoña on the occasion of the celebration here, in 1519, of the first and last chapter of the order of the Golden Fleece. The meeting, presided over by the Emperor Charles V—the Grand Master of the Order—was attended by the kings of England, Poland, Portugal, Denmark, Hungary and France; the coat of arms of England's Henry VIII is to be seen immediately to the right of the Emperor's, facing the high altar. The lower stalls, of less artistic interest, were executed by Macià Bonafè in 1456–62. Attached to the choir is a dazzlingly elaborate wooden **pulpit** of 1403 by Pere ça Anglada; this is reached by an early 15C stone stairway which was built by Jordi Johan and adorned with a traceried ironwork balustrade incorporating lily motifs. The splendid Renaissance **choir-screen**, or retrochoir, was begun in 1519 by Bartolomé Ordóñez (assisted by the Italians Simone de Bellano and Vittorio de Cogono), and completed in 1564 by Pedro Villar; Ordóñez himself was responsible for the exquisitely worked Italianate reliefs of Sant Sever, Santa Eulàlia, and the scenes of Santa Eulàlia's proclamation of her faith and martyrdom at the stake.

In between the choir and the presbytery are steps leading down to the **crypt chapel**, where you will find the most venerated object in the cathedral—the sarcophagus containing the remains of the 4C co-patroness of the city, Santa Eulàlia.

Santa Eulàlia, the virgin daughter of wealthy merchants from Sarriá (which is still a very prosperous district of Barcelona), was so shocked by the corruption of the Roman city that she was converted to Christianity by at least the age of 12. Described by one of her early chroniclers as being 'extraordinarily beautiful', she has inspired a great number of legends, many of which relate to her gruesome sufferings at the hands of the Roman governor of Barcelona, Dacian. Aged only 13, she was forced by Dacian to worship the false idols in the Temple of Augustus, to which she responded by throwing a handful of sand at the altar. Thrown into a tower next to the Call, she was then subjected to a series of progressively crueller tortures of a type which the Marquis de Sade would have greatly approved. Eventually she was killed at the stake, some say on the site of the Boquería Market, others at the Plaça de l'Àngel or the Plaça de Sant

Pere. Doubts about the existence of the saint have frequently been voiced, and some even claim that she was a Catalan appropriation of the Mérida saint of the same name.

Whatever the authenticity of the contents, the **Sarcophagus of Santa Eulàlia** is a particularly fine alabaster work of 1327, intricately carved by a Pisan artist who clearly had a close knowledge of the work of Giovanni Pisano; the previous sarcophagus—made immediately after the discovery of the remains in 877—has now been placed on the wall at the back of the crypt. Radiating like a sun in the middle of the star-shaped vault is a huge boss of 1371, carved with a relief of Santa Eulàlia and the Virgin and Child. Altogether the crypt provides the cathedral with the note of climax which is at present so lacking in the raised presbytery above. The *presbytery was radically altered in 1970, the 14C Bishop's chair being moved from the side to a central position at the rear. To accommodate this change the 14C gilded reredos above the High Altar was taken away to the church of San Jaume, leaving as the main embellishment of the presbytery today an uninspired bronze by Frederic Marés of the Exaltation of the Holy Cross. Placed above the south wall of the ambulatory are the wooden *sarcophagi of Ramón Berenguer I (died 1025) and his wife Almodis. The third apsidal chapel contains a retable of 1450 by Bernat Martorell, with heavily gilded scenes representing the Life of Christ. Under the 16C organ in the north transept there hung until recently a cardboard Moor's head known as the *carassa*, which, on certain feast days, used to eject sweets from its mouth.

To many visitors the greatest pleasure of a tour of the cathedral comes from the **cloisters**, which lie off the south transept. Though begun by Bernat Roca in the late 14C, they were not completed until late in the following century, and have much Flamboyant Gothic detailing, such as the ironwork grilles entwined with floral motifs. The luxuriant character of the cloisters is due above all to the rich vegetation in the centre, featuring orange-trees, aloes and palms hovering over a large pool and fountain. However, unusually for places such as these, the cloisters cannot be described as a haven of peace, not only because of the large crowds of tourists, but also because of the squeals made by the geese that have been kept here over the centuries. Originally 13 in number, these geese (now thankfully reduced to six) are thought to have had a symbolical significance, though this has yet to be satisfactorily explained. Richard Ford believed that the canons of the cathedral, inspired by the geese on the Roman capitol, installed the geese here as a reminder of the greatness of Barcelona in Roman times. Though Ford's explanation makes you wonder why no such animals are to be found today in Tarragona—a far more important Roman city than Barcelona—it has been widely accepted, and there are several guidebooks that continue to refer to the cathedral's 'Capitoline geese'.

The fountain which feeds the cathedral's pond is protected by a mid 15C tabernacle decorated inside with a boss representing St. George and the Dragon. The *Cathedral Museum, situated off the north side of the cloisters, partially occupies the chapter house, and features numerous silk altar frontals and many indifferent religious paintings and sculptures. Two 15C works stand out, however, one being a retable by Jaume Huguet painted for the Guild of Esparto Workers (Gremio de Esparters). The other, and more impressive of the two, is Bartolomé Bermejo's signed and dated **Pietà** of 1490, which was formerly in the chapel of the nearby Casa de l'Ardiaca, (Archdeacon's House). Bermejo, a Cordovan-born artist who worked mainly in Catalonia and Aragón, is regarded as one of the greatest painters of the so-called Hispano-Flemish School. His superb Pietà reveals strong

Flemish influence in the wealth of naturalistic detail to be found in the extensive landscape background; however, the angularity, harsh realism and expressiveness of the whole is inherently Spanish.

Leaving the cathedral by the west portal you will find yourself in the PLAÇA DE LA SEU, where every Sunday from midday onwards a small band provides the music for the Catalan national dance known as the *Sardana*. In its stateliness and complete absence of sensuality, the *Sardana* is comparable to the English Morris-dance. Anyone can join in, but before doing so you would be well advised to read John Langdon-Davies's scholarly and entertaining study, *Dancing Catalans* (London, 1929), which gives a detailed description of the movements.

The square itself was formed in 1421–22 by the pulling down of houses belonging to the deacon and canons, and of a section of the Roman wall; a stairway was created leading down to the Carrer de la Corríbia, a street which has now been replaced by the modern and bustling AVINGUDA DE LA CATEDRAL. On the site of one of the destroyed buildings there was erected later in the 15C the *Casa de la Pia Almoina, which survive in a heavily restored state on the northern-eastern side of the square, and are soon to house a *Diocesan Museum. Further changes to the square, involving the demolition of other houses facing the cathedral, were made in 1943; one of these houses—belonging to the medieval guild of Shoemakers—was subsequently rebuilt in the nearby Plaça de Sant Filip Neri. From the Avinguda de la Catedral and the adjoining Plaça Nova, a good view càn now be had of both the west front of the cathedral and of the long section of Roman wall attached to the back of the Casa de l'Ardiaca (Archdeachon's House; see below).

Before resuming a tour of the Barri Gòtic, you should take a look at the tall modern block at No. 5 Plaça Nova, which was built by Xavier Busquets i Sindreu in 1958–62. This dreary and incongruously situated structure—a sad advertisement for the Collegi d'Arquitectes de Catalunya which it houses—is of interest largely for its long frieze inscribed with linear child-like murals designed by Picasso and executed in 1960 by the Norwegian Carl Nesjar; there are two further Picasso murals inside, one of which represents the *Sardana*. Architectural enthusiasts might also like to visit the college's outstanding bookshop, which is housed in the basement.

Back on the Plaça de la Seu head down the Carrer Santa Llúcia, passing to your right the *Casa de l'Ardiaca or Archdeacon's House. Built in 1479–1512, and partially remodelled in 1548–59, this was adapted early this century for use as a Barristers' College, the architect responsible being the leading modernist, Lluís Domènech i Montaner; the building is now occupied by the city's History Archive. The street façade is marked by an elegant Renaissance portal of c 1510–12, to the right of which is a delightful letter-box designed by Domènech i Montaner in 1902; the box is decorated with swallows and a tortoise, presumably a witty reference to the erratic nature of Spain's postal service. Behind the portal is a charming small patio comprising a fountain and arcades of basket arches. On the other side of the street, attached to the western side of the cathedral's cloisters, is the small *Capella de Santa Llúcia, which was built in 1257–68, during the bishopric of Arnau de Gurb; possibly intended as the chapel of the neighbouring Bishop's Palace, it was soon afterwards incorporated into the cathedral complex. The façade has the characteristic severity of the Catalan Romanesque, the ornamentation being concentrated solely on the portal, which is decorated almost entirely with vegetal and geometric motifs; one of the capitals has worn carvings of the Annunciation and Visitation. The dark barrel-vaulted interior features the late 13C sepulchre of Bishop Arnau de Gurb (protected today by a glass panel), and a floor extensively paved with tomb slabs. Walking towards the western end of the Carrer de Santa Llúcia you will see directly in front of you—on the western side of the CARRER DEL BISBE—the *Palau Episcopal or Bishop's Palace, which dates back at least to the time of the Bishop Arnau de Gurb, but was extensively remodelled after 1681. The surviving and much restored parts of the original Romanesque palace are to be seen in entrance courtyard off the Carrer del Bisbe, and include an arcade of elegantly ornamented arches, and rows of paired and triple openings on the second floor. The façade of the palace overlooking the Plaça Nova is a neo-classical work of 1784 by the brothers Mas, while that on the Plaça Garriga i Bachs was added as late as 1928.

The Plaça Garriga i Bachs, on one side of the Bishop's Palace was created in 1929 with the demolition of the houses separating the palace from the Palau de la Generalitat to the south. On the western side of the square, attached to the side façade of the church of Sant Sever (see below) is a monument of 1929 to the city's victims of the Napoleonic wars; it features bronze and stone figures executed respectively by Josep Llimona and Vincenç Navarro, as well as ceramic tiles reproducing a series of historical prints of the early 19C.

Before making your way to the Palau de la Generalitat, you should make a short detour west of the square along the dark and alley-like CARRER MONJUÏC DEL BISBE, which was originally a path leading to the cemetery of that name; though the cemetery has gone, the former solemn nature of the street is recalled in a couple of shops specialising in religious objects. In place of the cemetery is the small and shaded **Plaça de Sant Felip Neri**, which appears to be a particularly atmospheric and well-preserved corner of the old town, though in fact is largely a modern sham incorporating old elements.

The Irish heroine of Colm Tóibín's novel *The South* (1990) finds herself one night in this square and believes that she has stumbled at last on the 'real Barcelona': 'I had been in Barcelona for about a week and suddenly I felt as though I had found the place I had been looking for: the sacred core of the world, a deserted square reached by two narrow alleyways, dimly lit, with a fountain, two trees, a church and some church buildings'.

The only two buildings actually to have been intended for the square are the former Residence of the Secular Priests of the Oratory (the Filipenses) and the attached Church of Sant Felip Neri. The former, founded in the late 17C, was austerely remodelled in the second half of the 18C. The present church, begun in 1721, was not completed until 1751. Its severe exterior, with its flanking giant pilasters and crowning rounded pediment, is one of several in Barcelona inspired by that of the Ciutadella church; meanwhile the single-aisled interior, featuring interconnected side chapels, and a dome above the crossing, is of a type derived from the Gesù in Rome.

The pock-marked masonry on the lower level of the church's exterior is a result of the bomb which was dropped on the square during the Civil War. In the course of the square's subsequent restoration two fine Renaissance buildings were brought here from other parts of the city. Next to the church is the much-travelled *Casas del Gremi de Calderers, which was originally situated on the Carrer de la Bòria; after having been removed to the distant Plaça Lesseps in 1911—following the creation of the Via Laietana—it finally ended up on its present site. The elegant Renaissance detailing on its exterior dates from the time that this former private house was acquired by the Guild of Coppersmith Workers. The Guild of Shoemakers was responsible for the construction in 1565 of the adjacent *Casa del Gremi dels Sabaters, which was one of the houses taken down in 1943 during the relaying of the area in front of the cathedral's west façade. On its façade is a relief of the lion of St. Mark, the patron of shoemakers. The building now houses the *Museu del Calçat Antic, an entertaining collection of Catalan shoes from the medieval period up to the 19C.

Heading down the short CARRER SANT FELIP NERI, you will emerge at the intersection of the Bajada de Santa Eulàlia and the Carrer de Sant Sever, two charming quiet streets lined with modest 17C and 18C houses. The former street would not have had such pleasant associations for the saint whom it commemorates, for it was down here that she was supposedly rolled naked in a barrel filled with pieces of glass; a mosaic incorporated into a small tabernacle on one of the houses commemorates this event. At the junction of the Carrer de Sant Sever and the Plaça Garriga i Bachs is the *Església Sant Sever, which was built in 1698–1705 to the designs of Jaume Arnaudies. The decoration on the modest façade is limited to the portal, which supports a niche containing a statue of Sant Severus executed by Jeroni Escarabatxeres in 1703. Little hint is given by this façade of the rich interior, which though simple in plan, contains some of the most elaborate baroque decoration to be seen in Barcelona; as with the cathedral, the church was spared by anarchists during the Civil War thanks to the constant vigil of the *Generalitat*. The decoration of the three-aisled interior is comparable to that which once adorned the Betlem church on La Rambla (see p. 45), and includes a richly sgraffitoed vault and elaborate gilded screens in the galleries. The dazzlingly sumptuous *high altar, set in front of an apse painted with illusionistic architecture, was designed by Escarabatxeres. The church is rarely open, but you can usually gain access by calling at the house at No. 9 Carrer Sant Sever.

Back at the Plaça Garriga i Bachs you should turn right and walk down the Carrer del Bisbe towards the Plaça de Sant Jaume. As you make your way along this narrow and elegant pedestrian street, you will flank the eastern side of the enormous palace of the *Generalitat*, and pass under a neo-Gothic bridge which connects this palace to the rambling complex comprising the *Cases dels Canonges. The latter was formed by the joining together of a group of canon's houses dating back to the 14C; this complex—used today as the official residence of the Presidents of the *Generalitat*—was heavily restored in 1924–25, three years before the construction of the bridge. Beyond the bridge you will see to to your right the magnificent medieval entrance to the **PALAU DE LA GENERALITAT**.

The *Generalitat*, or Government of Catalonia, has its origins in the *Corts Catalanes* (Catalan Parliament) founded during the reign of Jaume I (1213–76), the monarch who was also responsible for the elevation of St. George (Sant Jordi) into the patron saint of Catalonia. St. George achieved this honour after having been sighted by the king at the siege of Mallorca in 1229, making a posthumous appearance in order to lead the Catalans into victory. The effigy of this mythical saint was later to be the principal ornamental and symbolical motif of the Palau del Generalitat.

In 1283 Pere II the Great restructured the Corts Catalanes, and divided it into bodies representing the clergy, army and citizenry. The committees created by this parliament in 1289 to collect the royal taxes were to form the basis of the Generalitat de Catalunya, which were given permanent status in 1359 by Pere III the Ceremonious (1336–87). Under Pere III, the *Generalitat* became an administrative council for Catalonia comprising three deputies from each of the three bodies that made up the Parliament.

Though one of the first governing bodies in Europe with the authority to mitigate the absolutism of a sovereign, it was not to be given its own premises until the early 15C. These premises—the nucleus of the present palace—were created in 1403–34 by the joining together of a group of houses on the Carrer de Sant Honorat that had been confiscated from wealthy Jews; the principal architect in charge of the works was Marc Safont. The acquisition of another house early the following century led to the extension of the palace to the north, the works being mainly carried out by Tomàs Barsa and Pau Mateu, who built the original Pati dels Tarongers (Courtyard of the Oranges). Pere Ferrer extended this courtyard northwards in 1570–91, and in 1610–30 Pere Pau Ferrer provided the building with its present north façade, overlooking the Plaça Garriga i Bachs. The most important of the later additions was the Hall of St. George, which forms the building's southern and main façade, and was conceived originally as a new chapel to accommodate the ever growing cult of St. George.

In 1714, following Catalonia's support for the Habsburgs during the Spanish War of Succession, the *Generalitat* was suppressed by the Bourbon monarch Philip V, and its palace was turned into the city's Law Courts. The palace was to remain as such until 1908, during which period it saw the trials of most of Barcelona's notorious anarchists, including Santiago Salvador (the man responsible for the Liceu attack), and Joaquín Miguel Artal, who was condemned in 1904 to 17 years' imprisonment for his assassination attempt on the minister Antonio Maura: at the moment of his arrival at the Law Courts, he had received a clamorous ovation from a group of anarchists standing outside. Among those sentenced to death here was the murderer Isidro Monpart, whose sentence was carried out in 1892 by the infamous Nicomedes Méndez, who was able to use for the purpose a special garotte which he had invented himself but had yet been able to try out; the garotting was later the subject of a popular painting by Ramon Casas now in the Museum of Modern Art in Madrid.

After serving after 1908 as local government offices, the palace became once again the seat of the *Generalitat* with the restoration of this institution in 1931. The first President of the new *Generalitat* was Francesc Macià, who in 1934 was succeeded by Lluís Companys. A Statute of Autonomy issued by Macià gave Catalonia its own Parliament, judicial administration and police force. After the Civil War the *Generalitat* was once again outlawed, and went into exile. Companys—sent back to Spain by the government of Vichy France—was executed in 1940, but was replaced as 'President in exile' first by Josep Irla and later by Josep Tarradellas. Tarradellas, together with the *Generalitat*, was able to return to Catalonia following the death of Franco in 1976. A new Statute of Autonomy, passed in 1979, greatly increased the power of the *Generalitat* by making Catalonia one of the three Spanish regions known as 'historical autonomies' (the other two being Galicia and the Basque Country). Since 1980 the *Generalitat* has been led by the appropriately named Jordi Pujol, whom some like to compare to the pugnacious St. George, but who was controversially referred to by the designer Mariscal as a 'dwarf' because of his diminutive physical stature.

The entrance to the Palau del Generalitat on the Carrer del Bisbe is that of the medieval palace, and was built by Marc Safont in 1416–18. The low exterior wall, which shields the smaller of the old palace's two courtyards, is distinguished by an exquisitely worked Gothic parapet, lined with gargoyles, topped by finials, and incorporating an outstanding carved *Roundel of St. George by the sculptor Pere Joan; the *Generalitat* was apparently so pleased with this work that the sculptor was paid twice the amount that he had asked for. The early 17C façade on the Plaça Garriga i Bachs is in an austere classical style inspired by that of Juan de Herrera, while the late 16C main façade, on the Plaça de Sant Jaume, recalls Michelangelo's design for the Palazzo Farnese in Rome. Two later additions to the latter façade were the statue of St. George (a modern work by the sculptor Aleu), and the balcony, which was added in 1860. From the balcony Francesc Macià proclaimed the short-lived Catalan Republic in 1931 (it lasted one day!), while Josep Tarradellas, on his return to Catalonia in 1977, greeted the crowds with the memorable words, *'Ja sóc aquí !,* 'I am here!'

The rich and wonderfully varied interior of the palace is officially open to the public only on the afternoon of St. George's Day (23 April; see below), when the patios are filled with roses, and popular Catalan songs are played continuously on the palace's bells. However, the place can be visited on written application, preferably some time before your intended visit; the address to write to is, Protocol, Palau del Generalitat, Plaça de Sant Jaume, 08002, Barcelona. The excellent tour of the palace—led by one of the uniformed guides of the Generalitat—begins with the medieval palace, which is one of the best preserved civic buildings of its period in Europe. The core of the medieval building is the **Inner Courtyard**, where a staircase sprung at a daringly low angle leads up to a Gothic arcade of exceptional lightness and elegance, dating from 1425; above this is an upper arcade of basket arches crowned by finials and gargoyles attributed to Pere Joan. The two Corinthian columns supporting the arch at the top of the staircase have finely carved banding of classical inspiration. Directly in front of these is the entrance to the **Chapel of St. George**, which was built by Marc Safont in 1432. The entrance itself is one of the most elaborate and exuberant examples of the Gothic style in Catalonia, with pinnacles and ogee arches, and a riot of tracery which extends up from the portal and flanking windows to cover the whole wall and cornice; such Flamboyance is in marked contrast to the austerity of the Catalan Gothic in general. The chapel itself was altered and extended in 1620 and given a cupola decorated at each corner with four suspended capitals, a feature peculiar to Barcelona. The furnishings are particularly fine and include numerous scenes of St. George and the Dragon, among which are a late 15C altar frontal embroidered in relief by Antoni Sadurni, and an Italian silver reliquary of c 1500 featuring the first known representation of the saint on foot.

Attached to the northern side of the inner courtyard's Gothic arcade is the long **Courtyard of the Oranges**, the southern end of which was begun by Pau Mateu in 1532. This southern end is given a brilliant colouring not only by its orange trees but also by the pink columns with Renaissance capitals that support the lower Gothic arcade. The narrower northern end, dating from the late 16C, is far more austere, but has been made to harmonise with the other half by carrying through the whole length of the courtyard a Gothic upper arcade of basket arches, gargoyles and finials. Among the rooms off this courtyard is the so-called **Gilded Hall**, which is named after its gilded ceiling of 1578, a resplendent coffered structure from which are suspended two 18C Murano chandeliers; the walls of the room are lined with 16C Flemish tapestries representing allegorical scenes from Petrarch. Nearby is a small room containing early 20C frescoes by J. Torres-Garcia that were originally painted for the Hall of St. George; these classical allegorical works, full of overtones of the art of the French Symbolist painter Puvis de Chavannes, are typical examples of so-called Noucentisme. More recent art to be found in the palace includes a room with walls adorned with bizarre Post-Modern reliefs by the present-day sculptor Josep Maria Subirachs; another room is being decorated by Tàpies. The tour of the building ends in the **Hall of St. George** (Saló de Sant Jordi), the church-like interior of which—complete with central dome—is a reminder that this reception hall was originally planned as a replacement to the chapel of St. George. The decoration, comprising heavy gilding and conventional historical scenes, was executed in 1928 during the dictatorship of Primo de Rivera, which explains why most of the scenes depicted are of Spanish rather than specifically Catalan subject-matter.

The PLAÇA DE SANT JAUME, the symbolical heart of Barcelona, and by far the largest square of the old town, dates back to Roman times, when it marked the junction of two roads. However, from the Middle Ages onwards most of the area which it now covers was occupied by the church of Sant Jaume and a building known as the Bailia, which was where taxes on goods imported into the city were administered. The destruction by fire of the church of Sant Jaume in 1822 provided the impetus for the creation of the present square, which was laid out by 1850 and given a predominantly classical look. As with Madrid's Puerta del Sol, this is not today a square where people generally come to linger, though the inevitable Sardanas are danced here on Sunday evenings. The place is undoubtedly seen at its most animated on St. George's Day (23 April), when stalls of books are laid out around it, and crowds queue up to buy roses from the courtyard of the Palau de la Generalitat. This feast-day in honour of Catalonia's patron saint was instigated in 1436 (later than in either Valencia or Mallorca), and coincided with another popular festivity of 15C origin, The Festival of the Roses. The old custom of men presenting women with roses on this day is still enthusiastically maintained, and has been enhanced by the rather more recent tradition of women giving books to the men in exchange: this last tradition goes back only to 1926, when St. George's Day was chosen additionally as the Day of the Book, in commemoration of the death of Cervantes.

On the southern side of the square, directly facing the Palau de la Generalitat, is the city's other main civic building, the **Casa de la Ciutat** (City Hall), the main seat of the *Ajuntamient*. Whereas the *Generalitat* is responsible for administering the whole of Catalonia, the *Ajuntamient* deals purely with the city of Barcelona, though in practice there is a certain degree of confusion concerning their respective spheres of influence. This situation has been complicated by the present political confrontation between the two institutions, the former being essentially right-wing, and the latter being much more to the left, many of its supporters being found among the city's large colonies of Andalusian workers.

Despite the importance of medieval Barcelona, its citizens were not given the right to elect their own councillors and aldermen until as late as 1249, when a constitution of civilian rights was introduced by the enlightened Jaume I. The subsequently formed municipal assembly, which later developed into the *Consell de Cent* (Council of One Hundred), met up to begin with in various places, and did not have a permanent home until the construction by Pere Llobet in 1373 of the Saló de Cent, which was the nucleus of the present city hall. Between 1399 and 1402 Anau Barguès, with the assistance of Francesc Marenya, extended the building through the creation of the façade on the Carrer de la Ciutat. A large courtyard was created in the 1550s, while the present façade on the Plaça de Sant Jaume was built in 1830–47, the works being carried out in conjunction with the relaying of the square itself. The visit of Isabel II to the city in 1860 led to the construction of a new sessions chamber and the extension and redecoration of the original Saló de Cent. Numerous other changes and additions have been made to the building since then, including work executed by Domènech i Montaner in preparation for the World Exhibition of 1888, when the City Hall came also to serve as a royal residence. The Exhibition of 1929 inspired a further series of major works, including an ambitious redecoration campaign involving an iconographic programme drawn up by the historian Duran i Sanpere. A large modern extension was added in 1958, and in 1982 the courtyard and vestibules were adorned with modern sculptures.

The City Hall's main façade on the Plaça de Sant Jaume is a grand but brutally austere neo-classical structure by Josep Mas i Vila. A typical work of the progressive Barcelona government of the 1820s, it aroused enormous controversy in its day, and certainly forms a dramatic contrast to the surviving parts of the Gothic building which it so incongruously shields.

Most visitors today are somewhat surprised and relieved when they dis-
cover, on the adjacent Carrer de la Ciutat, Arnau Barguès' Gothic façade
of 1399–1402, a quaintly irregular work with delicate tracery in the arches
and parapet. The Gothic courtyard and arcades to be found inside the
building are largely 19C and 20C work, but there survives here a Gothic
loggia of the mid 16C. Members of the public are allowed freely to wander
around this area, where you will find sculptures by Francesc Marés, Josep
Clarà, Joan Miró and others. To visit the rest of the building permission
must be had from the Protocol here, but this can usually be obtained on the
spot, the only requirement being a passport or some other form of identification. The parts of the interior that you are shown have an altogether dark
and heavy character, and lack the immediate appeal of the rooms of the
Palau del Generalitat. A late 16C portal of Solomonic columns leads into
the late 14C Saló de Cent, a vast heavily restored hall in the style of the
Saló del Tinell, with enormous round arches supporting a wooden beam
ceiling; two of the arches were added in 1848, while the neo-Gothic
furnishings are of 1914. The present council chamber, dating from the reign
of Isabel II, is a gloomy panelled structure with dark oak seating arranged
in a hemicycle. The most outstanding of the building's decorations—though
sadly little appreciated by most of those who come here today—are those
by Josep Maria Sert decorating the **SALÓ DE LES CRÓNIQUES** (Hall of
the Chronicles). These enormous murals, painted on canvas in Paris in 1928,
were among the palace's many decorations executed for the Exhibition of
1929; they represent scenes of Catalan exploits in 14C Greece and Asia
Minor. Sert, who is not to be confused with the moderniste architect of this
name, enjoyed a deservedly large international reputation in the 1920s,
when he received such prestigious commissions as the decoration of the
Palace of the League of Nations, and of New York's Waldorf Astoria; largely
for his having supported Franco, he went out of fashion after the Civil War,
and was an almost completely forgotten figure after his death in 1945. The
murals he executed in the Saló de les Cróniques are painted solely in ochre,
gold and sepia, and show a compositional and illusionistic bravura worthy
of his great idol, the Venetian 18C painter G.B. Tiepolo.

West of the Plaça de Sant Jaume is a district known as the Call, which
extends all the way to the street marking the western boundary of the
Roman city, the Carrer Banys Nous. The name Call, first mentioned in a
document of 1241, is derived from the Hebrew word *quahal*, which means
a meeting-place. Up to 1492 this was the centre of Barcelona's thriving and
distinguished Jewish community.

Though Jews had probably settled in Catalonia by Roman times, the earliest mention
of them here is a document of 889 attesting to their presence in Girona. The Barcelona
community, which had become firmly established in the Call by the 11C, experienced
its heyday between the 12C and 14C, when it not only played a leading role in the
commercial history of Catalonia, but also became the country's undisputed centre of
learning and culture, boasting most of the great doctors of the time, as well as a Jewish
College which for a long while was Catalonia's only institution with the character of
a university. Among the more celebrated figures of the community were the poet Ben
Rubén Izahac, the astronomer Abraham Xija ('Hanasi') and the philosophers Abraham
Ben Samuel Hasdai, Rabbi Salomón Arisha and Bonet Abraham Margarit.

Enclosed by the Roman wall to the west and to the east by a wall which ran parallel
to the present Carrer Sant Honorat, the Call was turned into a ghetto in 1243, the
entrance to which was on what is now the Plaça de Sant Jaume. With the creation of
this ghetto, laws were issued preventing Christians from entering here other than on
days when goods were displayed on its streets; furthermore the Jews were forced to
wear large capes and hats, and to place red or yellow bands around their heads. Jaume

I, who had been responsible for these segregation laws, was also one of the Jews' great benefactors, and he offered them special privileges in return for their financial support. Royal favour and protection—implemented in Barcelona by the *Consell de Cent* (Council of One Hundred)—were to be extended to the Catalan Jews up to 1400, eventually being undermined by growing anti-semitism.

The first attacks on the ghetto were recorded at the very end of the 13C, but it was not until 1391 that the Jewish community came seriously under threat. A wave of anti-semitic rioting spread that year from Seville to Valencia and eventually to Barcelona, where the Consell de Cent organised a force of 1000 men to defend the Call. This force was in place by 17 July, but, believing after about a fortnight that the danger had passed, was unprepared for the attack on the Call made on 5 August, when men bearing torches put fire to the houses, and killed all those whom they found in the streets. Orders given by the Consell de Cent to execute ten of those responsible for the outrage only increased the fury of the mob, and in a subsequent attack 300 Jews were reputedly murdered in the space of an hour. Joan I ordered the execution of 15 more of the offenders, and arranged that taxes should be paid to the surviving Jews for a period of 30 years. However, the ghetto had by now been effectively destroyed, and was to survive for only a short time afterwards. The smaller of its two synagogues was turned into a church in 1395, and in the following year the remaining one was rented out to a stone-mason; all Jewish synagogues and cemeteries in Catalonia were suppressed in 1401, and the stones acquired from these places were later used for such buildings as the palaces of the *Generalitat* and *Lloctinent*. Expelled from the Call in 1424, the remaining Jewish families were to stay on in Barcelona until 1492, when they were thrown out of Spain itself. Jews only began returning in significant numbers to Barcelona after 1930, the number of Jewish families increasing from 400 at the beginning of the decade to 5000 by 1935. In 1931 the first Jewish synagogue since the 15C was opened in Barcelona (situated in the Eixample, at the corner of the Carreres de Balmes and Provença). The triumph of Franco during the Civil War, however, led to a further Jewish exodus, and the Barcelona synagogue was not to be reopened until 1948.

The attractive dark and narrow streets comprising the present-day Call feature a number of 14C to 16C buildings, and a jumble of antique shops. From the north-west corner of the Plaça de Sant Jaume, you should head along the winding CARRER DEL CALL, which was the main street of the Jewish ghetto. A mosaic plaque at No. 14 records the site of the shop founded in 1591 by the printer and bookseller Cormellas; this establishment, which was mentioned in Cervantes' *Don Quixote*, achieved particular renown through its late 16C commemorative edition of Ovid's *Metamorphoses*, a work referred to in the façade's sgraffitoed decoration of 1780. The first street to the right is the CARRER DE SANT DOMÈNEC DEL CALL, which was where the main Jewish synagogue was situated. The house at No. 5, occupied by a *pension*, has retained much of its 13C to 15C structure, and has a delightful small courtyard decorated with ceramic tiles designed in 1900 by the Modernist architect Antoní María Galissa Soqué. The *Vinateria del Call*, at No. 9, is a pleasant traditionally decorated wine bar renowned for its selection of wines and *tapas*. At No. 15 a plaque records the site where St. Dominic of Guzmán founded the first Dominican monastery in Barcelona in 1219.

Returning down the street, turn right into the CARRER DE MARLET, where you will find, at No. 1, a 19C house bearing a stone of 1314 inscribed in Hebrew with the enigmatic words, 'Holy Foundation of Rabbi Samuel Hassardi, whose life is never-ending' (implying that his holiness was immortal); this stone, which features the date 692 of the Jewish calendar, possibly came from the nearby former synagogue, and is the sole remaining testimony to the Jewish presence in the Call in medieval times.

Heading down the CARRER SANT RAMON DEL CALL, you will come back to the Carrer del Call, where you should continue heading west. The next street to the right is the CARRER DELS BANYS NOUS, the name of which (the New Baths) refers to the Jewish baths that were founded here in 1160 at the junction of this street and the Carrer del Call's continuation, the CARRER DE LA BOQUERÍA; at No. 20 is the barrel-vaulted *Bodega Portalón*, one of the finest of Barcelona's few surviving traditional wine cellars.

Leave the Call and continue on the Carrer de la Boquería, a street originally lined with butchers, and now featuring a number of modest 16C, 17C and 18C houses; the 18C house at No. 12 has a delightful turn-of-the-century portal in a Flamboyant Gothic vein. You are now in the district of the Pi, an area of ancient origin which grew up outside the Roman walls and derived its name from the great pines which were once to be found here. Immediately to the north of the Carrer de la Boquería is the PLAÇITA DEL PI, one of three interconnecting squares surrounding the large church of **Santa Maria del Pi**. This impressive building, erected on the site of a much earlier church, was begun in 1322, but not completed until the late 15C, under the supervision of the master mason Bartolomeu Mas. One of the most characteristic examples of the Catalan Gothic, this is a box-like structure notable for its austerity and great width. The west façade, on the Plaça del Pi, is articulated by two prominent string courses, which give it a pronounced horizontal character; above the portal is a vast rose window, said to be the largest in the world. The echoing single-aisled interior was gutted in 1936 and lost most of its original stained-glass windows, which were subsequently replaced by rather brash copies.

The squares surrounding the building, marking the site of two cemeteries, are among the most pleasant in Barcelona's old quarter. There are few better places in the city centre to sit outside at than the café tables belonging to the popular and modest *Bar del Pi*, on the west side of the shaded Plaça Sant Josep Oriol. On the adjoining square to the north, the PLAÇA DEL PI, numerous street artists, musicians and other performers gather on Saturday and Sunday mornings; a lively artisans' market, selling cheeses, sausages and other local produce, is held here on the first Friday of every month. The large and solitary pine at the centre of the Plaça del Pi, though planted comparatively recently, is a reminder of a famous, ancient tree which once stood here; the house on the western side of the square, at No. 3 (originally the premises of the Guild of Retailers), is covered with sgraffito decorations dating back to 1685.

Due north of the Plaça Sant Josep Oriol runs the CARRER DEL PI, where you will find the *Cercle de Sant Luc, an art academy which was founded at the turn of the century in opposition to the prevailing radical tendencies of the time. Its founder members, of stong symbolist and mystical tendencies, included Gaudí and the sculptor Josep Llimona; during the First World War Joan Miró studied drawing here, finding himself in the same class as the ageing Gaudí. Towards the end of the street, at No. 16, is the *Xarcutería la Pineda*, a famous delicatessen and bar dating back to the early years of the century.

Running north-west of the Plaça del Pi is the narrow CARRER DE PETRITXOL, its old houses adorned with balconies overflowing with plants. Though widely admired today for its shops and general prettiness, this street was not so fondly remembered by the Madrilenian playwright and poet of the Romantic era, Leandro Moratín (1760–1828). This Francophile writer stayed here at a squalid *pension*, which he described in a letter of 18 July 1914: 'I am staying at a terrible lodging-house in an alley called the 'Carrer de Petritxol'; this house, with service, bed, breakfast, lunch and dinner, costs me three pesetas, and from this you can infer that the food is quite evil; but it's time to make economies'. Living here in somewhat grander style later in the century was another playwright and poet, Àngel Guimerà (1849–1924), who wrote in Catalan and was named in 1877 the *mester en gai saber* (master troubadour) in the Jocs Floraux; his house, marked by a plaque, is the elegant early 19C building at No. 4. At No. 5 is the *Sala Parès, which was founded in 1884 as the city's first art gallery. At this establishment—later owned by the children of the poet Joan Maragall—the 20-year-old Picasso exhibited a series of pastels that had mainly been executed in Paris; the exhibition met with an enthusiastic response from his circle of friends at *Els Quatre Gats*, and led to an article on the artist by Miguel Utrillo. One of the earliest of the city's pastry shops, and two old cafés specialising in hot chocolate, are also to be found on this street.

Returning to the Plaçita del Pi, head south along the CARRER DE ALSINA and CARRER DE RAURIC until you reach the CARRER DE FERRAN, the animated street which connects the Rambla with the Plaça de Sant Jaume. Designed by Josep Mas i Vila in 1820–23, in connection with the relaying of the Plaça de Sant Jaume, it became in the late 19C one of the most fashionable of Barcelona's streets; a fine survival from its turn-of-the-century heyday is *Wolf's*, at No. 7, a shop with an exuberant Moderniste façade. Half-way along the street, on its southern side, is the *Church of Sant Jaume, founded for converted Jews in 1394, on the site of the smaller of the Call's two synagogues. The much restored portal is of 1398, but the appearance of the interior is due largely to remodelling carried out between 1866 and 1880 by Josep Oriol Mestres; the high altar bears today a magnificent retable of 1357 commissioned by Pere III for the Cathedral.

Continuing along the street, you will find, also to your right, the entrance to the *Passatge del Crèdit, an elegant passage built by Magí Rius i Mulet in 1875–79, and featuring cast-iron columns and girders in imitation of fashionable Parisian shopping arcades. The painter Joan Miró (1893–1983) was born at an apartment at No. 4, where his father kept a successful jewellery shop; the apartment was to remain in the family's possession until 1944, and Miró was to keep a studio here for much of this time, working apparently in such cramped conditions that he had to crawl on his stomach under the stacks of canvases. The artist is commemorated here by a mosaic plaque erected in 1968 on the occasion of his 75th birthday.

South of the Passatge del Crèdit, extends the district of Palau, a district of quiet and narrow streets bordered to the west by the Carrer d'Avinyó and to the east by the Carreres Ciutat and Regomir. The name is derived from the medieval Palau Menor (Lesser Palace), which was built on the site of a large Roman fortress, and occupied by the queens of Catalonia. The palace was demolished in 1858, and only its chapel remains, at No. 4 of the Carrer d'Ataülf (immediately below the modern, southern extension of the Casa de la Ciutat); this much altered chapel, remodelled in the mid 16C, has a 19C façade incorporating a 13C side portal. A partial compensation for the destroyed royal palace is the fine **Palau Centelles**, which is situated at 8 Bajada de Sant Miquel (turn left on to this street at the end of the Passatge del Crèdit). Built c 1514 for Lluís de Centelles, this palace came in the mid 19C into the possession of Maria Pignatelli, a descendant of the Gonzagas; it is now owned by the *Generalitat*. Though the interior cannot be visited, you are allowed to wander around its beautiful small courtyard, which mingles Gothic and Renaissance elements, and has an open staircase supporting a slender arcade.

Leaving the palace and walking to the western end of the Bajada de Sant Miquel, you will come to the CARRER D'AVINYÓ, to the west of which begins a large and seedy area frequented by numerous prostitutes and figures of the Barcelona underworld. The street itself, with a number of imposing 17C and 18C palaces bearing witness to smarter days, went into a sharp decline towards the end of the 19C. The building at No. 27 marks the site of a well-known brothel frequented by Picasso, who was possibly referring to this street in the title of his pioneering Cubist work *Les Demoiselles d'Avignon* (others believe that this title derived from a ribald suggestion that the Avignon grandmother of the poet Max Jacob had posed for one of the figures). In 1899, one year before his first trip to Paris, the 19-year-old Picasso had a studio at No. 1 of the parallel street to the west of the Carrer d'Avinyó, the dark and narrow Carrer dels Escudellers Blancs; this studio was a small room in the apartment of the brother of the young sculptor Josef Cardona. Other rooms in this building were used in Picasso's time as workshops for the making of ladies' underwear; Jaume Sabartés—whose first meeting with Picasso took place here—recalled how the artist, 'in his idle moments, entertained himself by making eyelet holes in the corsets with the appropriate machines'.

Walking down the Carrer d'Avinyó, you will pass on your left, near the street's far end, the entrance to the short Carrer de Milans, an impressive example of town planning conceived in 1849 by Francesc Daniel Molina: near its centre the street swells out into a tiny round space (known as the Plaça dels Lleons) before changing course and heading east, the overall effect resembling a snake which has swallowed a large object. Continuing along the Carrer d'Avinyó the next street to your left is the CARRER D'EN GIGNÀS, where at No. 16 is one of the city's better known restaurants, *Agut*: opened in 1924, this place has maintained over the years a reputation for excellent food, remarkably modest prices and increasingly long queues to get inside. The Carrer Avinyó ends immediately to the south of this street, at the junction of the long CARRER AMPLE. The word *ample* means 'wide' in Catalan, and this street was known as such because it was wide enough for horses and carriages to parade along. This was once the most aristocratic street in Barcelona, and a remarkably distinguished group of people have lived or stayed here, including the kings of Hungary and Bohemia, the Emperor Charles V and his wife Isabel of Portugal, the viceroys of Catalonia, and the future wife of Charles VI of Germany, Isabel Cristina of Brunswick (the mother of Maria Theresa). From the mid 18C onwards the street became the favourite residential district of the city's upper middle classes, but decline set in with the construction of the Eixample in the mid 19C. This whole area lying behind the Passeig de Colom (see p. 98) has today a rough but lively character, with much animation provided by the wealth of modest bars providing a great variety of wines and *tapas*; this is a popular district to come to for the Barcelona equivalent of a 'pub crawl', and in the evenings is filled with people moving from one bar to another.

Heading south-west down the Carrer Ample from the Carrer d'Avinyó, you will skirt to your left the former monastery *Church of La Mercè, the façade of which overlooks the elegant Plaça de la Mercè. Founded by the Mercedarians in 1267, the monastery was dissolved in 1835, and its main building was taken over as the premises of the Capitanía General (see p. 99). The present church, which now serves the parish, was built in 1765–75 by Josep Mas d'Ordal, its sculptural ornamentation being carried out by Carles Grau. Its most remarkable feature is its façade, which, though restrained in its decoration, is the only one in the city to employ the theatrical and characteristically baroque device of placing curved walls on either side of a straight frontispiece. The square which it faces was created in 1982 with the demolition of a group of houses in the centre, and the placing here of a 19C fountain of Neptune, originally from the port. Returning north-east along the Carrer Ample, and walking beyond the junction with the Carrer d'Avinyó, you will see to your right, at No. 28, the finest of the street's remaining 18C and early 19C palaces. This, the *Palau Sessa Larrard**, was built in 1772–78 for the Viceroy of Catalonia, the Duke of Sessa, but was acquired only one year after its completion by the banker and Danish consul, J.A. Larrard; the architects were Josep Gaig and Joan Soler, who worked to a plan drawn up by Josep Rivas i Margarit. The building displays a late baroque classicism similar to that of the Palau de la Virreina (see p. 46), and is distinguished, on its main façade, by an elegant portal comprising Corinthian columns supporting a superlative ironwork balustrade, executed, like the surrounding sculptural ornamentation, by Carles Grau.

Continuing along the Carrer Ample, you will pass to your right the entrance to the Carrer de la Plata, the street where Picasso had his first studio, in 1888. Traditionally it is thought that this studio was situated on the fifth floor of the attractive house at No. 4; however, certain experts believe that the room was located instead in the basement of No. 5. In any case a commemorative plaque to the artist has been placed outside No. 4, where you will also find an art gallery named the Cambra Picasso.

Further along the Carrer Ample you should turn left into the bar-lined CARRER DEL REGOMIR and enter the small district of this name, which up to the 13C was one of the 'vilanoves' or new towns at the edge of Barcelona; its name is due to its having once been crossed by an irrigation canal built in the 10C by Count Rego Mir. The second street to your right as you walk up the picturesque and decayed Carrer del Regomir is the CARRER CORREU VELL, where at No. 5 is an early 16C palace containing a fine courtyard with exuberant late Gothic motifs. At its eastern end, beyond a small round tower from the Roman walls (uncovered in 1968), this street joins the CARRER HOSTAL D'EN SOL, the name of which is derived from a famous inn which once stood here; one of the guests at this inn was 'Count Calgiostro' (Giuseppe Balsamo), the 17C Italian adventurer whose exploits were to inspire Alexandre Dumas and other novelists.

Back on the Carrer del Regomir and continuing north, you will skirt to your right the quaintly irregular complex (at Nos 11–19) forming the 14C *Casa dels Gualbes. Elements of the original structure have survived, but the most impressive feature of this building is the early 18C portal (at No. 13), a baroque structure of an elaborate kind rare in Barcelona; for many years the building has been used as a studio by one of the most successful of Catalonia's recent sculptors, Josep Maria Subirachs. Further along, also to the right (at No. 5) is the *Chapel of Sant Cristòfol, which was built in 1530, but given a neo-Gothic interior in 1899; every year, on St. Christopher's Day (10 July), cars queue up along the already congested street to be blessed outside the chapel. Originally the chapel was attached to a 15C palace, the decayed and much altered remains of which can be seen by turning right, into the narrow cul-de-sac of the Carrer de Sant Simplici. At the end of this alley is an arch marking the entrance to the palace's courtyard, known today as the *Pati d'en Llimona, one of the more evocative hidden corners of old Barcelona. The courtyard's outstanding feature is a late 15C gallery supported on corbels carved with a number of life-like heads.

Turning right at the top of the Carrer del Regomir, and walking to the end of the short Carrer Cometa (named after the sighting of Haley's Comet in 1834), you will come out at the lower end of the CARRER DE LLEDÓ, which dates back to the 13C, when permission was given to build alongside the Roman walls. You are now in the district of Sant Just, which is quieter and more sophisticated than that of Regomir, but similarly decayed. The narrow Carrer de Lledó, which was one of the wealthiest and most aristocratic streets of the late medieval city, is surpassed only by the Carrer de Montcada (see p. 83) in evoking what Barcelona must have been like in its medieval heyday. However, in contrast to the latter street, its appearance today is characterised by an overall shabbiness, and though it has miraculously retained a remarkable number of palaces of medieval origin, these have been much altered and poorly maintained. The palace at No. 13, remodelled in the mid 19C, has kept on its façade two fine Renaissance medallions of female heads. Further up, at No. 11, is a former 18C palace (now occupied by a college of Carmelite nuns) with an unusual open staircase in its courtyard. The columns of this staircase are truncated in a way which leaves their upper section suspended in mid-air; possibly the architect was just showing off, but in any case the idea for these columns certainly derives from the suspended capitals to be found elsewhere in Barcelona (for instance in the Palau de la Generalitat). The oldest of the street's palaces date back to the 14C and are concentrated at the street's upper end, beginning with the one at No. 7, which was largely remodelled in the 18C. Marginally better preserved is the palace at No. 6, a building which has been described as having belonged to Queen Elionor of Sicily for no other reason than that it adjoins the street of this name; on the side façade is a Renaissance window with an architrave supported by tiny carved corbels. The neighbouring palace, at No. 4, has a run-down courtyard with a Gothic window featuring further corbel figures, these being possibly the work of a follower of Pere Joan. In the late 14C this was the palace of Joan Fiveller, a town councillor of legendary character whose intransigence was such that he is supposed to have compelled King Ferdinand of Antequera to pay a municipal tax on fish consumed by his retinue. Another celebrity associated with this street was the court poet and translator Joan Boscà Almugaver (1487?–1542), who was born here; Boscà, an important force in the introduction to Spain of the literature and ideas of Renaissance Italy, was the Spanish translator of Castiglione's *Courtier*, a work to which he had been introduced by his poet friend Garcilaso de la Vega.

The street ends at the small and charming **Plaça de Sant Just**, at the entrance to which is a fountain donated to the city in 1367 by Joan Fiveller, whose love of hunting is alluded to in a carving of a falcon; the fountain, which was not operational until 1427, was given a neo-classical remodelling in 1831. The square itself was created in the early 19C following the closure of the small remaining section of the ancient cemetery of Sant Just, which was reputedly the burial place of Barcelona's first martyrs. The **Church of Sant Just**, on the western side of the square, has the reputation of being the oldest church in the city.

According to legend the church of Sant Just has its origins in a 4C temple erected by Christians above the ruins of a Roman amphitheatre; however, the documented history of the church begins only with its reconstruction by Louis the Pious in 801. This royal church was made a dependency of the Cathedral in 965, and, from then up to the 15C, its rectors automatically became archdeacons of the Cathedral. The former importance of this church was shown by the special privileges that were bestowed upon it in the early Middle Ages. The most significant of these was the Right of Sacramental Wills, which allowed Barcelona citizens anywhere in the world to make a valid will—orally and without recourse to a notary—simply by getting a witness to come to this church within six months and validate the will's contents in front of the altar of Sant Feliu. This right, instituted reputedly by Louis the Pious, is first known to have been used by one Berenguer Sendret in 1082; remarkably, it still remains in force, and over 100 people have had recourse to it since 1939.

The present church, generally attributed to Bernat Roca, was begun in 1342 and completed up to the fourth bay of the nave by 1363; the last bay was not finished until the late 15C. The austere façade is largely due to restoration and remodelling carried out after 1883 by Josep Oriol Mestres, who, with a view to enlarging the square in front of it, demolished various structures that had been added to the façade, most notably the parish archives; the semi-octagonal bell tower was built in 1559–72 by Pere Blay and Joan Safont. The single-aisled interior features on the nave vault a series of 14C poylchromed bosses carved with scenes of the life of Christ and the Virgin. The neo-classical High Altar of 1832 incorporates an image of the Virgin of Montserrat, who is reputed to have paid a visit to the church before appearing in the mountain which bears her name. By far the most remarkable of the church's furnishings is the altarpiece to be found in the **Chapel of Sant Feliú**, which is situated at the far left-hand side of the nave. The work was commissioned in 1525 by Joan de Requesens, who had been given permission to be buried here on the condition that he decorated the chapel. Comprising a central panel of the Pietà, this altarpiece was painted by the Portuguese artist Pero Nunyes; the intricate framework was the work of the Flemish craftsman Joan de Bruseles.

On the eastern side of the square is the late 18C *Palau Moixó, which is richly sgraffitoed with garlands and putti. From here a dark cul-de-sac leads east to the main entrance of the **Palau de la Comtessa de Palamós**, which was the largest private palace in medieval Barcelona. Dating back to the 13C, it incorporated on its eastern side the stretch of Roman wall which extends down the Carrer del Sots-tinent Navarro; the palace was greatly extended during the 15C, when it belonged to Galceran de Requesens, Count of Palamós, and Governor General of Catalonia. Its wonderful courtyard, which retains windows and masonry from the original 13C structure, has an open staircase leading up to a delicate 15C arcade. Since 1970 the palace has been the seat of the Academy of Fine Arts, and can only be visited by prior arrangement or on the third Sunday of each month, from 10.30–14.00. The interior, which was remodelled in the early 18C, houses the *Galeria De Catalans Illustres, a collection of paintings of famous Catalans, displayed in outstanding baroque rooms. North of the Plaça de Sant Just you rejoin the Carrer Jaume I, a few hundred metres to the west of the Plaça de l'Àngel.

C. The Barris de Santa Anna, Sant Pere and Santa Maria del Mar

The extension of Barcelona's walls during the reign of Jaume I embraced an especially large area to the east of the Roman city. This area, comprising the districts of Sant Pere and Santa María del Mar, has a similar wealth of narrow medieval streets as the Barri Gòtic, but without either the latter's museum-like character, or the overall seediness of other parts of medieval

Barcelona; it is lively and busy, its streets filled with artisans, shoppers and schoolchildren.

Walking to the Barri de Sant Pere from the Plaça de Catalunya (see p. 124), you will pass through the small Barri de Santa Anna, the medieval character of which has been largely lost through modern development. Indeed as you walk south from the Plaça de Catalunya on the tiny CARRER DE RIVADENEYRA, you might be surprised at coming across, incongruously hidden behind the modern blocks, an enclave of cypresses and flowers enclosing one of the city's oldest churches. This, the former monastery **Church of Santa Anna**, was founded by the Knights Templar shortly after their arrival in the city in the early 12C; the building was much altered and extended in later periods, most notably in the 15C, when the monastery was merged with that of Montsió. The single-aisled church, entered through a 13C portal, is in the shape of a Greek cross, and has an interior of exceptional simplicity and austerity, which was made more apparent through the loss of most of its furnishings during the Civil War. The main survivals of the Romanesque structure are the barrel-vaulted square apse and transepts, the original masonry being distinguished from the modern restoration by being in stone rather than brick; the nave was revaulted and extended in the 14C, while the crossing dome is a modern reconstruction of an unfinished 15C structure. The elegant two-storey Gothic cloister, which has been greatly enhanced by the luxuriant group of palms and other trees in its centre, was begun in the 15C but not completed until c 1590; off it lies a former chapter house (now a chapel), also dating from the 15C. The rest of the monastic complex fell into ruin shortly after the monastery's dissolution in 1835, and all that remains is a 15C door which once marked the entrance to the whole precinct. This door has been preserved at No. 29 of the CARRER DE SANTA ANNA, which follows the southern side of the church. At No. 21 of this same street is a fine Moderniste block of 1907, designed for Elena Castellano by Jaume Torres i Grau, and with exuberant floral motifs on the exterior; the vestibule is especially lavish, with stucco, stained glass, ceramic and sgraffito decorations.

Head east along the Carrer de Santa Anna until you reach the AVINGUDA PORTAL DE L'ÀNGEL, a busy shopping thoroughfare marking an old route which headed to the north of the city's 13C walls. The street significantly narrows towards its southern end, and eventually reaches an octagonal fountain which dates back to 1356 but was remodelled in the 19C and given a ceramic coating in 1918 by Josep Aragay. Walking south down the street you will note to your left at Nos 20–22 the ostentatious and eclectic façade of the *Catalana de Gas i Electricitat, which was built in 1893–95 by the Moderniste architect Josep Domènech i Estapa. On the southern side of the building is the entrance to the quiet and narrow CARRER DE MONTSIÓ, where you should turn left. At No. 3, on the left-hand side, is the **Casa Martí**, which was the first work in Barcelona of the leading Moderniste architect Josep Puig i Cadafalch. Built in 1895–96, it has a striking brick exterior, imitative of a medieval palace, but wholly fantastical in its overall effect. Certain elements such as the arcaded top-floor gallery recall Catalan Gothic architecture, but the Flamboyant Gothic windows below, as well as the pinnacled oriel window on the side façade, are of North European derivation. The virtuoso carvings are by Eusebi Arnau and include a coat of arms formed by the emblems of the textile industry, and—on the large corbel at the corner of the building—a lively carving of St. George and the Dragon, a motif which was thereafter to feature on nearly all of Puig i Cadalfach's works and serve almost as the architect's signature. Manuel

Ballarín was responsible for the splendid ironwork balconies on both the main façade, and on the gate closing off the lane in between this building and the one at No. 5 Carrer de Montesió (a structure of 1906 attributed to Puig i Cadalfach); the floral and other ornamental details of the ironwork are inspired by the railings in the cloister of Barcelona cathedral. The large Gothic openings on the ground floor mark the entrance to the former artistic tavern of **Els Quatre Gats**, the famed haunt of the city's avant-garde at the turn of the century.

The creation of *Els Quatre Gats* was due essentially to four individuals who had spent much time in Paris, where they had taken an enthusiastic part in the Bohemian life of Montmartre. Two of these figures were the painters Ramon Casas and Santiago Rusiñol. Another was Miquel Utrillo, who had gone to Paris in 1880 as an engineeering student, but had found himself drawn to the artistic circle which had gathered in a well-known Montmartre café called *Le Chat Noir*. At *Le Chat Noir*, Utrillo met the artist and model Suzanne Valadon, by whom he was to have an illegitimate child who was to become the painter Maurice Utrillo. He also acquired at this café a taste for shadow-puppet theatre, which was then very much in vogue in Montmartre. While still in Paris Utrillo worked as a puppeteer with an eccentric and flamboyant compatriot, Pere Romeu. Romeu, who was later to manage *Els Quatre Gats*, appears to have begun his career as a painter, but was later consumed by a dual interest in bicycling and cabaret. An enormous inspiration to him was the infamous *cabaretier* Aristide Bruant, whom he was to emulate both in his behaviour and attire, going around Barcelona dressed in a long waistcoat and flat-brimmed hat.

On his return to Barcelona, Romeu founded a gym which was attended by both Utrillo and Ramon Casas, who appear to have come more for the conversation than the physical exercise. With the arrival of Rusiñol into their group, the enthusiasm for the gym waned and a decision was made to found instead an artistic tavern. Remarkably, financial backing for this rather unworldly new project was provided by the same banker who had sponsored the construction of Barcelona cathedral's west façade, Manuel Girona; Girona's help might partially be explained by the fact that Romeu's sister-in-law had been a cook in his household.

Els Quatre Gats opened on the ground floor of Puig i Cadalfach's newly completed Casa Martí on 10 June 1897. The name *Four Cats* alluded not only to the *Chat Noir* in Paris, but also to the tavern's four founders; furthermore the Catalan phrase *quatre gats* has the additional meaning of 'a handful of people', a meaning which well conveyed the minority nature of Barcelona's *Moderniste* circles. As a tavern, *Els Quatre Gats* was famously informal, providing the city's cultural and intellectual élite with an environment far less sophisticated and elegant than that of other fashionable institutions of the time such as the Café Torino. It promoted itself for its high-quality French and Catalan food, but in fact appealed less as a restaurant than as a meeting-place for a late-night crowd composed largely of writers, journalists, artists, actors and musicians; these were people who talked far more than they consumed, but this appears not to have unduly worried Romeu. One of the visitors to the tavern in 1899 was the Nicaraguan poet Rubén Darío, who later wrote of this place that it was packed to capacity, and that 'a residual note of elegance was provided by a handful of young ladies—intellectuals, we were told—but these were types neither from Botticelli nor Aubrey Beardsley, for neither their clothes nor the way they wore their hair betrayed the slightest snobbery'. The place, he continued 'abounded in artistic types straight from the *Boul' Mich*; young, long-haired, with 1830-style cravates, and other types of cravate…'

The importance of *Els Quatre Gats* in the history of Catalan culture is due above all to the many and varied functions that were organised here. These included poetry recitals, musical performances (given by the likes of Albeniz and Granados), meetings of the newly-formed Wagnerian Society and shadow-puppet shows put on by Utrillo; following on from the example of *Le Chat Noir* in Paris, the tavern even came to publish its own art journal, which was eventually succeeeded by the influential *Pel i Ploma*, edited by Utrillo and Casas. Perhaps the most significant aspect of the place's activities was the holding of art exhibitions, its main room providing young artists with an informal alternative to the Sala Parès, which up to then had been the only private exhibiting institution in the city. The first of its exhibitions, held only one month after the tavern's opening, was devoted to the work of four of the younger generation of Modernistes, Nonell, Canals, Mir and Ramon Pichot; a later exhibitor, showing his work to the public for the first time, was Pablo Picasso.

The tavern, though enormously influential, was only to survive for six years. In July 1903, following the departure of Rusiñol to Paris, Romeu closed the place to devote himself wholly to his passion for the bicycle; he was to die a few years later, a victim to poverty and tuberculosis. Ironically, the tavern's premises were subsequently to be taken over as the headquarters and exhibition gallery of the Cercle Artístic de San Lluc (see p. 72), the members of which were politically conservative and deeply opposed to the atheist, left-wing tendencies associated with the tavern's previous habitués.

In recent years the original decoration of *Els Quatre Gats* has been recreated, and a bar and restaurant have been installed here, of distinctly un-Bohemian character; clean, smart and moderately expensive, it is frequented largely by a combination of tourists and office-workers. A visit here will at least give you some idea of the look if not the character of the place which Utrillo had described as a 'Gothic beer hall for lovers of the north, and an Andalusian patio for amateurs of the south, a house of healing'. A bright ceramic decoration on the walls, evocative of the south, competes with elements of northern medieval inspiration, such as the heavy wooden beam ceiling and the wooden chandeliers, the latter becoming a hallmark of Catalan Modernism; the wooden chairs, benches, long tables and other furnishings are reproductions of designs by Puig i Cadalfach. The walls have been decorated with copies of the works by Rusiñol and Casas that once hung here (the originals are now in the Barcelona Museum of Modern Art). Among these are a series of portrait sketches of the regular associates of the tavern (including Picasso), a large picture of Rusiñol swinging on one of the chandeliers and a mural-sized canvas of Casas and Romeu riding through Barcelona on a tandem (in 1900 this work had been replaced by a portrait of the pair in an automobile).

The parallel street to the north of the Carrer de Montsió is the CARRER DE COMTAL, a lively shopping street which includes among its varied shops *La Casa de Bacalao* (at No. 8), a place specialising solely in different cuts of dried and salted cod, all of which are displayed as if they were goods in a high-class confectioners. The house at No. 3 (and not at No. 2, as a plaque wrongfully indicates) was the birthplace of the influential Catalan essayist and philosopher, Eugeni d'Ors y Rovira (1882–1954), the leading spokesman of the Noucentisme movement.

At its eastern end the Carrer de Comtal emerges into the VIA LAIETANA, a busy thoroughfare which runs from the Eixample all the way south to the port, cutting in the process a great swathe through the medieval city. The street was conceived in 1868, but the construction work did not go ahead until 1907, amidst enormous protests from conservationists. As with Madrid's Gran Vía, with which it is almost contemporary, the street is lined with a number of tall blocks inspired by the Chicago School, a pioneering example of which is the one at No. 17, built by Albert Joan i Torner in 1918–28. The most eccentric of its modern buildings is the *Caixa de Pensions per a la Vellesa i d'Estalvis, which you will see rising up to your left as soon as you enter the street from the Carrer de Comtal. Built by Enric Sagnier Villavecchia in 1917–18, this structure was a self-conscious reaction to the emergent American influences of the time, and harked back to the neo-medievalism of Modernisme; its main façade, at the corner of the *CARRER DE LES JONQUERES, features a soaring, pinnacled spire which was intended to give the building the look of a cathedral, in this case a cathedral to money. On this same side of the street, but directly facing the entrance to the Carrer de Comtal, is a solitary survival from an earlier century, the *Casa Gremial Velers (No. 50). This was built by Joan Garrido i Bertran in 1758–63 as the headquarters of the Silk-workers' Guild, and its ostentatious sgraffito decoration of caryatids, columns and putti testifies to the economic and political power which the city's guilds once held. With the construction of the Via Laietana this building was almost pulled down, but was saved after being declared a national monument in 1913; it was extensively restored in 1928–31.

Running east from the Casa Gremial Velers is the CARRER DE SANT PERE MÉS ALT, which you should now follow. The first building which you will come to (at No. 11) is the **PALAU DE LA MÚSICA CATALANA**, the supreme expression of Catalan Modernisme, and certainly one of the most seductive and entertaining concert halls in the world.

The history of this building goes back to the foundation in 1891 of the private musical society known as the *Orfeo Català*. In 1904 the society commissioned Lluís Domènech i Montaner to design a building which would serve both as their headquarters and as a large concert hall; his brief was to design a 'Temple of Catalan art, a palace to celebrate its renaissance'. The first stone was laid in 1905, but already by October of the following year funds were running dangerously low, and a public appeal had to be made. This appeal, which played heavily on nationalist sentiments and Catalan pride, was enormously successful, and in February of 1908 the building was finally inaugurated. The place won for its architect the Town Hall prize for the best building of 1908, but by the late 1920s there was already much talk of pulling it down or at the very least of completely remodelling its interior. Architectural critics considered it then to be a decadent work, and one of them even wrote that it was 'a monument to the ostentatious vanity of an age filled with illusions'. The building, which managed fortunately to survive unscathed the critical onslaught of the 1920s, has recently been enhanced by an excellent modern extension containing offices, dressing-rooms, a library and rehearsal rooms. Built by Oscar Tusquets and Carlos Díaz in 1982–89, this extension was conceived as part of these architects' remodelling of the adjoining church of San Francesc de Paula.

In the Palau de la Música, Domènech i Montaner made the most of a cramped and awkward site by placing the auditorium on the first floor and turning the ground floor into a large vestibule which is linked to the street by a spacious arcade. The use of space is suggestive and fluid, with a brilliant play of light and shade, and a lack of rigid division between exterior and interior. Of more obvious appeal is the building's stunning decoration, which involved several of the finest craftsmen of the day, including the sculptors Miquel Blay and Pablo Gargallo, the mosaic artist Lluís Bru and the designer of stained glass, Antoni Rigalt. The mauvish-red brick exterior is crowned on its façade by a frieze of allegorical mosaics, below which, suspended in niches recalling the arcades of the Mosque at Cordova, are busts of Palestrina, Bach and Beethoven; further down is a forest of polychromed columns with exuberant floral capitals whose elaborate forms are taken up in the abstract decoration featured in Tusquet's and Díaz's extension on the north-western corner of the building. Especially remarkable is the sculpted group by Blay at the corner of the façade, a frothing mass of stone from which a knight in armour and a naked woman billow forth to proclaim an allegory of popular Catalan music. Within the auditorium itself all the stops of Modernisme are pulled out in the creation of a spectacular ensemble of breathtaking richness and colour, glowing under a great ceiling of stained glass. Water-lilies and nymphs provide some of this room's principal decorative motifs, but the most memorable features of the ornamentation are Gargallo's massive sculptural groups flanking the stage. The group to the left, lyrical in tone, features a bust of the Orfeo's founder, Josep Clavé, basking under the luxuriant shade of the Tree of Life; the right-hand group, incorporating a bust of Beethoven, shows with exceptional drama and a frightening degree of realism the horses of the Valkyries making a massive leap in the direction of the audience, an excellent device for keeping awake any somnolent listeners.

From the Palau de la Música you should continue heading along the Carrer de Sant Pere més alt, which will plunge you into the medieval heart of the Barri de Sant Pere. Near the street's eastern end, you will pass to your left (at No. 49) the birthplace of the outstanding muralist, Josep Maria Sert (1874–1945), whose many works include decorations in the Casa de la Ciutat (see p. 70). Beyond this you will come to an attractive small square dominated by the church after which this district is named, **Sant Pere de les Puelles**. This former monastery church, one of the oldest surviving monuments of the city, was founded in 945 by the Benedictines for the Counts of Barcelona; the site chosen was that of a Visigothic church dedicated to Sant Saturninus. Destroyed by Al-Mansur in 985 and again by the Almoravids in the early 12C, the church was rebuilt and recon-secrated in 1147. The building experienced various other changes before being gutted by fire in 1909 and again in 1936. The fortress-like main façade is a medieval pastiche of 1911, its only earlier feature being the 15C portal. The interior has preserved its 12C Greek plan, but owes its appear-ance largely to modern remodelling; a large fragment of the 12C cloisters— which were pulled down in 1873—can now be seen in the Museu de Arte de Catalunya in Montjuïc (see p. 117).

The Carrer de Sant Pere més alt is the highest of three parallel ancient streets which converge at their eastern end on the Plaça de Sant Pere. The street below is the CARRER DE SANT PERE MITJÀ , while further south is the CARRER DE SANT PERE MÉS BAIX, an especially lively shopping street lined with numerous old houses of medieval origin. A 16C nobleman's house near the western entrance of this street (at Nos 7–9) housed up to 1986 the pioneering *Institut de Cultura i Biblioteca Popular per a la Dona. This institution, founded by Francesca Bonnemaison de Verdaguer in 1909, was the first cultural society and library in Spain intended solely for women; on the ceiling of its main reading-room was a quotation by the medieval Catalan philosopher Ramon Llull, *'Tota dona val mes quan letra apren'* (every woman is worth more if she knows how to read). As well as its books, the institution also offered conference rooms, a restaurant, a hairdressers and—another novelty in pre-First World War Spain—showers. After the Civil War this former progressive institution was taken over briefly by the Female Section of the Falange before being incorporated into the Library of Catalonia; it is now the centre of a Theatre Institute. Another 16C building on this street, at No. 52, houses the former *Farmàcia Padrell (now Bernadas), a Moderniste pharmacy of 1890, with a remarkable stained-glass frontage by Juan Espinagosa.

At the eastern end of the Carrer de Sant Pere més baix, you should head south down the CARRER BASSES DE SANT PERE, which widens into a quiet and picturesquely irregular small square; from the Middle Ages up to the early 19C, this space was occupied by artificial ponds or '*basses*' serving a group of textile mills. At the lower end of the square, at No. 4, is a modest 14C house housing one of Barcelona's many milk bars or 'Granjas'; there is a popular tradition that Christopher Columbus was once imprisoned in this building. Beyond this the Carrer Basses de Sant Pere reaches the decayed PLAÇA DE SANT AGUSTÍ VELL, where you should bear right and head in a south-westerly direction down the CARRER DE CARDERS. The second street which you will pass to your right is the CARRER SANT JAUME GIRALT, where the great Catalan poet Joan Maragall (1860–1911) was born and grew up; the exact house of the poet's birth is not known, and claims have been made for Nos 5, 7 and 4. The street is recalled in one of Maragall's poems: 'When I was a boy/I lived timidly/in a dark street./The walls were damp/but the sun was joy'. Another inhabitant of this same street was the actress Margarita Xirgu (1888–1969), who lived as a child at No. 36; one of the greatest Spanish actresses of her day, Xirgu is best remembered today for her association with García Lorca, which began with a production of *Mariana Pineda* in 1927.

Continuing down the Carrer dels Carders, you will reach eventually, at No. 2, a tiny Romanesque chapel of the 12C, the *Capella d'En Marcús. Built between 1166 and 1188, this is the sole survival of the Hostal de la 'Bona Sort', which was founded on the initiative of the merchant Bernardí Marcus in 1147, and served both as a travellers' hostel and hospital for the poor; the chapel, which is rarely open, was gutted by fire in 1909 and 1936, and has little of interest inside. On the other side of the street to the chapel's west façade is the entrance to the CARRER GIRALT I PELLICER, which leads to the large and lively *Mercat de Santa Caterina; this covered market, which was built in the early 19C on the site of a Dominican monastery, is uninspiring on the outside, but has an interesting interior of wooden beam ceilings. Taking instead the street which follows the chapel's southern side you will come almost immediately to the western end of the **CARRER DE MONTCADA**, which is the finest of all Barcelona's medieval streets.

The Carrer de Montcada formed originally the main route between the important commercial district of the Bòria with the ancient port of Vilanova de la Mar. Wider and straighter than the streets of the old walled city, it became in the 15C the favoured residential street of aristocrats and wealthy merchants. The maritime decline of Barcelona from the 16C onwards, the transference of the port to the south-western side of the city after 1768 and the creation of the Eixample in the late 19C, were all factors that contributed to the gradual decay of the street. Saved from further decay by being declared a national monument in 1947, it was gradually restored by the Municipality after 1953, and in the process several of its finer palaces were adapted as museums and other cultural institutions. Whereas the surrounding district has maintained a lively residential character, the Carrer de Montcada has been turned into a showpiece, and is noticeably quiet on Mondays, when its museums and galleries are closed.

Shortly below its northern end the Carrer de Montcada is intersected by the long CARRER DE LA PRINCESA, which was built after 1853 as the final phase of the plan conceived in 1820–23 to link La Rambla with the Ciutadella. At the time of its construction the Carrer de la Princesa was regarded as a marvel of modern town-planning, and for a short while was one of the most fashionable addresses in town. The city's chronicler at that time, Josep Coroleu, wrote of the street that 'it is one of the best and largest that have been built in Barcelona this century. This spacious thorough-fare…has got rid of a large number of gloomy and insalubrious alleys'. The painter Santiago Rusiñol was born here in 1861, at the height of the street's fashion. His family home, situated above the shop of his father's textile factory, was at No. 37 (near the intersection of the Carrer de Montcada); the birthplace is marked today by a plaque calling Rusiñol 'a symbol of his age'. A delightful account of Rusiñol's childhood is to be found in *Santiago*

Rusiñol y su época (Barcelona, 1989) by the leading Catalan writer Josep Pla.

The outstanding section of the Carrer de Montcada begins immediately below the Carrer de la Princesa. From here all the way down to the Born, the street is lined with a near uninterrupted series of medieval palaces; much of the Gothic detailing has been lost on the façades through later remodelling (particularly in the 17C), but many of the buildings have retained their original courtyards. One of the first buildings to your left, at No. 17, is the **Palau Berenguer d'Aguilar**, which dates back to the 13C; among the fragments discovered here of the original structure were a series of murals depicting the conquest of Mallorca (these are now in the Museu d'Art de Catalunya; see p. 117). The palace was entirely remodelled in the 15C, and features a magnificent Gothic courtyard comparable to the inner courtyard by Marc Safont in the Palau de la Generalitat, and possibly by the same architect. Adjoining the palace, at No. 17, is the *Casa del Baró de Castellet, an 18C building with 15C fragments, and a sumptuously decorated neo-classical salon; the next door building, at No. 17, is the Palau Meca, an 18C remodelling of a 14C structure. All three palaces have now been linked to form the premises of Barcelona's most popular museum, the *MUSEU PICASSO.

Born in Málaga in 1881, Pablo Picasso spent three years as a child in the Galician town of La Coruña, where his father taught at the local art school. In 1895 the father was appointed Professor of Fine Arts at the Academy of Art in Barcelona (La Llotja), and the family moved here from Galicia in September of that year, staying apparently to begin with at a *pension* at No. 4 Passeig d'Isabel II (see p. 101). In the summer of 1896 the family settled in an apartment on the Carrer de la Mercè, in a building which was recently pulled down to make way for the Plaça de la Mercè (see p. 74). Already having his own studio by 1896 (in the Carrer de la Plata; see p. 75), Picasso later worked at No. 1 of the Carrer dels Escudellers Blancs (seep. 74), where, in 1899, he had his first meeting with the man who was later to found this museum, Jaume Sabartés i Gual (1881–1968). The myopic Sabartés, who was to be Picasso's life-long friend and future secretary and collaborator, was the constant Barcelona companion of the artist during the years when they frequented *Els Quatre Gats* (see p. 79). Picasso, followed shortly by Sabartés, went to Paris in 1900, but was back again in Barcelona in 1902, working first at 10 Nou de la Rambla (see p. 95), and later at 28 Carrer del Comerc (see p. 87); these were the years of the artist's so-called Blue Period. Picasso settled permanently in France in 1904, and subsequently made only the occasional short visit to Barcelona, where his parents continued to live. One of these visits—in the company of Diaghilev and the Ballet Russe—was in 1917, following a five-year absence from the city; his father had died in the meantime, and his mother had moved in with her daughter Lola and son-in-law Juan Vilató to a house on the Passeig de Gràcia. Picasso, who stayed on that occasion in a hotel on the Passeig de Colom, was warmly received by his friends and admirers, who put on numerous parties for him, and took him to Flamenco sessions held in the music-halls of the Paral-lel. On that same visit Picasso showed a large oil painting entitled The Harlequin—a work clearly inspired by the world of the Ballet Russe—at an exhibition organised by the Municipality; two years later this painting would be the first of his works that he was to present to the city of Barcelona.

Many years later Barcelona's Museum of Modern Art—to which The Harlequin had been given—was to create a Picasso room, incorporating a further donation from the artist in 1937, as well as works from two important collections acquired respectively in 1932 and 1953, the Plandiura and Garriga i Roig Collections. For most of the Franco period Picasso was to have little contact with Spain, and was unresponsive to the attempts made by the Spanish Government to lure him back to the country at the beginning of the 1960s, when there was a lessening of the official hostility towards him; the Government was at one time even willing to accept his controversial painting of Guernica, but the artist was resolute in not allowing this work to be shown in Spain until the return of democracy there. However, Picasso was rather more flexible in his dealings with Catalonia, regarding this region as a country in its own right, and harbouring a particular affection for Barcelona. In 1962 he accepted an invitation from a group of young Barcelona architects to produce designs for their new College of Architecture (see p. 64). He also gave full support to Sabartés when the latter proposed to offer his extensive collection of the artist's work to Barcelona on the condition that a Picasso Museum was established here. Thanks to Sabartés' persistence this museum was finally opened in the Palau Berenguer d'Aguilar on 9 March 1963. Sabartés, in declining health for several years, had been unable to attend the opening, and was to die five years later. As a commemorative gesture to his old friend Picasso presented 58 works to the museum in 1968, including a famous series of paintings and oil sketches relating to Velásquez's Las Meninas. In 1970 the museum was further enhanced when Picasso gave to it an enormous group of works that had been executed in his youth and been kept over the years in his sister's flat on the Passeig de Gràcia. After the artist's death in 1973 his heirs, carrying out the conditions of his will, donated to the museum a large body of his graphic work; to this was added in 1981 a collection of 141 ceramics owned by his widow Jacqueline. From 1970 up to 1981 the premises of the museum were gradually expanded to include first the Casa del Baró de Castellet and then the Palau Meca.

The perpetually crowded Museu Picasso, for all the donations that it has received over the years, can barely compete in the number and range of its works with the Musée Picasso in Paris. Its great strengths lie in its exceptionally beautiful setting—an imaginative blending of the old and the new—and its unrivalled holdings of the artist's early works. Academic drawings carried out as a child in Málaga and La Coruña put to the test the artist's later boast that he could draw like Raphael at the age of ten; you can also appreciate here the close similarities between the works of his early years and those of his Barcelona circle, in particular Nonell. Experiments with Impressionism, Pointillism and Symbolism gave way after c 1901 to the development of a more personal style first in the so-called Blue Period and then in the Rose Period. Both these periods, which are excellently represented in the museum, drew inspiration from scenes of poverty and hardship, as observed in the streets of both Paris and Barcelona; several of the Blue Period works were executed in his studio at No. 10 Nou de la Rambla (see p. 52), which is was situated on the edge of Barcelona's notorious Barri Xinès. The museum's holdings of later stages in Picasso's art are far from being representative, with only a Head of 1913 to testify to the Cubist years. Apart from the superb Harlequin of 1917—a work heralding the onset of his classical phase—the highpoint of the later collections is the series of 44 interpretations of Velázquez's Las Meninas; Picasso's fertility of imagination and creative energy are fully revealed as he explores all the compositional possibilities of Velázquez's multi-faceted painting, making you see the work in a completely new light. As a final attraction, the museum puts on outstanding temporary exhibitions of modern art in its rooms in the Palau Meca.

Directly facing the Museu Picasso, at No. 12 Carrer de Montcada, is the *Palau de los Marqueses de Lió, a palace of 14C origin with a combination of Gothic and Renaissance windows and a baroque entrance portal. The building was restored in 1969 to house the excellent **Museu Tèxtil i de la Indumentària** (Textile and Costume Museum). The texile collections range from 4C Coptic fabrics to 16C Flemish tapestries and modern Catalan embroideries; there is a large group of liturgical vestments from the 13C to 20C. The costume collections were mainly the legacy of Manuel Rocamora i Vidal, and comprise a wonderfully varied representation of male and female wear from the 16C up to the 1930s; additional items include fashion plates, toys and dolls. The museum has recently been extended by the acquisition of part of the adjoining *Palau Nadal (No. 14), which dates back to the 15C; another part of this building houses one of the many exhibition halls run by the Fundació Caixa de Pensions.

Continuing down the street, you will see to your right, at No. 20, the Palau Dalmases, which, though featuring fragments of the original 15C structure, owes its present appearance essentially to late 17C remodelling; the court-yard has an impressive open staircase with Solomonic columns and an elaborate balustrade. In 1699 the Catalan cultural society known as the *Academia dels Desconfiats* (literally the 'Academy of the the Mistrustful') was founded here, and was to hold its meetings in the building during the early years of the 18C; since 1962 the palace has housed the Omnium Cultural, which was founded by Félix Millet in 1961 and is likewise devoted to the promotion of Catalan culture. On the other side of the street, at No. 25, is the early 16C *Casa Cervelló Giudice, the only palace on the street to have retained its original façade and entrance portal. The building now houses the *Maeght Gallery, which is run by the same art dealers who created the famous modern art foundations at St. Paul de Vence in southern France; the gallery hosts outstanding temporary exhibitions of modern art.

Near the southern end of the Carrer de Montcada you should turn right into the CARRER SOMBRERERS, which follows the northern side of the church of **SANTA MARIA DEL MAR**. Situated at what was once the heart of maritime Barcelona, and erected during Catalonia's heyday as a seaborne empire, this magnificent church of cathedral-like proportions is one of the most eloquent examples of the Catalan Gothic style. The origins of the building are traditionally thought to be in a temple built to house the remains of Santa Eulàlia, though the first documented mention of the church dates back only to 988. It served at first as the parish church of an outlying district composed mainly of fishermen, but was later made the church of an archdiocese following the extension of the city's walls in the 13C, and the arrival here of numerous noble families, wealthy shipbuilders and merchants. The present structure, attributed to Berenguer de Montagut, was initiated by Canon Bernat Llul, who in 1324 was appointed archdeacon of Santa María. Building began in 1329, and this imposing building was completed in less than 50 years, which helps to explain its remarkable unity.

No other Catalan church of its size has such a perfectly preserved exterior as Santa Maria del Mar, an exterior which, furthermore, encapsulates the essential characteristics of the Catalan Gothic style, such as a preference for horizontal proportions and large areas of unadorned masonry. Two tall octagonal towers flank the west façade, at the centre of which is a portal decorated with statues of St. Peter and St. Paul, and a tympanum representing Christ between St. John and the Virgin; the rose window above is a mid 15C replacement of a window destroyed in an earthquake in 1428. The interior was gutted by fire during the Civil War and lost its central choir and many of its furnishings, a loss which had at least the advantage of making you appreciate all the more the extraordinary harmony and spaciousness of the architecture. Without transepts, and with aisles of almost the same height as the exceptionally wide nave, the interior closely resembles that of a hall church; the slender piers form in the apse an arcade of stunning elegance which makes the apse of Barcelona's cathedral seem clumsy by comparison. The beauty of the interior is enhanced by the wealth of 15C to 18C stained glass, including a scene of the Coronation of the Virgin in the rose window of the central façade.

The surroundings of Santa Maria del Mar include some of the more picturesque corners of the old city. The intimate PLAÇA SANTA MARIA, on the western side of the church, was created in 1807 on the site of one of the church's two cemeteries. At its north-western corner is a *Gothic fountain built by Arnau Bargués in 1402, and restored in 1962. Behind this runs the diminutive **CARRER DE LES CAPUTXES**, one of the most toy-like of Barcelona's medieval streets, complete with archways, timber beams and projecting floors supported by columns, the whole forming a quaintly asymmetrical ensemble. Through the archway at the southern end of the street you will emerge again at the Plaça Santa Maria. Heading east from here along the southern side of the church, you will come immediately to the Fossar de les Moreres, which marks the site of a cemetery where those who defended Barcelona in the siege of 1714 here buried. The place inspired some famous lines dedicated by the 19C poet Pitarra to the 'martyrs of 1714':

Al Fossar de les Moreres
no s'hi enterra cap traidor
Fins perdent nostres banderes
serà l'urna de l'honor

(At the cemetery of the Mulberries no traitor is buried. Even though losing our flags, their tomb will be an honourable one.)

In 1989 the FOSSAR DE LES MORERES was turned into a small square by the pulling down of a number of decrepit buildings attached to the eastern side of Santa Maria; as with so many of Barcelona's recent public spaces, this square features a large expanse of brickwork tilted at a slight angle. At its northern end, just beyond the apse of the church, you will reach the long rectangular square known as EL BORN, the name of which is derived from the Catalan word for tournament. From the 13C to the 18C this was the city's main square, a place where tournaments were held in the Middle Ages, and later a scene of carnivals, processions, evening promenades of the aristocracy, and glass and metal markets, the latter being enthusiastically described by the 17C Madrilenian dramatist Tirso de Molina. As with La Rambla, which eventually superceded it in importance, El Born came to be synonomous with Barcelona, and gave rise to a well-known saying, *'Roda el món i torna al Born'* (Go round the world and come back to the Born). The buildings that surround this pleasantly shaded square date mainly from the late 18C and early 19C, the one survival from the Middle Ages being the heavily restored 14C house at No. 17.

Near the eastern end of the square you will find to your right the entrance to the CARRER DEL REC, where there is a curious group of porticoed buildings that served originally as shops; the buildings were reconstructed after 1797, but their porticoes are probably closely similar to those of the original 15C structures. The Born emerges at its eastern end into the long and broad CARRER DEL COMERC, which is dominated on its eastern side by the *Market of the Born, a pioneering ironwork structure designed in 1873 by Josep Fontserè i Mestres, who was also responsible for the construction of the flanking commercial buildings; the market itself is now used for the occasional exhibition, though its future is uncertain. Parallel to the market to the east runs the PASSEIG DE PICASSO, which skirts the western side of the Parc de la Ciutadella (see p. 103). A line of trees overlooking the park shades a row of pools centred on a controversial *Monument to Picasso by the contemporary artist Antoni Tàpies. This remarkable monument comprises a large glass box in which old furniture and other objects have been placed, the whole being obscured by jets of water that shoot up against the glass sides. The water was in fact added later as a cooling device, the original box having cracked under the heat.

Monument to Picasso by Tàpies, Passeig de Picasso

D. The Raval

In between La Rambla and the circuit of avenues to the west extends an area known as the Raval. Originally an outlying district with a scattering of hospitals and religious institutions set among fields and orchards, the Raval was embraced in the 14C by the third and final extension of the city walls. Up to the late 18C it continued to be an area especially favoured by hospitals, charitable institutions and other such buildings, but its present-day character is due largely to radical redevelopment in the 19C, when it became the cradle of industrial Barcelona. The northern and more respectable part of the Raval is sometimes referred to as the Raval de Ponent, an excellent description of which in the 1950s and early 1960s is to be found in *El día que murió Marilyn* (The Day that Marilyn Died), a semi-autobiographical novel by Terenci Foix, who was brought up here.

Beginning a tour of the Raval de Ponent at the Plaça de la Universitat, you should head down the CARRER DELS TALLERS, the name of which is a reference to the slaughterhouses that were found here from the 12C onwards, the trade of cutting meat being one that was originally not allowed within the walls of the city. The street leads shortly to the PALÇA DE CASTELLA, on which stands the former monastery church of *Sant Pere Nolasc. The Paulist monastery to which this belonged was converted in the early 19C, first into a tobacco factory and then into a military hospital serving French troops; only the church survived when the complex was pulled down in 1943. The church, built in 1710–16, is a baroque structure which has been given a dreary neo-classical look in the course of numerous remodellings and alterations; its chief interest lies in its dome, which was decorated inside with a scene of the Coronation of the Virgin by Joseph Flaugier (1757–1813), a pupil of David.

Behind the building, on the CARRER TORRES I AMAT, is the pale pink block of the **Dispensario Anti-tuberculoso** (Anti-tuberculosis Clinic), one of the more important early examples of Rationalist architecture in Spain. Commissioned in 1934 by the *Generalitat* as part of their pioneering scheme to nationalise hospital and other social services, the building was designed by the Le Corbusier-inspired architectural team known as GATCPAC, whose main members were Josep Lluis Sert i López, Josep Torres i Clavé and Joan B. Subirana i Subirana. The building, described by the Spanish architectural historian Oriol Bohigas as 'the masterpiece of our Rationalism, and one of the most important buildings of its kind in Europe', was completed at the height of the Civil War and thus little appreciated in its time; after the war GATCPAC was dispersed, and all Moderniste trends in architecture came to be regarded as ideologically suspicious.

The Carrer Torres i Amat emerges at its western end at the entrance to the CARRER DE JOAQUIM COSTA. Known to the older members of this district as the Carrer de Poniente, this is one of the liveliest and best preserved streets in the Raval de Ponent, and is lined on both sides by tall 19C tenements adorned with metalwork balconies. As you walk down the street, you will pass to your right the entrance to the CARRER DEL TIGRE, where you will find at No. 27 a famous and very popular dance hall known as *La Paloma*; founded in 1904, it has retained its original interior by Salvador Alarma, and features a long and profusely gilded hall, surrounded by balconies on all sides, and with elaborate ceiling decorations and a central chandelier. Continuing down the Carrer de Joaquim Costa, you will come at No. 32 to the *Casa Riera*, which has had the reputation for many years as one of Barcelona's cheapest restaurants. Another traditional establishment is the *Casa Almirall*, a wonderfully old-fashioned night-time bar situated at the junction with the Carrer de Ferlandina; founded in 1860, the place was used in 1966 as the setting of José María Nunces' film, *Noches de Vino Tinto* (Nights of Red Wine).

Turning left into the CARRER DE FERLANDINA, you will enter a part of the city which is at present undergoing radical redevelopment to accommodate a complex of cultural institutions. On the Carrer de Ferlandina itself are the offices of the future **Museu d'Arte Contemporani**, which is planned to open in 1994. Surprisingly, Barcelona has had up to now no museum which has adequately reflected the vital role which the city has played in the history of modern art. The so-called Museu d'Arte Modern in the Ciutadella (see p. 104) is now devoted exclusively to Catalan art of the turn of the century, but has never devoted much attention to contemporary art. Its meagre holdings of the Catalan avant-garde are to be given to this new museum, the nucleus of which will be made up of works amassed by a contemporary art foundation which was established in 1987; the collection so far comprises works by Catalan artists such as Antoni Tàpies and Miquel Navarro, and leading foreign masters such as Beuys, Calder, Caro, Dubuffet, Fontana, Klee, Merz and Oldenburg. The building has been designed by the American architect Richard Meier and will incorporate part of the former Casa de La Caritat, the main façade of which takes up much of the adjacent CARRER MONTALEGRE (turn left at the end of the Carrer de Ferlandina). The Casa de la Caritat has its origins in a 14C convent for Franciscan nuns, which in 1598 was converted into a Tridentine seminary, and later into a hospice. The present structure dates back to the early 18C, but is now being dramatically remodelled. Apart from the long façade on the Carrer de Montalegre, the main survival of the 18C building is the Pati Manning, a two-storey courtyard built in 1743 and containing charming ceramic decoration on the upper level. This courtyard, reached from the entrance portal at No. 5, now belongs to the cultural department of the Diputació, and is used for occasional exhibitions. The entrance at No. 3 leads to what is now being turned into a vast cultural centre, expected to be completed by 1993; the centre will include exhibition and concert halls, a theatre and conference rooms.

At its southern end, below the junction with the Carrer de Ferlandina, the Carrer Montalegre widens into the Carrer dels Àngels, the name of which is derived from the former Convent dels Àngels, a Dominican monastery which moved to the Raval in 1497. The monastery church—which you will see to your right as soon as you enter the street—is a late Gothic structure of 1562–66; the church and adjoining buildings were used as an arms storeroom by the former Francoist mayor Miquel Mateu, but are now being adapted by Carlos Díaz and Óscar Tusquets for use as a municipal archive and library. Behind the monastery is a large newly built square, underneath which is an underground car park.

The Carrer dels Àngels ends at the lively CARRER DEL CARME, where, on turning left, you will come at No. 24 to the *Lencería 'El Indio'*, a draper's shop founded in 1870 and with a delightful Moderniste exterior executed by the decorators Vilaró i Vals in 1922. By far the greatest attraction of the street, however, is the former hospital complex directly facing the Carrer dels Àngels, at Nos 47–49. This complex—which extends south all the way to the Carrer de l'Hospital—dates back to 1402, when the Consell de Cent decided to rationalise the city's hospital system, and bring together all the city's hospital institutions to form the **Hospital de la Santa Creu**. In 1629 the city councillors laid within the precinct of this hospital the first stone of the **Casa de Convalescència**, and in 1760 there was established alongside this the **Colegi de Cirurgia** (College of Surgeons). The buildings of these last two institutions are the first that you see when approaching the complex from the Carrer de Carme. The Colegi de Cirurgia, at No. 49, is the only part of the complex which still has a medical role, the place having served since 1929 as the seat of the Royal Academy of Medicine. The building was designed by the great neo-classical architect Ventura Rodriguez, and has an exterior of exceptional severity, with mouldings and window frames of great simplicity, and a virtual absence of decoration, the whole being articulated by bare pilasters, niches and blind windows. The design is centred on two large windows that give light to the **Anatomy Theatre**, which is the outstanding feature of the interior. This oval room, used initially for the training of students and now as a ceremonial hall, has a gilded rococo interior featuring a bust of Charles III, a marble dissecting table and a Venetian crystal chandelier presented in 1929 by Alfonso XIII.

The eastern façade of the building overlooks a tiny garden named after the Scottish discoverer of penicillin Sir Alexander Fleming, whose memory is commemorated in virtually every Spanish town and village; a bust of him, with the inscription *'Barcelona a Alexander Fleming'* is attached to the wall of the Royal College of Medicine. The western façade of the college is separated by an alley from the Casa de Convalescència, at No. 47 of the Carrer del Carme. Walking down this alley is like entering an Oxford or Cambridge college, and you will find yourself in a peaceful enclave which seems far removed from the bustling city outside. The strong university character is largely explained by the fact that both the Casa de Convalescència and the Hospital de la Santa Creu have now been taken over by the Library of Catalonia and the Institute of Catalan studies. The construction of the former building, though begun in 1629, was delayed by a fire in 1638, the War of the Harvesters of 1641–53, and epidemics of plague and famine in 1650–54; under the supervision of Andreu Bosch and Josep Juli the building was eventually brought to completion in 1680. The entrance to the building is from the alley directly in front of the College of Surgeons, and leads to a vestibule richly decorated with ceramic scenes of the life of St. Paul executed by Llorenç Passoles in 1679–82. At the end of the vestibule you emerge into a splendid Renaissance-style courtyard dominated in the middle by a statue of St. Paul sculpted in 1678 by Lluís Bonifaci; this same sculptor was also responsible for the gargoyles above the courtyard's upper arcade, an ornamental feature which harks back to the Gothic period. The upper floor is reached by staircases adorned with ceramics of fruit and flowers by Bernat Reig. The main attraction of the upper floor is the chapel, which is profusely decorated with ceramic murals attributed to Josep Bal and Llorenç Passoles. The gilded altarpiece, with its Solomonic columns, is attributed to Lluís Bonifaci.

From the upper floor access is also gained to the three surviving wards of the former Hospital de la Santa Creu. The vast wards, now used as library halls, date back to the 15C, and are typical structures of the Catalan Gothic, with large pointed arches supporting timber roofs.

Returning to the entrance of the Casa de Convalescència and turning right you will come to the hospital's main courtyard, a beautiful space shaded by trees and incorporating at its northern end three wings of an early 15C cloister by Guillem d'Abiell. A baroque cross stands on the site of the cloister's south wing, which was demolished in 1509 so as to extend the space southwards; the southern half of the courtyard is made up of a variety of interconnected structures dating from the 16C to the 19C, the whole being extensively restored after 1930, when the place was finally abandoned as a hospital. Through the arch at the southernern end of the courtyard you will emerge on to the CARRER DE HOSPITAL, a narrow but busy commercial street; the entrance to the hospital from this street (at No. 56) is marked by a curious Renaissance portal featuring a tympanum incorporating the arms of the hospital within the scallop shell of St. James. Turning left you will come to the former hospital chapel, which was built originally as a free-standing structure in 1406–44; extensively remodelled in the 18C, the dark and simple barrel-vaulted interior of the chapel is now used for art exhibitions.

On the other side of the street is the small PLAÇA DE SANT AGUSTÍ, on which stands the former Augustinian *Monastery of Sant Agustí. The Augustinians were given this site in c 1726 following the demolition of their previous monastery to make way for the Ciutadella (see Rte 1E). The church, begun in 1728 to the design of Alexandre de Retz, is an example of the Catalan baroque at its most austere. Especially impressive is the unfinished west façade, which features a porticoed atrium articulated by giant Ionic columns; the interior, heavily remodelled in the 19C, has lost most of its original decoration as a result of a series of arson attacks.

Heading west up the CARRER DE L'HOSPITAL you will pass on your left, at No. 109, the *Farmàcia Dr Sastre i Marquès*, a pharmacy which was founded in 1855 and remodelled by Puig i Cadalfach in 1905; the much decayed Moderniste exterior—which has recently been deprived of an elaborate ironwork lamp—features sgraffito decorations of garlands and flowers. At the western end of the street you will come out at the PLAÇA DEL PEDRÓ, a narrow, hemmed-in square marking the junction of the Carrer de l'Hospital and del Carme. At the intersection of the two streets is the Romanesque *Capella de Sant Llàtzer which belonged formerly to a lepers' hospital which Bishop Guillem de Torroja had had built on the outskirts of the city in 1141. The chapel, which was deconsecrated in 1913, has been largely engulfed by the surrounding dwellings, and to see its Romanesque apse— the finest surviving feature of the original structure—you have to walk through the vestibule of the house at 105 Carrer del Carme (the keys to this can be had from the neighbouring store); the interior of the chapel was considerably modified in the 18C. At the centre of the square is a famous *Statue of Santa Eulàlia, which was commissioned in 1670 by the Consell de Cent to commemorate the site where, according to tradition, the saint's crucified body was laid out. The statue is claimed as Barcelona's oldest surviving public monument, though the work of today is largely a reconstruction of 1951 by Frederic Marés. The original statue, in wood, was replaced in 1685 by a stone monument executed by C. Tremulles and Ll. Bonifaç. The revolutionary municipal government of 1823 wanted to demolish the statue, but a public outcry led to its being saved, and three years later a fountain was erected at its foot. The work was attacked by anarchists in 1936, but its head was saved by two brothers who later presented it to the Museu d'Història de la Ciutat.

From the Carrer de l'Hospital all the way south almost to the port extends what is sometimes described as the largest red-light district in Europe; referred to increasingly by the innocuous name of the Raval de Sant Pau, it is popularly known as the Barri Xinès (Chinatown), a name which has traditionally inspired a mixture of fear, revulsion and fascination.

The term 'Barri Xinès was coined in the 1920s in reference to the small district lying between the Carrer Nou de la Rambla and the Carrer Portal de Santa Madrona; later the term came to be loosely applied to the entire seedy area lying to the south of the Carrer de Hospital. This red-light district, serving Barcelona's port, has nothing to do with the Chinese, but appears instead to owe its name to the writer Miguel Toledano, who wrote under the pseudonym Manuel Gil de Oto. Following a journey to the United States in 1924, Toledano wrote a colourful book entitled *Los Enemigos de America* ('The Enemies of America'), which included a lurid description of the Chinatown of some North American city; a young journalist called Angel Marsá, reporting on a den of thieves to be found on the Carrer del Cid, remembered Toledano's book and likened the surrounding area to a 'Chinatown'.

The squalid and corrupt aspects of the area have attracted the Bohemian elements in Barcelona society, and the place has always held a strong romantic fascination for foreign visitors to the city. The French writers Georges Bataille and Genet were the authors of some of the most vivid descriptions of the area, most notably Genet in the powerful opening pages of his *Thief's Journal*. More recently the area has been described at length by the Barcelona-born writer Juan Goytisolo, whose self-confessed 'fervour for slum areas' undoubtedly developed as a result of having been brought up in the smarter middle-class areas of the city. Lengthy accounts of Goytisolo's youthful experiences in the Barri Xinès feature in his controversial biography, *Forbidden Territory* (English translation, Quartet Books, 1989):

Alone or with Carlos, I carefully explored the bars and dives on the back streets between Conde de Asalto (Nou de la Rambla) and Atarazanas: the Criolla had disappeared after being frequented by the author of *Journal du Voleur*, but other haunts exuding filth and dirt still justified the reputation of that Barcelona opposed forever to the homogeneous, paternalist, limp ideal of its petty bourgeoisie and the magnetic attraction the city held for writers like Genet or Bataille. Cigarette girls, blackmarketeers, cripples, dope peddlers, vile, ill-lit bars, adverts for permanganate baths, contraceptive shops, grotesque sights from the Bodega Bohemia, rooms let by the hour, six-peseta brothels, the entire Hispanic court of miracles imposed a brutal reality that burst the bubble around me with one blast. The public whore-houses of Robadors and Tapias (Carrer de les Tàpies), the opulent, sometimes obese shapes of the women queuing on the benches, their legs wide apart, half-naked, preoccupied, in a posture of innnocent bestiality, attracted me not only because of a consciously perverse Baudelairean aesthetic but because of their tangible, disturbing promiscuity.

The Barri Xinès still has a notorious reputation, and the well-dressed tourist carrying expensive camera equipment should take care while walking down some of the smaller streets, particularly after dark. However, the area is rapidly changing and, in preparation for the Barcelona of 1992, a programme of intensive urban renewal has been initiated which has already led to the pulling down of many of the more seedy parts. Foreign tourists continue to search out the picturesquely sordid, though with a sense of increasing nostalgia for a disappearing Barcelona. For an excellent if now sadly out-dated guide to the life of this area you should consult José María Carandell's perversely detailed *Nueva guía secreta de Barcelona* (Barcelona, 1982), which contains fascinating information about brothels, venereal clinics, drug addicts, rubber shops, cabaret shows, decadent bars and other alternative aspects of the city.

Immediately south of the Plaça del Pedró is the dark and narrow CARRER DE LA CERA, which is one of the main streets associated with the city's gypsy population. The *Bar El Salsichón* is a popular meeting-place for the gypsies of the area, while the modest restaurant *Can Lluís* (No. 49) has been popular over the years with artists and writers. The small and atmospheric cinema known as Cine Pedrí (No. 31) has its origins in the turn-of-the-century music-hall, *Ambigú Barcelonés*; at present closed and decayed, it awaits an uncertain future. Next door, at No. 33, a plaque commemorates the birthplace of the popular singer Emili Vendrell.

From the Carrer de la Cera you should head south down the CARRER DE LA RIERETA, which is lined on both sides with old workshops; appropriately, for this strong working-class district, the trade union known as USO (Unió Sindical Obrera) has its headquarters at No. 31. Continuing to walk south you will pass on your right the short CARRER DE SANT PACIÀ, where you can admire a bizarre shop specialising in old-fashioned orthopaedic footwear. At the southern end of the Carrer de la Riereta you will emerge on the long CARRER DE SANT PAU, which runs all the way from La Rambla to the western boundary of the Raval. This is the main artery of the Barri Xinès, though this is also the street which is likely to be the most affected by the great changes that are happening to this district. The architectural jewel of the eastern end of the street is the **Hotel España**, at Nos 9–11. A one-time luxury hotel which later went slightly to seed as a result of its situation in the Barri Xinès, this has remained for many years a modestly priced establishment with a pleasantly intimate character. The hotel dates back to the late 19C, but owes its architectural distinction to reforms carried out on the ground floor by Domènech i Montaner in 1902–03. The highpoint of the interior are the two dining-rooms, both of which have retained much of their original Moderniste furnishings, including elaborate ironwork candelabra; one of the rooms has extensive ceramic decorations, while the other has curious classical-style murals of mermaids by Ramon Casas, as well as an interesting frieze of ceramic roundels inset in a wooden framework imitative of bamboo-work. The small hotel bar has suffered the most from insensitive remodelling in the 1950s, but is none the less worth visiting for its magnificent fireplace, which was expressively sculpted by Eusebi Arnau (with the assistance of Pau Gargallo) with allegorical figures and the coat of arms of Spain; among its amusing details is a cat making its way to the fender.

The decayed heart of the Carrer de Sant Pau lies to the west of the Hotel España. At No. 65 is the *Bar Marsella*, a once notorious haunt of Barcelona low-life now favoured increasingly by foreigners with a yearning for the Barri Xinès of old. As its name suggests, this spacious wood-panelled bar of the early years of this century was created in self-conscious imitation of a typical bar of Marseilles (another such establishment is the nearby Pastís; see p. 55); the particular attraction of the Marsella is its absinthe, a drink now illegal in most western countries.

The former monastery of **SANT PAU DEL CAMP**, the most important of Barcelona's surviving Romanesque monuments, stands at the western end of the street. Vázquez Montalbán, commenting on this monastery's unexpected presence within the Barri Xinés, likened the building to 'an abandoned Christian mission', though today the incongruity of its situation has been somewhat lessened by the pulling down of neighbouring slum-dwellings and houses of ill-repute to make way for a large park and sports centre.

A tombstone of 912, and Visigothic capitals on the portal of the monastery church, indicate that the foundation of Sant Pau del Camp dates back at least to the beginning of the 10C. Possibly destroyed by Al-Mansur in 985, it was almost certainly set fire to by the Almoravids in 1114–15, for the place was refounded by the viscounts Geribert and Rotlandis in 1117. In 1528 the monastery was taken over by friars from the Chapel of Montserrat, and in 1672 was turned into a Benedictine novitiate. During the Peninsular War the place served as a hospital and shelter for Royalist troops, and following a fire in 1835, the monastery buildings were converted into a barracks, while the church was temporarily designated as parish of the Raval. The demolition of the whole complex was later prevented through the intervention of the Associació Catalana d'Excursions, who, with the support of the politician Víctor Balaguer, succeeded in having it declared a national monument in 1879. Restoration work was begun in 1896, and renewed in 1922 and 1930; in the course of the last two restoration campaigns, baroque and later structures were demolished with a view fully to expose the Romanesque church and cloister, which now stand within a small garden.

Entering the precinct of the former monastery, you will see to your right the much restored 14C Abbot's House (now the rectory), which is joined to the 12C church by a brick school building of 1932. The exterior of the church, decorated with Lombard arcades, has a portal incorporating marble capitals from an earlier structure, and corbels and reliefs crudely carved with the emblems of the Evangelists; a Latin inscription on the lintel refers to SS. Peter and Paul, and also to the unidentified Renardus and Raimunda. The church, shaped like a Greek cross, has an octagonal crossing tower crowned by an 18C belfry. The simple, barrel-vaulted interior was largely refaced following damage caused during the 'Tragic Week' of 1909. A door through the south transept leads into the early 14C Chapter House (now a chapel), where you will find on the east wall the tombslab of the early Catalan leader, Guifre Borrell (947–992). From here, you can enter the tiny cloister, one of the more enchanting corners of old Barcelona. Centred around a garden and fountain, this Romanesque structure of the 13C has arcades of Moorish-inspired polylobed arches, the capitals of which are decorated with vegetal and grotesque motifs.

Shortly to the west of Sant Pau del Camp, the Carrer de Sant Pau reaches the western boundary of the Ciutat Vella (Old Town), a boundary marked today by the junction of the RONDA DE SANT PAU with the long, wide and ugly AVINGUDA DEL PARAL-LEL. The surrounding district, with its various night clubs, music-halls and other places of entertainment, enjoyed its heyday in the early 20C, when it was regarded as the Barcelona equivalent of Montmartre. On the western side of the Avinguda, immediately behind the metro station Paral-lel, is the *Molino*, a celebrated nightclub dating back to 1909 and at one time referred to as the Moulin Rouge; the atmosphere of the place today is tackily old-fashioned, and its mildly erotic shows appeal to a largely elderly audience, who eagerly respond to the taunts of the similarly aged chorus girls. Further south down the Avinguda del Paral-lel is the PLAÇA RAQUEL MELLER, which is named after a popular singer of the early 20C who made her début in 1911 in the neighbouring music-hall called *El Arnau*; a full-length statue of this singer, by Viladomat, stands on the northern side of the square, and shows her in the pseudo-rustic costume appropriate to the type of song which made her famous, the *cuplé*. Behind the statue are the entrances to two of the livelier streets of the Barri Xinés, the Carrer de les Tàpies and the Carrer Nou de la Rambla (see also Rte 1A). The former, which runs immediately to the south of the monastery of Sant Pau del Camp, was at one time famous for its beggars and prostitutes, though has recently been smartend up. A sign of the changing times is the recent transformation of the late 19C printers at No. 4 into a workshop intended to help the city's young and unemployed; one of the survivals from older times is the cabaret *Barcelona de Noche* (Barcelona by Night), which specialises in shows with a strong camp element. The western end of the CARRER NOU DE LA RAMBLA has been especially affected by the recent programme of urban renewal, though you will still find here, at No. 103, the infamous *Baghdad*, which has had the reputation for many years of putting on one of Europe's most pornographic shows, featuring live sex acts and audience participation.

From the Plaça Raquel Meller, you could take the old funicular which climbs up the hill of Montjuïc (see Rte 1F); alternatively you could continue walking south-east down the Avinguda Paral-lel until you reach the stretch of the city walls attached to the Museu Marítim Drassanes (see pp. 97–8).

E. Maritime Barcelona and the Ciutadella

One of the much-repeated sayings about Barcelona was that after its maritime heyday in the Middle Ages the city had turned its back on the sea. However, as part of the radical urban transformation of Barcelona in preparation for 1992, elegant maritime promenades have been laid out, and long stretches of beach have been reclaimed, so that the place can now boast one of the finest sea-fronts of any European city.

The obvious starting-point for a tour of maritime Barcelona is the PLAÇA PORTAL DE LA PAU, a large seaside square created in 1849 through the opening of the stretch of medieval walls which blocked off the southern end of La Rambla (see p. 42). At the centre of the square is the 60m-high **Monument a Colom** (Monument to Columbus), the most prominent and

The Monument to Columbus in the Plaça Portal de la Pau

popular of the city's commemorative monuments. There is a certain irony in the fact that such a work should celebrate the man whose achievements effectively demolished Barcelona's maritime economy by diverting trade to Seville.

The idea for a monument commemorating Columbus' alleged visit to Ferdinand and Isabella in Barcelona in 1493 was that of a local merchant called Antoni Fages i Ferrer, who obsessively pursued this idea with the authorities. Eventually the project was taken up by the mayor, Rius i Taulet, who claimed it as his own, and established in May 1881 a commission which set about raising funds and organising a competition to decide on the architect. The competition, after initially failing to find a winner, was won in September 1882 by the architect Gaietà Buïgas i Monravà, who proposed a cast-iron column resting on an elaborate stone plinth; while cast-iron columns of this sort had been relatively common since the time of the July Column in Paris, Gaietá Buïgas had the novel idea of creating a lift-shaft within the monument. The construction of the monument, delayed for several years through lack of funds, was eventually made possible through the diversion of money from a special municipal budget, and through the donation by the State of a number of old cannons from the castle at Montjuïc that were to provide, when melted down, over 30 tons of bronze. Cast in the engineering workshop of Alexander Wolhguemuth, the column was finally inaugurated on 1 June 1888, shortly before the opening of the first World Exhibition. Extensive restoration has been carried out in recent years.

Antoni Miralda, a Barcelona-born conceptual artist who has lived for many years in New York, has planned for 1992 a special event entailing the marriage of the Christopher Columbus monument with New York's Statue of Liberty. This characteristically witty idea of Miralda's, involving vast expense on an international scale, has been hailed as both brilliant and infantile. Various countries have made different contributions to the wedding, the ring being supplied by the city of Liverpool.

A group of bronze lions by Vallmitjana Abarca surround the base of the monument, while behind them are eight copper reliefs of scenes from Columbus' life, four of the scenes being the work of Josep Llimona, the others being by Antoni Vilanova. Placed in front of the buttresses of the plinth are stone figures by Carbonell, Gamot, Atché and Carcassó representing the kingdoms of Catalonia, Aragón, León and Castile; the bronze detailing on the plinth is by Rossend Nobas and includes decorative forms featuring the figure of Fame and the prow of a caravel. Representations by Francesc Pastor of the Four Continents are to be found on the capital of the column, and the whole is crowned by a massive crown supporting a bronze statue by Rafael Atché of Columbus pointing to the sea. You can climb by lift right up to the base of the crown, but the views are somewhat obscured by the ironwork.

On the north-western side of the Plaça Portal de la Pau are the extraordinary former shipyards or **DRASSANES**, the most important medieval shipyards to have survived anywhere in the world, though extensively altered in the course of many centuries of use.

The royal shipyards were the place where the galleys of the Crown of Aragón and later of Spain were not only built and repaired, but also put into dry dock. The first mention of the yards is of 1243, but it was not until 1284, during the reign of Pere II the Great, that they were built on their present site. Their subsequent history is exceedingly complex, and it is not easy today to sort out the various phases in their construction, particularly as the same building system seems to have been favoured over the centuries. This system appears to have been evolved during the reign of Pere II's great-grandson, Pere III the Ceremonious, who in 1378 decided to alter and enlarge the shipyards through the creation of eight parallel aisles formed of rounded arches supporting pointed roofs. These aisles both extended the yards to the north and covered part of the large open courtyard comprising the nucleus of the original structure. By the early 17C this courtyard had been almost entirely covered by additional aisles, and in 1613–18 three further ones were built to the east. The façade of the building overlooking the sea was created in the early 18C, and at the same time the two central aisles were joined together to form a large single one.

The decline of the shipyards set in during the 17C, and was to culminate with the dissolution of the royal galleys in 1748. The building, which had already served as an ammunition store, barracks and fortress during the War of the Harvesters, was eventually taken over entirely for military purposes. In the late 19C numerous plans were proposed entailing the demolition of the building, and it was not until the 1920s that the future of this remarkable complex was finally assured, thanks to a large extent to an eloquently persuasive article written in 1926 by an artillery colonel called Joaquín. This article, which appeared in the newspaper *La Vanguardia*, referred to the shipyards as a 'priceless jewel which is completely unknown'. In 1936 plans were made to transform the oldest part of the yards into a Maritime Museum, which was finally opened in 1941.

Seen from the Plaça Portal de la Pau the shipyards could almost be mistaken for a vast 19C warehouse were it not for the odd medieval tower peering over the sea of long parallel roofs; the western side of the building, overlooking the Avinguda del Paral-lel, is in fact attached to the longest surviving stretch of the city's 14C to 15C defensive walls. The **Museu Marítím** installed within the shipyards is entered from a tower on the south-eastern side of the building; this is one of the four corner towers belonging to the structure built in the late 13C by Pere II the Great. The museum is the finest of its kind in Spain and certainly compares favourably with the ramshackle Maritime Museum in Madrid. However, the lasting impression of a visit here derives unquestionably from the setting, which, with its forest of enormous arches and columns, can almost be described as a secular version of the Mosque at Cordova. The setting is especially memorable if visited at dusk, when the dramatic spot-lighting of the museum's exhibits, contrasted with the cavernous gloom of the vast surroundings, creates mysterious chiaroscuro effects of a Piranesi-like character. Among the exhibits are amphorae, navigational maps, objects relating to Columbus, ship models, coats of arms of distinguished maritime families and a colourful and entertaining group of 19C figureheads. However, the pride of the collection is the red and glisteningly gilded life-size reproduction of Don John of Austria's flagship, *La Real*, which rises up like an apparition in the enormous central aisle.

Directly facing the main façade of the Drassanes, on the south-western side of the Plaça Portal de la Pau, is the pompous H-shaped block of the *Duana Nova (Customs House), a neo-Renaissance structure articulated by a giant order of columns and crowned by a row of griffins; it was built in 1895–1902 by Enric Sagnier i Villavecchia and Pere Garcia Fària i Monteys. Adjacent to this, on the southern side of the square, is the landing-stage of the *'Golondrinas'*, pleasure boats that specialise in regular tours of the port and go as far as the pier of Rompeolas, where there is a massive lighthouse, and a curious abstract sculpture by Salvador Aulèstia, *Sideroploide* (1963), which was made from pieces of metal recovered from the sea; evocative descriptions of the now rapidly changing port are to be found in Juan Goytisolo's autobiographical work, *Forbidden Territory* (English translation, 1989), and in his short story, *Otoño, en el Puerto, cuando llovizna* (Autumn, in the Port, when it Drizzles). Usually moored alongside this landing-stage is the Museu Marítím's reconstruction of Columbus' caravel, *Sta. María*, which has recently been making a number of journeys as part of the 1992 celebrations.

The parallel promenades of the Passeig de Colom and the Molls Bosch I Alsina (Moll de la Fusta) extend north-east of the Plaça Portal de la Pau, forming what is now the grandest and most elegant stretch of Barcelona's sea-front. The former, situated the furthest back from the sea, was created with the demolition in 1878–81 of a large section of the medieval walls. Located in what was once the aristocratic part of Barcelona, it became during the World Exhibition of 1888 the city's main thoroughfare. At its entrance there once stood Domènech i Montaner's extraordinary Hotel International, which was built specifically for the Exhibition and taken down soon afterwards; built in 53 days with the help of a daily workforce of up to 2000, it daringly featured foundations floating on water, an aspect of the building which led to numerous cartoons in the press, most notably of the whole structure sailing out to sea. The buildings that line the northern side of the Passeig today are heavy, unimaginative structures of the late 19C and early 20C. Half-way along you will pass on your left the PLAÇA DUC DE MEDINACELI, a small landscaped square which was laid out in 1849 by F.D. Molina. Molina, together with Lluís Rigalt, was also responsible for the design of the memorial *column to the Catalan admiral Galceran Marquet, which stands in the middle of the square, surrounded by tall palm trees; the memorial, executed in 1851, was sculpted by Anicet Santigosa Vestraten, and was the first commemorative monument in the city to employ cast iron.

Further down the Passeig de Colom, at No. 14, is the *Capitanía General (Military Headquarters), which occupies the former Mercedarian Convent, the church of which adjoins the Carrer Ample (see p. 74). The building, constructed by Jeroni Santacana in 1605–53, was transformed into the Capitanía General in 1846, and given its present façade by Adolf Florensa i Ferrer in 1926–29; this colossal and overwhelmingly pompous classical façade was built as part of the city's preparations for the Exhibition of 1929, and was clearly influenced by the architecture of Mussolini's Italy. Florensa remodelled as well much of the interior, but fortunately left untouched the magnificent 17C cloister, which is comparable to that of the contemporary Casa de Convalescència (see p. 90) and is likewise richly decorated with ceramics; written permission to visit the interior is essential. At 6 Passeig de Colom is a fine Renaissance house with corner towers and a patio sadly altered through having been appropriated by a Chinese restaurant. Architecturally less interesting is the 16C house at No. 2 (at the very end of the avenue, overlooking the Plaça d'Antoni López), which is known as the *Casa Cervantes* for the belief that the author of *Don Quixote* stayed here.

Running along the southern side of the Passeig de Colom and spreading all the way down to the waterfront is the newly created **MOLL DE LA FUSTA**, one of the more spectacular examples of recent European town-planning. In the 1920s the waterfront had come to be shielded from the Passeig de Colom by a group of drab warehouses serving the port; despite numerous public protests, these structures were not finally to be taken down until the 1960s, and it was not until 20 years later that a new scheme for improving this whole area came finally to be implemented. Built in 1981–87 under the supervision of Manuel de Solá-Morales, the wide thoroughfare of the Moll de la Fusta was designed to provide Barcelona with a dignified maritime façade complete with bar facilities, and also to alleviate the traffic congestion of what has been described as 'the densest kilometre of urban seafront on the Mediterranean'. The thoroughfare features two parallel promenades, the one nearest the sea being at a lower level and lined with rows of palm trees. A dual carriageway, partially covered by the upper promenade, separates the two levels and is spanned by two colourful red draw bridges inspired by Van Gogh's *Bridge at Arles*. Along the upper promenade are five wavy-roofed huts serving as *chiringuitos* or beach bars. The decoration of the easternmost of these bars was assigned to the architect Alfredo Arribas and the designer Javier Mariscal, both of whom have collaborated on some of the most adventurous and amusing of Barcelona's 'designer bars'. Their bar on the Moll de La Fusta, known as *Gambrinus*, was created in 1988, and was their most extravagant joint effort prior to the Torres de Ávila on Montjuïc (see p. 116). The exterior of the bar is dominated by a gigantic upright prawn which waves its claws in cheeky riposte to the Columbus Monument at the other end of the Moll de la Fusta. The metalwork of the outdoor seating, encrusted with marine life, is intended to suggest some epic shipwreck, while the interior features a large wooden bar-table shaped like the prow of a ship; port-holes and frosted glass inscribed with maritime doodles, complete the decoration of the bar, which specialises, understandably, in seafood *tapas*.

Mariscal's prawn at Gambrinus, on the Moll de la Fusta

North east of the Gambrinus is the PLAÇA D'ANTONI LÓPEZ, which marks the chaotic junction of the Via Laietana (see p. 57) with the Passeig de Colom and its eastern continuation the Passeig d'Isabel II. On the northern side of this square stands the *Edificio de Correos (Central Post Office), a modest building in comparison with that of Madrid, but exceedingly grand by any other standards. Designed in 1914 by Josep Goday i Casals and Jaume Torres i Grau (but not constructed until 1926–27), this massive classical structure features a central frontispiece articulated by giant Corinthian columns supporting four allegorical figures by the Noucentiste sculptor Manuel Fuxà. The Noucentiste painters Josep Obiols Labarta, Canyelles and Francesc Galí were responsible for the classical, Puvis de Chavannes-inspired frescoes adorning the lunettes of the building's echoing main hall, though these works are now so darkened and gloomily lit as to be barely decipherable.

The broad but short PASSEIG D'ISABEL II, which joins the Plaça d'Antoni López with the Pla de Palau, was created after 1835, following the first stage of the demolition of Barcelona's maritime defensive walls. Almost its entire southern side is taken over by the **Edifici de Llotja** (Stock Exchange Building), the neo-classical exterior of which blends well with the neighbouring ensemble of grand early 19C structures.

In 1339 the *Consell dels Vint*—a group of 20 merchants under the direction of a *cónsol* or judge—acquired a plot of land in the district of Ribera del Mar with the intention of erecting a building where all commercial transactions could take place; the money for its construction was to be raised by the levying of a 3 per cent tax on all goods entering and leaving the city. The original structure, built by Pere Llobet in 1352-57, appears to have been a simple porticoed structure, where the merchants carried out their business under the arches of the loggia. The original building, which had been damaged both by the sea and by an attack carried out by the Castilian Navy in 1359, was replaced in 1383 by a new structure commissioned by Pere III the Ceremonious from Pere Arbei. This new *Llotja*, apparently inspired by that of Valencia, comprised a courtyard and a large hall, the latter being the only part of it to have survived to this day.

By 1764 a large section of the building was threatening to collapse and, soon afterwards, a commission of works was established with a view to transforming the place into the seat of the Barcelona Chamber of Commerce. The remodelling was entrusted to Joan Soler i Faneca, who destroyed all but the hall, which he encased in a large neo-classical block; Soler supervised the work until his death in 1794, after which he was replaced by Joan Fàbregas and Tomàs Soler, who constructed the imposing pedimented façade on the Pla de Palau. After the dissolution of the Chamber of Commerce in 1847, part of the building was handed over to the Barcelona School of Fine Arts, which was to be based here until comparatively recently, and still keeps in the building a small museum of academic works in its collection. Picasso's father, José Ruíz Blasco, taught at the School at the end of the 19C, and Picasso himself was a pupil here. The hall of the original Llotja is now used by the Barcelona Stock Exchange.

Entering the Llotja from the Passeig d'Isabel II, you will find yourself in the neo-classical courtyard which replaced the original medieval one; 60 orange trees apparently covered the latter space, but all that the present courtyard has to offer are marble statues of the Four Continents by two pupils of the neo-classical sculptor Campeny, Bover and Oliver. A staircase lined with marble allegories by Salvador Gurri of Industry and Commerce (1802) leads up to the attractive 18C rooms of the former Board of Commerce, which can generally be visited in the mornings; elsewhere in the building is the Museu de la Reial Academia Belles Arts Sant Jordi, which puts on the occasional exhibition. However, the main object of a visit to the Llotja is to see the superlative if misleadingly named **GOTHIC HALL**, which lies off the eastern side of the courtyard, and was built by Pere Arbei in the late 14C as the Trading Hall. This impressively spacious structure is divided into three aisles by exceptionally tall and elegant arcades formed not of pointed but rounded arches, the whole covered by a wooden beam ceiling. Part of the fascination of this hall is that its trading activities have been almost continuous up to the present day, the place being used now as a Stock Exchange, the delightfully old-fashioned furnishings of which (including a large clock which records not only the time, but also the year, month and temperature) blend well with the surroundings.

Facing the Llotja, on the southern side of the Passeig d'Isabel II, are the *Cases d'En Xifré, a porticoed neo-classical block formed of five houses, the whole intended to harmonise with the Pla de Palau, which it overlooks on its eastern side. Promoted by Josep Xifré i Casas, a Catalan merchant who had made his money in America, it was built in 1836–40 by Josep Buixareu and Francesc Vila; articulated by a giant order of pilasters, it is richly decorated with terracotta and other reliefs attributed to Tomàs Padró, a pupil of Campeny. Whereas the three upper floors of the building were intended as homes, the rooms off the ground-floor arcade were used as commercial establishments, one of which, at No. 14, still survives to this day. This, the 7 *Portes*, is one of Barcelona's most famous restaurants, and has been patronised by such diverse personalities as Picasso, Einstein and Ava Gardner; the place, which was extensively restored in 1980, has been the subject of a book by José María Carandell. Picasso's family, who, immediately on arriving at Barcelona in 1895, had lived in a basement apartment at 4 Passeig d'Isabel II, moved shortly afterwards to a second-floor apartment at the back of the Cases d'En Xifré. This apartment was situated at 3 Carrer Reina Cristina, a street which has been turned today into a great electronics bazaar where televisions, computers, clocks, cameras and other mechanical devices can be bought at discount prices. Incongruously situated amidst all this is the *Xampanyeria* (at No. 7), a bodega specialising exclusively in the Catalan champagne known as Cava. At No. 7 of the waterfront street to the south, the Carrer Pas Sota Muralla, is the *Bar Pascual*, which makes the justifiable claim to serve the 'best coffee in the district'.

The large PLA DEL PALAU, laid out by José Massanés in 1836, constitutes one of Barcelona's grandest and most harmonious ensembles of early 19C buildings, even though it has lost the Royal Palace which gave the place its name; this was situated on the north-eastern corner of the square, and was burnt down in 1875. At the centre of the square is the *Font del Geni Català (The Fountain of Catalan Genius), which was designed by Francesc Daniel Molina in 1825, but not executed until 1855; the sculptors responsible were two Italians resident in Barcelona, Fausto and Ángel Baratta. The work commemorates the Marquis of Campo Sagrado and his bringing to the city of waters from Montcada; the central figure is an Allegory of Catalan Genius, while below are four seated figures representing the four Catalan provinces, the main rivers of which (the Llobregat, Ter, Ebre and Segura), are suggested by the four jets of water at their feet.

At the junction of the square and the Avinguda Marquès de l'Argentera (the eastern continuation of the Passeig d'Isabel II) is the former *Duana Vella or Custom House, which was built in 1790–92 in replacement of a previous custom's house which had been burnt down in 1777. Designed by the versatile Count of Roncali, then Minister of Finance, this cheerful stucco-coated structure is articulated by pilasters simulating coloured marble. The building, transformed in 1902 into the seat of the Civil Government, has retained sumptuous and extensive neo-classical decorations by Pere Pau Montañá.

Walking east along the Avinguda Marquès de l'Argentera, you will pass to your right the enormous *Estació de França, an enormous railway station which was built in 1926–29 as part of the city's urban improvements carried out in preparation for the International Exhibition of 1929; it replaced a station of 1848, the oldest in Spain. Its most striking feature is its vestibule—

decorated by Raimon Duran i Reynals and Salvador Soteras i Taberner—
which is covered by three coffered shallow domes, the whole having a
classical elegance in keeping with the tenets of Noucentisme; the station
has been closed for many years for extensive restoration and remodelling.
Beyond the station you will come to the main entrance of the **PARC DE LA
CIUTADELLA**, Barcelona's oldest municipal park and the site of the World
Exhibition of 1888.

The Ciutadella has its origins in a notorious fortress commissioned by Philip V in 1715,
following his successful siege of Barcelona in September of the previous year. His
attack on the city had been made through an opening in a north-eastern section of the
medieval wall, a section which for many years had been considered a potential military
weakness; from the middle of the 17C onwards the army had been pressing for the
construction here of a citadel which would counterbalance the hill-top castle of
Montjuïc, on the south-western side of the city. Philip V's decision to build the citadel,
however, was taken less for military reasons than for purely vindicative ones, for he
wanted to punish Barcelona for having supported the Habsburgs during the War of
Succession. His plans for the citadel entailed initially the destruction of the entire
Barcelona district of the Ribera, though in the end only the eastern half of this district
was pulled down. Even so no less than 61 streets disappeared completely, and the
owners of 1262 houses and churches were forced to demolish their properties at their
own cost and without any form of compensation.

The demolition of this half of the Ribera was carried out in 1715–18, and work on the
new citadel was begun in 1716. The design of the fortress was entrusted to Próspero
de Verboom, who produced a star-shaped plan inspired by Vauban; the construction
of the project was supervised by Verboom himself, together with Alexandre de Retz.
The walls and defensive ditches were completed by 1719, but work on the buildings
within the citadel continued until 1727, and was never entirely finished, for the plans
to construct a hospital, a barracks and an artillery foundry had eventually to be
abandoned. The place never functioned as a true fortress, and was captured with
considerable ease by the French in 1808. Its main role came to be that of a prison and
execution-ground for political criminals, acquiring a special notoriety during both the
Napoleonic occupation and between 1828 and 1830, the worst years of Ferdinand VII's
anti-Liberal reprisals.

No other place in Barcelona aroused such popular hostility as the Ciutadella, which
became the supreme symbol of the oppression of the Catalan people. Numerous
attempts were made to have it pulled down and, during the Regency of General
Espartero in 1840, the city's specially created Civilian Guard began its demolition on
the pretext that the place might have been appropriated by those members of the army
taking part in the anti-Espartero revolt of 1841. The crushing of this revolt, and the
Spanish Government's threat to bombard the city if the Ciutadella were to be taken
down, led not only to the demolition work being abandoned but also to the reconstruction of those parts of the citadel that had already been destroyed. With the decision
made in 1858 to pull down the remaining city walls and create the Eixample, the
Ciutadella lost all possible military significance. None the less it was not until the fall
of Isabel II in 1868 and the instigation of the revolutionary government of General Prim
that permission was finally given to demolish once and for all this hated monument.

The Ciutadella was handed over by the Spanish Government to the City of
Barcelona, and numerous plans were proposed for the development of the site, all of
which were forced to include some provision for a public park. Eventually, after a
protracted competition, the City decided to adapt a scheme proposed by Josep
Fontserè, who rejected the idea of creating any residential blocks on the site, and
concentrated his plan entirely on the park, which he believed would stimulate the
renewal of the old city; in his own words 'gardens are to a city what lungs are to the
human body'. Work on the park was begun under Fontserè's direction in 1872, but the
decision made in 1885 to hold the World Exhibition within its grounds entailed
considerable modification of the architect's original plans. Fontserè protested strongly
to Barcelona's newly appointed mayor, Rius i Taulet, and in consequence found himself
sacked for supposedly misappropriating funds. He was replaced as director of the
works of the park by his long-standing enemy Antoni Rovira i Trias; meanwhile the

design of the Exhibition grounds was entrusted to Elies Rogent. A lively and excellently researched account of the transformation of the once dreaded Ciutadella into the grounds of the World Exhibition is to be found in Eduardo Mendoza's fantastical novel, *The City of Marvels* (English translation, 1989).

The World Exhibition was officially inaugurated on 20 May 1888, and was closed on 9 December of the same year. Two of its main structures—Vilaseca's Arc del Triomf and Domènech's Café-Restaurant—were retained, but the park itself, despite plans to create here a zoo and a museum of archaeology and medieval art, came gradually to be neglected, the attentions of the municipal authorities becoming largely devoted to the Park of Montjuïc, the proposed site of the International Exhibition of 1929. A revival in the Ciutadella's fortunes came in 1932 when the former arsenal here was adapted as the seat of the Parliament of Catalonia, a function which was retained until 1939, and restored in 1980.

Entering the luxuriantly verdant Parc de la Ciutadella from the Passeig Marquès de l'Argentera, you should head straight down the broad alley which leads towards an equestrian monument to General Prim; the monument, executed in 1882–87 by Lluís Puigjaner, was destroyed in 1936 and reconstructed in 1945 by Frederic Marés. Beyond this monument are to be found the main survivals of the original Ciutadella, beginning with the *chapel, an austerely simple structure of 1718–27 by the military engineer Alexandre de Retz. Inspired in its restrained classical detailing by the architecture of the French late baroque, the building was in turn to influence a number of later Barcelona churches, in particular in the use of a rounded pediment on the west façade (see for instance the Church of the Betlem on La Rambla); the place is still used by the army for services. Adjoining the chapel is the former *Governor's Palace, which was built by Jorge Próspero de Verboom in 1716–27 and is now the premises of a school; as austere and French in its architecture as the chapel, it is surmounted by the Bourbon coat of arms.

Immediately beyond the two buildings is the former parade ground or PLAÇA D'ARMES, which in 1916–17 was landscaped in a formal French style by the distinguished and appropriately named French landscape designer Jean C.N. Forestier. Forestier's classically simple arrangement of hedges and flower-beds centred around an oval pool is fully in the spirit of Noucentisme, a spirit reinforced by the beautiful white sculpture by Josep Llimona which lies in the centre of the pool, surrounded by water-lilies; entitled *Desconsol* (Disconsolate), this marble sculpture of 1917 (based on a model of 1903) is of a recumbant female nude staring at the water in a pose reminiscent both of Narcissus and the repentent Magdalene. The pool and its sculpture forms an elegant foreground to the former arsenal, another work of 1716–27 by Jorge Próspero de Verboom. The palatial aspect of this building is because it was adapted as a royal residence in 1889–95 by Pere Falqué i Urpí, who added the grand, pedimented frontispiece. Further changes to the building, including the addition of two wings, were made in 1904–15, when the place was converted to house the combined collections of Barcelona's museums of fine arts and archaeology. These collections were transfered to Montjuïc in 1932, when the former arsenal was turned into the seat of the Catalan Parliament. After 1939 the place served as a barracks before being transformed, in 1945, into the **MUSEU D'ART MODERN**, which has remained in the building to this day, though occupying a smaller part of it than before as a result of the return here of the Catalan Parliament in 1980.

The name of the Museu d'Art Modern is a misleading one, and those coming here expecting a representative and international collection of modern art will be disappointed (such a museum does not at present exist in Barcelona, and will not do so until the opening in the Raval of the Museu d'Art Contemporani; see p. 89). This particular museum has its origins in the Museu Municipal de Belles Arts, which was founded in 1891, and had as its nucleus a group of works acquired during the World Exibition of 1888, as well as paintings and sculptures executed by artists who had received bursaries from the municipality to visit Rome. The museum, which had been housed originally in the no longer extant Palau de Belles Arts, developed a particular speciality in Catalan medieval art after having been moved to the arsenal of the Ciutadella in 1904. The holdings of medieval, Renaissance and baroque art were to form the basis of the Museu d'Art de Catalunya in Montjuïc, while its post-18C collections—mainly composed of the works of Catalan artists from the Romantic period up to the early 20C—were brought together in 1945 to create the Museu d'Art Modern. From October 1990 to January 1991 a major exhibition of Catalan Modernisme was held here, after which the museum was closed for four months for a radical rehanging of the collections. The museum is now devoted exclusively to Catalan art from c 1860–c 1930, dwelling in particular on those artists associated with Modernisme and Noucentisme. The earlier holdings will eventually be incorporated into the Museu d'Art de Catalunya, while the later ones will be presented to the Museu d'Art Contemporani. The fate of the few works by non-Catalan artists such as Sorolla and Sisley is still uncertain.

The Museu d'Art Modern was at one time a pleasantly rambling institution, unsystematic in its layout, and with no attempt made to separate the odd outstanding work of art from a myriad of mediocre if often entertaining works. Today all has changed, and within the now tastefully modernised rooms by can be found a streamlined and thoughtfully laid out selection of works, which, without the assistance of information panels or documentary material, is intended to provide a clear account of the development of what the museum's curators believe to be the greatest period in Catalan art since the 15C. An indication of the new, rational spirit of the museum is the provision within the entrance lobby of a number of computers supplying—and even printing out, if so required—information relating to all aspects of the collection. The greatness of Catalan art of the turn of the century has been revealed by the new display as it never was before, but in other respects the museum has been diminished. The criteria for selection have been motivated by rigid aesthetic judgements that will soon prove to be out-dated and by nationalistic biases that might turn out to be parochial and petty-minded. There is no room in the new humourless and reverential display for the charming works of an artist such as Francesc Galí, who, despite his historical importance as the teacher of Miró and others, has been ignored for not meeting the high artistic standards required of the curators. More shamefully, the large collection of oil sketches, maquettes and mural fragments by Josep Maria Sert—one of the greatest European decorators of this century—has been left out altogether on the grounds that the achievement of such an artist can only be judged from his finished decorations (this collection will probably be presented to the projected Sert Museum at Vich). One suspects that the real reason for Sert's omission lies in the fact that his highly idiosyncratic art falls outside the categories of both Modernisme and Noucentisme, which the curators consider as representing the quintessential Catalan genius.

The museum's selection of Catalan works opens with a room devoted to the Reus-born Marià Fortuny (1838–74), who is treated here as a precursor of Modernisme. In terms of subject-matter, Fortuny was little different to the academic artists of his time, his greatness as a painter lying essentially in the vividness of his technique, which comprises rapid brush-strokes and brilliant colouring. The first Catalan artist to achieve a truly international reputation, he spent much of his working life in Italy, dying in Rome at the age of 36; the museum to him in Venice is housed in his beautifully preserved studio in the 18C Palazzo Pesaro degli Orfei. The Fortuny room in Barcelona is dominated by an enormous scene of the Battle of Tetuan, a minutely detailed work which takes up almost an entire wall and powerfully conveys the dust and chaos of war. Flanking this room are two rooms dedicated to late 19C 'Realism', a category which is composed mainly of Catalan artists active in Paris, Barbizon and Rome; among the works here are Italianate paintings by Roig i Soler (1852–1909), Parisian scenes by Romà Ribera (1848–1935) and Francesc Miralles (1848–1901), landscapes by the Barbizon School followers Joaquim Veyreda (1843–94) and Josep Berga (1877–1914), and the Manet-inspired El Marne by Eiseu Meifrèn (1858–1940).

Rooms 4 to 8 contain works by what the museum describes as the 'First Generation' of Modernistes, including Symbolist canvases by Tamburini (1856–1932) and Joan Brull (1863–1911), highly expressive sculptures by Miquel Blay (1866–1936) and a richly detailed sculpture of The First Communion by Josep Llimona (1864–1934). The dominating artists of this first generation were the painters Ramon Casas (1866–1932) and Santiago Rusiñol (1861–1931). Among the former's works here are those that decorated the famous artistic tavern of *Els Quatre Gats* (see p. 79), most notably a series of pencil portraits of the tavern's associates (including the young Picasso), an oil sketch showing Rusiñol suspended from one of the tavern's wooden chandeliers, and the no less celebrated double portrait of Casas himself riding a tandem with Pere Romeu. The most important of Casas' paintings were his large oils of contemporary political and social events, all of which were painted with a vivid life-like technique which combined compositions inspired by photography with a startling fluency of brushstroke derived from his experiences as a plein-air landscapist. The Museu d'Art Modern is missing two of his finest works of this type (The Garotting of Santiago Salvador and Mounted Policemen Dispersing Protesters; these are to be found respectively in the Museu de Arte Moderno in Madrid and in the Museu d'Olot at Olot), but in compensation has the richly detailed Corpus Procession Departing from the Church of Santa Maria del Mar. As an example both of the photographic boldness of Casas' compositions and his painterly fluency you should note in the latter work the feathered plumes of the soldiers' helmets, which stand in isolation in the painting's left-hand corner.

Rusiñol, while occupying a central position in the history of Modernisme through his organisation of the '*Festes Modernistes*' at his house in Sitges (see p. 156), was a less powerful and original artist than Casas. His reputation as a painter lies mainly with his charming landscapes and genre-like portraits, of which the Museu d'Art Modern has a particularly fine selection. Prominent among these works are those that he executed during his first stay in Paris in 1889, most notably his indoor scene entitled The Romance (the pianist in which is none other than Eric Satie), and two scenes set in the famous Montmartre Beer Garden of the Moulin de la Galette: one of the latter is a view of the garden from the kitchen, while the other is a full-length portrait of his Catalan friend and colleague Miquel Utrillo. Whereas Renoir in the 1870s had portrayed the Moulin de la Galette with vibrant colour, Rusiñol represented the place in a more sober way, with an overall grey tonality inspired by the art of Bastien-Lepage, whose works were then at the height of their popularity. After flirting with Symbolism on his return to Catalonia (a phase in his art which can only be appreciated in the museum to him at Sitges; see p. 157), Rusiñol considerably brightened his palette and came to devote himself largely to the portrayal of gardens. His garden scenes, which tend towards the facile and sentimental, ensured Rusiñol's popular appeal if not his critical reputation.

Following an important exhibition of '*Modernismo en España*', which was held here in 1970, the Museu d'Art Modern acquired a collection of furniture, jewellery and architectural furnishings from the Moderniste period. These are excellently displayed in Rooms 9–12, though it has to be said that many of the works can only be appreciated fully when seen in the original architectural context for which they were created. Among the works are decorative elements from buildings by the great Moderniste trio, Domènech i Montaner, Puig i Cadafalch and Antoní Gaudí, the latter represented by ironwork railings from his Casa Vicens in Gràcia (see p. 146).

Paintings and sculptures by artists of the 'Second Generation' of Modernisme occupy Rooms 13–16, and reflect the influence in Catalonia of French Impressionism and Post-Impressionism. Two artists misleadingly referred to as Catalan Impressionists were Francesc Gimeno (1860–1932) and Nicolau Raurich (1877–1945). The former was the author of ochre-coloured landscapes of great expressive power and technical freedom, in particular his scenes set in and around the mountain village of Torroella de Montgroí. Raurich's landscapes, mainly of coastal scenes, are characterised instead by their startling use of lurid colours such as oranges, deep pinks and vivid purples, and by the remarkable relief-like effects created by the thick application of paint. A more genuinely Impressionist artist than either of these was Ricard Canals (1876–1931), whose works reflect the influence of Degas and, above all, Renoir. Joaquim Mir (1873–1940), the leading figure of the so-called Olot School of landscape artists, painted in a colourful decorative manner akin to that of Vuillard, and is also represented in the museum by a seductive stained glass window which he designed. The most original of all these artists was Isidre Nonell (1873–1911), who, inspired by a combination of Daumier and Japanese prints, achieved effects of decorative simplification and luminous colouring. Among the many works of his in the museum are some near abstract still lives (executed in the last years of his short life) and a series of huddled gypsy women which appears to have strongly influenced Picasso in the latter's so-called Blue and Pink Periods.

Rooms 17–19 are taken up by works of artists associated with Noucentisme, a movement initiated in 1906 by the writer and philosopher Eugeni d'Ors. Noucentisme, which was to be the prevalent Catalan style right up to the 1930s, represented both a return to classical models and a reaction against the stylistic eccentricities of Modernisme. One of its leading associates was the sculptor Josep Clarà (1878–1958), whose classically simplified and smoothly modelled female nudes closely recall the works of Aristide Maillol. The leading painter of the movement was Joaquim Sunyer, whose art combines the linear grace of Matisse with the colouring, composition and faceting technique of the great Noucentiste hero, Paul Cézanne.

The works in the museum's last two rooms are of some of the more avant-garde artists working in Catalonia in the second and third decades of the century. Particularly remarkable are the playful sculptures of Pau Gargallo (1881–1934), which include a caricature stone head of Picasso of 1913, and such lively metal cut-outs as his Great Dancer of 1929. There is also a portrait of mesmerising power by the young Salvador Dalí. It represents—without recourse to Dalí's later surrealistic devices—the artist's father, Salvador Dalí i Cusí, whose stern forbidding features express the scorn which he is known to have felt for his son's activities.

Leaving the museum and heading south, you will skirt the part of the arsenal which is now occupied by the Parlament de Catalunya. Immediately to the south of this is the entrance to the *Parc Zoològic (Zoo), which takes up much of the southern half of the Ciutadella. Founded after the Civil War, it is laid out on the pioneering principles of England's Whipsnade, with moats rather than cages separating the spectators from the elephants, bears, lions and other animals. Its attractions include a whale and dolphin show, and a series of glass panels where these mammals can be seen on other occasions swimming under water. But for many years the zoo's greatest claim to fame has been its gorilla called *Snowflake*; the only known albino gorilla in the world, this animal is now of venerable age, its white fur being greatly in need of restoration. For the cultural tourist the zoo offers the delightful attraction of Roig i Soler's sculpture of 1885 entitled *Lady with Umbrella, an evocative survival from the time of the World Exhibition, and a work which served almost as a symbol of Barcelona before the arrival of Mariscal's Cobi.

Returning to the former arsenal and heading north you will reach—immediately beyond the Plaça d'Armes—an *artificial lake featuring a grotto on its northern side. Entering the grotto you would originally have found yourself behind a great sheet of water which cascaded from the elaborate **monument** which rises behind the lake; the cascade has been inactive for many years, awaiting the complete overhaul of the park's water system. The lake and monumental cascade, which were created by Josep Fontserè between 1875 and 1881, were closely inspired by a neo-baroque complex (the Château d'Eau) designed in the 1860s by H.J. Esperandieu for the grounds of the Palais Longchamp in Marseille. The monumental cascade has as its centrepiece a triumphal arch raised high above the ground, flanked by great sweeps of steps, and adorned and surrounded by an over-abundance of statuary, including works by most of the leading Catalan sculptors of the day. A gilded bronze Chariot of Aurora (by Rossend Nolas) crowns the central arch, while below is a beautiful group designed by Venanci Vallmitjana of Venus and the Naieads; in addition there are works by Francesc Pagès, Josep Gamot, Manuel Fuxà, Joan Flotats and Rafael Atchè, the whole forming a composition which was criticised at the time for being ludicrously crowded. Though the static and conventional overall design was by Fontserè, the boulders and the animated decorative detailing in the ironwork and elsewhere are often attributed to the young Antoni Gaudí, who, while still an architectural student, is known to have worked for Fontserè. Gaudí, who is also thought to have been responsible for the ironwork gates at the two entrances to the park, certainly had a hand in the design of the building enclosing the original water supply for the cascade. This brickwork structure, erected in 1874–77, overlooks the northeastern edge of the park, and is entered at 48 Carrer de Wellington. The story goes that Gaudí was asked by Fontserè to do the technical calculations for this building. Afterwards Fontserè showed these to Joan Torras, a professor of structural engineering in the School of Architecture where Gaudí was studying; Torras was apparently so impressed with the student's work that Gaudí was passed in his course without having to attend a single class. The building is at present being remodelled for future use as a museum.

Just to the east of the monumental cascade is a children's play area, in front of which has recently been placed an enormous *bronze cat by the witty Columbian artist Botero, who is famous for his naïf overblown figures; the cat, shown with tail stretched out behind, has whiskers in the form of gilded bronze cylinders. To the west of the cascade is a *Monument to Bonaventura Carles Arribau, which was erected in 1884; this work features a statue of the poet by Manuel Fuxà (replaced by a bronze copy in 1934), and an eclectic pedestal designed by Josep Vilaseca, possibly with the help of Antoní Gaudí.

Botero's bronze cat in the Parc Zoològic

Four important buildings of the 1880s line the north-western border of the park, overlooking the Passeig de Picasso (see p. 87). The earliest of these is the *Museu de Geologia (Geology Museum), which was built in 1879–82 to house an important geological collection presented to the city by an amateur archaeologist and naturalist with the appropriate name of Martorell i Peña (the second of his names means 'stone'). The architect originally chosen for the building was Josep Fontserè, but his design of 1874 was later turned down in favour of one by Rovira i Trias, who had attacked Fontserè for not having had an academic architectural training. The building which eventually went up is a worthy but unexciting neo-classical structure, comprising two long wings flanking a colonnaded frontispiece; the interior, barely touched since the last century, has a musty institutional character with collections of interest purely to the specialist. On the southern side of the building is the glasshouse known as the *Umbracle, a work of 1883–84 by Josep Fontserè; its monumental side façades are of bare brick, while the main area features ironwork columns, steel beams and wooden louvers. Another glasshouse, the *Hivernacle, stands on the northern side of the Geology Museum. This light and elegant ironwork structure was built by Josep Amargós i Samaranch in 1888, and differs from the English prototypes established by Paxton in having an open central aisle.

Immediately to the north of the Hivernacle, in the north-western corner of the Ciudadella, rises the park's largest and most interesting structure, built by Domènech i Montaner in 1887–88 to serve as the **Café-Restaurant** of the World Exhibition. With its large expanses of bare, undecorated brickwork, and its undisguised framework in laminated steel, this building occupies a pioneering position in the history of Functionalist architecture, anticipating by over ten years Berlage's Stock Exchange building in Amsterdam. As with Modernisme in general, however, the building combines daring modernity with a fantastical medieval element. Its corner towers, crenellations, Mudéjar-style windows and upper row of ceramic plaques imitative of medieval shields (executed by Joan Llimona, Josep-Lluís Pellicer and Alexandre de Riquer), give the building the look of a fortress dreamt up by some science fiction illustrator. In its day the building came to be known as the Castell dels Tres Dragons (The Castle of the Three Dragons), after a popular contemporary play by Pitarra. Furthermore, in the course of its construction, jokes appeared in the local press suggesting that the waiters who were to work there would have to put on chain mail and armour. As it happened, the building was not completed in time for the World Exhibition, and so never functioned as a café/restaurant. Instead, on Domènech's suggestion, the place was made to house not only his own architectural studio but also what were among the earliest craft workshops in Europe dedicated to the revival of traditional ceramic and ironwork techniques; these workshops were to play a vital role in the renascence of the Catalan decorative arts at the turn of the century. Since 1917 the building has housed the Museu de Zoologiá, a drab and old-fashioned display of insects and stuffed animals; much of the original interior decoration has disappeared, including most of the painted ceiling panels, and all the stained glass.

Leaving the Ciutadella by its northern gates, you will find in front of you a long and broad landscaped promenade named after Lluís Companys. This dates back to the end of the 18C, but was transformed in the late 19C as one of the two main approaches to the World Exhibition. Until recently, the promenade had retained its original mosaic pavement and ironwork lamps by Pere Falqués, but these were inexcusably removed during the construction of a large underground car-park. The promenade's main monuments have been kept, however, including—directly in front of the Ciutadella's entrance gates—an obelisk designed by Falqués in 1897 to commemorate the mayor who promoted the World Exhibition, Francesc de P. Rius i Taulet; the sculptural elements, including a bronze bust of the mayor, and allegorical figures of Fame, Science and Art, are by Manuel Fuxà. On either side of the obelisk are statues of the medieval hero Roger de Llúria and the baroque painter Antoni Viladomat, the work respectively of Josep Reynés (1888) and Torquat Tasso (1880). In the middle of the promenade stands a bronze copy of an 1880 statue by Rafael Atché of the Catalan patriot Pau Claris; this work, removed from its pedestal in 1947, was not put back again until 1977. Josep Vilaseca's superb and highly original **Arc del Triomf** dominates the northern end of the promenade, and was built as a monumental entrance to the World Exhibition. In his creation of a triumphal arch appropriate to the modern age, Vilaseca radically departed from classical prototype, and produced a structure of which John Ruskin would have approved, achieving effects of monumentality through the use of such a humble building material as brick. Though he was prevented by Elies Rogent from carrying out his initial plan of placing crenellated towers at either side of the arch, the work still manages to have more of a medieval than classical character, the elaborately detailed brickwork recalling the techniques of the medieval Moorish craftsmen known as the Mudéjars. The sculptural decoration, executed by Josep Llimona, Josep Reynés, Torquat Tasso and Antoni Vilanova, has as its theme the welcome extended by the city of Barcelona to those participating in the Exhibition, and features a matronly figure handing out emblems representing the various Spanish provinces.

As you walk towards the Arc del Triomf, you will pass to your right the massive *Palau de Justicia, a heavy eclectic structure in grey Montjuïc stone designed in 1887 by Josep Domènech i Estapà and Enric Sagnier i Villavecchia, and completed in 1908. The exterior has fantastically complex sculptural decoration and exuberant ironwork detailing, while inside are some early mural decorations by Josep Maria Sert. At the end of the promenade you should turn right into the AVINGUDA DE VILANOVA, where you will find at No. 12 (at the junction with the Carrer de Roger de Flor) the *Hidroelèctrica de Catalunya, one of the most important works by Pere Falqués. Built in 1896–97 as an electrical plant, this brick and ironwork structure was closely inspired both in its detailing and use of materials by Domènech i Montaner's Editorial Montaner i Simón (see p. 128); the building, for which the architect had originally planned two large pyramids for the roof, has recently been adapted as the headquarters of the Catalan Electricity Company, and its ironwork painted a dark turquoise. Blocking off the eastern end of the Avinguda Vilanova is the former *Estació del Nord. Dating back to 1861, this railway station was remodelled by Demetri Ribes Marco in 1912–13 and given its splendid Moderniste ironwork. Abandoned as a station in 1972, the building has recently been saved from decay by being transformed into a sports centre, which will be inaugurated in 1992 with the Olympics' table-tennis championships. A curious modern park has been laid out on the southern side of the building, featuring sloping lawns and a pyramidical sculpture by B. Peppers. To the north of here extends a large wasteland which is currently the object of a massive redevelopment campaign intended to bring new life to this hitherto neglected area of town. The focal point of this new development will be the National Theatre of Catalonia, which will occupy a site alongside the Plaça de les Glòries Catalanes, at the intersection of the Avingudas Diagonal, de la Meridiana and de les Corts Catalanes. The theatre, which has yet to be started, has been designed by Ricardo Bofill and will take the form of a Post-Modernist temple with an outer glass shell and a concrete inner structure, the whole flanked by colonnades and approached by a monumental flight of steps.

If you wish to visit the district of **Barceloneta** and the adjoining **Vila Olímpica**—a tour mainly of interest to those wishing to swim or eat in a fish restaurant—you should return to the Pla del Palau. South of this square, projecting into the sea, extends the popular maritime district of Barceloneta, which was built as a replacement to that part of Barcelona which had been pulled down after 1714 to make way for the Ciutadella. The architect of the citadel, Próspero de Verboom, was responsible for the initial plan which, in keeping with the latest principles of town-planning, took the form of a regular grid divided into short narrow blocks so that every house could have windows overlooking the street. The construction of the district was only begun in 1753, and the original stipulation that every house should be no higher than two storeys so as to ensure the maximum amount of light in the streets was eventually dropped. The grid, lined today with narrow monotonous rows of tall, dirty houses, offers little of architectural interest with the possible exception of the church of Sant Miquel del Port, a late baroque structure of Roman inspiration which was designed by Pedro M. Cermeño in 1753. The church, which serves the parish of Barceloneta, stands on the small Plaça Barceloneta, a short walk from the Pla de Palau down the harbourside Passeig Nacional. The whole seafront of Barceloneta is currently being radically altered with the construction of a new promenade, which has led to the demolition of many of the illegally built restaurants and bars that once gave to this area so much of its remarkable animation.

Near the western end of the Passeig Nacional you will come to the lowest of the two tall and flimsy-looking ironwork structures which support the cable-car linking Barceloneta with the hill of Montjuïc (see Rte 1F). The cable-car was devised by Carles Buigas in 1926 with a view to providing the city with another means of access to the site of the International Exhibition of 1929; however, financial backing for the enterprise was only found in 1928, thus resulting in the completion of the cable-car two years after the closure of the Exhibition. The lower tower, the *Torre de Sant Sebastià, resembles an old-fashioned oil rig, and features a lift which will take you to an upper platform from where the journey by cable-car begins. The whole system seems so antiquated that you might feel as if you are taking your life into your own hands as you hover high above the port, passing at a height of over 100 metres the top of the *Torre de Jaume I; the latter, the more elegant of the two towers, is comparable in its design to the Eiffel Tower in Paris, and has tapering ironwork supports holding up an octagonal platform.

Barcelona's long line of recently tidied beaches begins immediately below the Torre de Sant Sebastià, near the junction of the Passeig Nacional with the promenade which runs the whole length of the eastern side of Barceloneta, the Passeig Marítim. Public beaches, private beach establishments with changing cabins, segregated beaches for women, fish restaurants and beach bars known as *chiringuitos* characterise this side of Barceloneta, and provide the city with one of its main Sunday attractions. The Passeig leads north east to what was once an industrial semi-wasteland of gasometers, railway shuntings and warehouses. This is now the site of the *Vila Olímpica, a luxury residential and hotel district which will feature its own large park and marina. The creation of this new maritime district was proposed by Barcelona's former mayor Narcís Serra following the city's decision to put itself forward as a candiate for the 1992 Olympic Games. Serra's successor, Pasqual Maragall—the mayor of Barcelona since 1982— keenly championed the idea, and in 1985, at a time when it was still not known whether or not the city would host the Games, the architects Martorell, Bohigas, Mackay and Puigdomènech were entrusted with the design of the overall project. Quite apart from providing residential and other facilities for the Games, the project was intended to transform the industrial district of Poble Nou, a district—known as the 'Catalan Manchester'—which had not only fallen into decay but also been cut off from the rest of the city. The luxury flats that are nearing completion here have nearly all been sold, and at prices far higher than those of comparable residences in other parts of Barcelona. Dominating the district, and already two of the more prominent landmarks of modern Barcelona, are Spain's two highest skyscrapers, one of which (by Iñigo Ortiz and Enrique León) will serve as the MAPFRE office building, and the other (by the architectural studios of S.O.M. and G.C.A.) as the Vila Olímpica Hotel.

The irony of the Vila Olímpica, and indeed of the whole of Barcelona's new maritime development, is that it borders on what are likely to remain for many years to come some of the poorest parts of the city. The residential heart of Poble Nou, which lies to the east of the Vila Olímpica, is as run-down as ever, despite the smartening up of its maritime façade, which was once famous for its gyspy musical establishments. An evocative and decayed survival of old Barcelona is the *Cemeteri Vell de Barcelona (Old Cemetery), situated at the eastern end of the AVINGUDA D'ICÀIA, a large thoroughfare linking Poble Nou with the Pla del Palau. Founded by Bishop Climent in 1773, the cemetery was totally destroyed by the French in 1808 and rebuilt in 1818–19 by the Italian architect Antoni Ginesi. This symmetrically arranged neo-classical complex, featuring an entrance portal flanked by obelisks, mausolea in the form of pyramids and a pedimented chapel reminiscent of Hansen's cathedral at Copenhagen, was an expression of the Enlightenment ideals of the city's planners of the early 19C. In its present deserted, overgrown and crumbling state, it is as pathetic a testimony to the vanity of urban ideals as the Vila Olímpica will probably be in 200 years time.

F. Plaça d'Espanya and Montjuïc

Whereas the Ciutadella evokes the World Exhibition of 1888, the Plaça d'Espanya and the park of Montjuïc are essentially the legacy of the International Exhibition of 1929.

Plans for a sequel to the World Exhibition of 1888 were first formulated in 1907, by a group composed of councillors and representatives of the city's main businesses. The decision was made to hold the exhibition in 1914 on the mountain of Montjuïc, the landscaping of which had already been proposed in the 1890s. Work on the projected Exhibition was abandoned almost immediately, and was only taken up again five years later, as a result of pressure exercised by the young and rapidly expanding electrical industry. The new plans for the Exhibition involved postponing the event until 1917 and dividing it into two separate parts, one being an international exhibition on the theme of electricity, the other a general Spanish exhibition devoted mainly to the arts and crafts of the country. Puig i Cadafalch was entrusted with the overall design of the Exhibition, while the French landscapist Jean Forestier was commissioned to transform the slopes of Montjuïc into a lush park. Forestier, one of the leading landscapists of his day, had worked extensively in Spain, and was laying out the magnificent Maria Luisa Park in Seville at the time that he received the Barcelona commission.

Economic and political crises led to further postponements of the Exhibition, while the coming to power of Primo de Rivera in 1923 resulted in the downfall of Puig i Cadalfach both as a politician and as the Exhibition's main architect. The dictator's political ambitions provided another powerful motive for the Exhibition, which was finally inaugurated by Alfonso XIII on 19 May 1929. Though based to a large extent on Puig i Cadalfach's initial designs, the Exhibition which was eventually put on was far more ambitious than the one originally planned, and comprised four main sections, devoted respectively to the industries in general, the arts in Spain, agriculture and sports.

After the closure of the Exhibition at the end of 1929, the permanent structures were put to a variety of different uses, the ones at the foot of Montjuïc remaining to this day the venue of trade exhibitions. Some of the buildings on the mountain itself, including the main pavilion or Palau Nacional, were turned into museums, while another—the former Palau de l'Agricultura—was recently converted into a theatre; in addition Barcelona was left with a large sports stadium and the so-called Poble Espanyol, a walled village made up of buildings from all the different Spanish regions. By the early 1980s the park of Montjuïc still remained one of the main recreational centres of Barcelona, but the whole area lacked coherence and many of its structures were in a decayed and neglected state. With the choice of Montjuïc as the main sports area for the 1992 Olympics, new life has been given to the mountain. Buildings have been restored, road access greatly improved and spectacular new structures erected.

In Cerdà's 1855 plan for the expansion of Barcelona, the PLAÇA D'ESPANYA featured as an irregular space at the junction of the Gran Via de les Corts Catalanes with the old road to Madrid. The grand, semicircular square of today was planned by Puig i Cadalfach as the monumental approach both to the International Exhibition and to the park of Montjuïc; eventually the space was intended, in the words of the architect Rubió i Tudurí, as the 'nerve centre of Barcelona'. The various postponements of the Exhibition led to work on the square being delayed until the mid 1920s, and it was still not complete by the time the Exhibition opened in 1929. The large fountain in the middle, commissioned as late as 1928 to mark the entrance to the Exhibition, was designed by the former collaborator of Antoní Gaudí, Josep M. Jujol. In this work, Jujol departed radically from his previous Moderniste style to create a pedantic classical structure in keeping with the Noucentiste spirit of the Exhibition. Inspired by the fountains of baroque Rome, it has as its centrepiece a triangular-shaped structure formed of three Corinthian columns flanking niches adorned with statuary by Miquel Blay. The fountain was intended as a celebration of water, and the sculptural groups in the niches represent the three seas which surround the Spanish peninsula. Three winged Victories by the sculptor Llovet rise above the entablature, while at the base of the fountain are groups by Miquel and Llucià Oslé portraying Navigation, Public Health and Abundance.

   The oldest of the buildings around the Plaça d'Espanya, and the one exception to the prevailing classicism of the ensemble, is the bull-ring of *LES ARENES, which stands on the north-eastern side of the square. Built by August Font i Carreras in 1899–1900, it is in the pseudo-Islamic style characteristic of many of Spain's bull-rings, and has as its main source of inspiration the Great Mosque at Cordoba. Bull-fights are no longer put on here (they are held intead in the Plaça de Toros Monumental; see p. 135), and the ring is now used for concerts and other such activities. What was supposedly the first political demonstration in Europe in which handker-chiefs were waved in the air took place in the ring in 1906, in protest against a new law; in 1966 The Beatles performed here for the first time in Spain, an event which is often regarded as a key moment in the gradual liberal-isation of the country during the last years of Franco's rule. Immediately to the north of the ring extends a large formal park named after the artist Joan Miró and planned in close collaboration with him. A competition to design the park was held in 1981, and won by Andreu Arriola, Beth Galí, Màrius Quintana and Antoni Solanas; interestingly, a project put forward by the leading Post-Modernist architect Ricardo Bofill was turned down by Miró on the grounds that the classical temple which it featured was 'antiquated and dehumanised', a throw-back to the Franco days. Miró himself was to have provided a 'forest of sculptures', but was prevented by his death from executing all but one of these works, a massive phallic-like object which dominates the north-western side of the park; a library for children, attrac-tively situated among ramps and ponds, has recently been opened on the park's eastern side.

On the eastern side of the bull-ring runs the CARRER DE LLANÇÀ, where you will find at No. 20 (near the corner with the Gran Via de les Corts Catalanes) an interesting Moderniste apartment block built by Josep Graner Prat. The building is known as the Casa de la Papallona (House of the Butterfly) because of the butterfly-shaped crowning-piece adorning the otherwise sober façade. This extraordinary crowning-piece, covered all over with an abstract ceramic decoration in blue, green, white, red and yellow, gives a good idea of the extent to which Joan Miró was influenced by his city's Moderniste past.

The western and north-western sides of the Plaça d'Espanya are taken up by two large and austerely classical blocks built by Nicolau M. Rubio in 1928–29. These blocks, which served at first as hotels for the International Exhibition, were designed with the intention of being converted afterwards into apartments, this being part of Rubio's scheme for the city to profit from the investments put into the Exhibition; in the end the larger of the two blocks was given over to the Municipal Institute of Education, while the other was converted into a school. Running south west from the Plaça d'Espanya is the broad and landscaped AVINGUDA DE LA REINA MARIA CRISTINA, which joins the square with the park of Montjuïc and was built as the main thoroughfare of the Exhibition. The buildings that line the avenue are still used for trade fairs, and include two enormous pavilions with curved colonnnaded façades overlooking the southern side of the Plaça d'Espanya. One of these (to your left as you approach the avenue) is the recently restored *Palau del Treball, which was built in 1927 by Josep M. Jujol and André Calzada Echevarría; the other is the contemporary *Palau de Comunicacions i Transports, the work of Fèlix d'Azua and Adolf Florensa. In between the two buildings, at the very entrance to the avenue, stand two tall towers built by Ramon Reventó i Farrarons in 1927 and inspired by the campanile of St. Mark's in Venice. Walking down the avenue towards the looming mass of the Palau Nacional you will pass to your left the *Plaça de l'Univers, which was laid out originally by Forestier, but remodelled in 1985 by Pep Bonet i Bertran; in the centre of this largely bare space has been placed a sculpture by Josep Llimona entitled Forjador (The Foundry Worker), which was donated by the artist to the city on the occasion of the May Day celebrations of 1930.

The Avinguda de la Reina Maria Cristina emerges at a grand square lying directly at the foot of Montjuïc, and named after the engineer responsible for the ingenious electrical installations of the International Exhibition, Carles Buïgas. One of Buïgas' most successful creations was his Magic Fountain or **Font Màgica** of 1929, which dominates the square and was intended as the centrepiece of an electrical show involving beams projected from behind the Palau Nacional, large lamps placed the whole length of the Avinguda de la Reina Maria Cristina, and an obelisk fitted with coloured lighting. The fountain, with its central jet shooting over 50 metres into the air, is sometimes illuminated to the accompaniment of mainly baroque music; this popular show generally takes place at 21.00 on summer weekends, holidays and Thursdays, and at 20.00 on winter weekends.

A monumental flight of steps climbs from behind the fountain towards the Palau Nacional, and is flanked by the twin pavilions of Alfons XIII and Victòria Eugènia, which were built in 1923–28 to the designs of Puig i Cadafalch, and feature ornamental elements derived both from the baroque and the Viennese Secession. Recently-built escalators on either side of the steps considerably lighten the long and steep climb up to the Palau Nacional, a walk which can be very daunting owing to the glare from the white stone and the almost entire lack of shade. A longer and gentler way to the palace, and the one used by those driving there, is along the Avinguda del Marquès de Comillas, which begins at the north-eastern corner of the Plaça de Carles Buïgas and winds its way around the bosky slopes of Montjuïc. At the beginning of the avenue, on the left-hand side, is the **Pavelló d'Alemanya**, a reconstruction in its original location of Mies van der Rohe's German Pavilion for the International Exhibition of 1929. The abstract simplicity of this horizontally-based marble and glass structure, its fluid use of space and lack of rigid separation between interior and exterior, form a striking contrast to the pompous classicism of most of the official architecture of the Exhibition. The excellent reconstruction, carried out in 1985 by the leading Barcelona architects Cristià Cirici, Ferran Ramos and Ignasi de Solà-Morales, has had a significant impact on recent Catalan architecture and design, and has revealed to the full the richness and sensuality of a building known to the present generation only through black-and-white photographs.

You might well experience a sense of bathos as you make your way from the calming Minimalism of Mies van der Rohe to the busy kitsch of the **Poble Espanyol**, which lies half-way up Avinguda del Marquès de Comillas, surrounded on all sides by trees. The Poble Espanyol, which formed the part of the International Exhibition devoted to the crafts of Spain, was built in 1926–29 by the architects Francesc Folguera and Ramon Reventós, the painter Xavier Nogués and the art critic and former associate of *Els Quatre Gats*, Miquel Utrillo. Though enjoying from the beginning the status of one of the city's main tourist attractions, this pseudo-Spanish walled village developed over the years an exceedingly tacky character, and came to be frequented until recently only by foreigners. A complete restoration of the complex was begun in 1987 by Sen Tato, and at the same time the village has radically changed its image in the last few years through being turned into one of the centres of Barcelona's night-life. A number of popular night-time bars have now been opened here, including what is currently the most fashionable and extraordinary one in the whole city, the *Torres de Ávila*. This is situated at the main entrance to the village, within the reconstruction of one of the medieval gates of the Castilian town of Ávila. Opened in 1990, the bar is another creation of the architect Alfredo Arribas and the designer Mariscal, the latter modestly listing it as his favourite place in Barcelona. A bar guide issued in 1991 by the design magazine *Ardi* thought that no other bar could surely equal the Torres de Ávila in the amount of 'design per square metre'. The interior, featuring a number of differently sized and shaped bar areas, does achieve a certain magical quality through its baffling spatial complexity and scenographic lighting. The whole place is centred around a huge egg-shaped area, but the highpoint of the bar is its roof terrace, situated among the crenellations of the towers, to one of which the designers have added a dark and luminous dome, sparkling with stars and crowned by a crescent moon. The views of night-time Barcelona are magnificent, though the atmosphere of the whole bar is so dominated by the design as to be positively morgue-like, despite the crowds who queue up at weekends to get in here.

Entering the Poble Espanyol through the Ávila Gate, you will come immediately to the arcaded Plaça Mayor, which is made up of buildings taken from all over Spain. The sloping streets to the east of here lead eventually to a Catalan Square, and include streets from Aragon, the Basque Country and Extremadura, a flight of steps copied from ones in Santiago de Compostela, and a tiny but charming *Barrio Andaluz inspired by the Barrios Judio and de Santa Cruz in Cordova and Seville. With age the whole complex has acquired a remarkable authenticity in the sense that the places that it imitates, with their plethora of souvenir shops and over-restored quaintness, appear today to be no more genuine than the copies. An added attraction of the complex was once the *Museu d'Arts, Indústries i Tradicions, a folk art museum which was installed in the buildings around the Plaça Mayor; though the offices of this museum are still functioning, the collections themselves have been closed to the public for many years, and are likely to remain closed for many years to come.

From the Poble Espanyol the Avinguda del Marquès de Comillas leads eventually to the Olympic stadiums, which are situated above the Palau Nacional. To reach the palace you should turn left at the western end of the Poble Espanyol and climb up the Passeig Simón Bolivar until you reach the AVINGUDA DELS MONTANYAS, where you turn left again. The *Palau Nacional was conceived by Puig i Cadafalch as a vast domed building to act as the dominant element of the monumental vista leading from the Plaça d'Espanya down the Avinguda de la Reina Maria Cristina. His basic intentions were respected, though the building itself was not to be built until 1926–29, and to the designs of Enric Català i Català and Pedro Cendoya Oscoz. The end result was an eclectic structure of remarkable heaviness and pomposity, with elements derived from Spanish baroque and neo-classical architecture. The vast central dome is painted inside with frescoes by Francesc Galí and covers a hall which was originally used for the official ceremonies connected with the International Exhibition. The rest of the structure had been planned by Puig i Cadalfach to display exhibits celebrating electricity, the main theme of the exhibition which had originally been conceived. The redesigned building was to house instead the sections of the International Exhibition relating to art and archaeology; since 1934 it has served as the seat of the outstanding **MUSEU D'ART DE CATALUNYA**.

The desire to create in Barcelona a museum devoted to the fine arts goes back to the late 19C and was realised on the basis of works amassed during the World Exhibition of 1888. Founded in 1891, this museum was known originally as Museu Municipal de Belles Arts, and contained mainly modern works. In 1904 it was transferred from the no longer extant Palau de Belles Arts to the former arsenal in the Parc de la Ciutadella (see p. 103), where it soon developed a speciality in medieval Catalan art. The first important medieval acquisitions—a group of Romanesque capitals and altar frontals from Tavèrnoles—were acquired between 1906 and 1908 under the directorship of the architect and historian Josep Pijoan. However, the nucleus of the medieval collection was built up during the long directorship of Pijoan's successor, Joaquim Folch i Torres, who was greatly assisted by Puig i Cadalfach, then the President of the Confederation or Junta of Barcelona Museums. After 1907 the Junta, in combination with the Institut d'Estudis Catalans, began the work of copying, photographing and publishing the numerous Romanesque frescoes to be found in the isolated churches of the Catalan Pyrenees. The Catalan Romanesque had been largely ignored until around the middle of the 19C, and even then the interest had been entirely concentrated on the sculpture rather than on the painting of this period. The appreciation of Romanesque painting in Catalonia was initiated with the inauguration in 1891 of the Museu Episcopal at Vic, and became ever more widespread as a result of the publicity generated by the investigations carried out after 1907. The techniques that had recently been developed in Italy for the removal of frescoes from walls gave antique dealers the idea of buying the Romanesque frescoes from the local civic and ecclesiastical authorities and selling them abroad. Fortunately the Junta intervened at this stage and, with the exception of the apse frescoes from Mur (which ended up in the Fine Arts Museum in Boston), managed to secure for the Museu de Belles Arts all of Catalonia's important Romanesque frescoes, which were removed from their original settings between 1919 and 1923.

In 1934 the medieval, Renaissance and baroque holdings of the Museu de Belles Arts were separated from the modern collections and transferred to their present position in the Palau Nacional in Montjuïc, the resulting museum being given the name of the Museu d'Art de Catalunya. In 1985 a complete re-organisation of the museum's collections was begun, and the architects Gae Aulenti and Enric Steegmann were entrusted with the task of remodelling the interior of the Palau Nacional. The museum is expected to reopen in 1992.

The reputation of the Museu d'Art de Catalunya as the finest museum of medieval art in Spain, if not in Europe, is due essentially to its unrivalled holdings of Catalan Romanesque art, which used to take up no less than 33 rooms to the right of the main entrance. Among these holdings are numerous altar frontals and other painted panels and wood carvings (including the 12C 'Battló Majesty', a richly coloured work featuring a tunic adorned with Islamic motifs), statues in polychromed wood of the Virgin and the Crucifixion, and exquisitely carved capitals from the 11C church at the Pyrenean village of Tavèrnoles and from the church of Sant Pere de les Puelles in Barcelona itself (see p. 82). But the Romanesque holdings are remarkable above all for the frescoes, which have always been displayed in rooms emulating the shapes of the churches from which they were taken. Of these frescoes, there are three cycles that are especially remarkable, one being from one of the side apses of the Mozarabic parish church at **Sant Quirze de Pedret**: dating back to the late 11C or early 12C, this cycle features the Virgin and Child in the cupola, underneath which are animated scenes representing the Wise and Foolish Virgins. The most extensive and among the best preserved of the frescoes are those from the apse and walls of **Santa Maria de Taüll**, a church which was consecrated in 1123. The figure of the Virgin presides over the apse, while the side walls include scenes of the Three Kings, the Nativity and a remarkably realistic and gruesome portrayal of Hell; on the wall facing the apse there feature David and Goliath, the Last Judgement and two peacocks (symbolising immortality) drinking from the fountain of Paradise. Most memorable of all are the apse frescoes from the 12C church of **Sant Climent de Taüll**, which are dominated by a Christ in Majesty of mesmerising power: the expressiveness in the use of line, and the bold foreshortening and simplification of forms, reveal an artist of great individuality, and one who appears to have had a significant influence on the early development of both Picasso and Joan Miró.

Next in importance after the Romanesque holdings come the museum's extensive collection of Catalan Gothic art, which will probably continue to be shown in the rooms to the left of the main entrance. The earliest works in this section, dating back to the end of the 13C, show clearly the influence of French art, and include various sarcophagi and painted panels, a polychromed relief of the Calvary, and the recumbent tomb statue (from the Barcelona convent of San Francisco) of Sibilla de Fortià, the fourth wife of Pere the Ceremonious. Italian influence, in particular from Florence and Siena, reached Catalonia by way of the papal court at Avignon, and was very apparent in the leading Catalan artist of the early 14C, Ferrer Bassa. The main Italianate artists working in Catalonia in the second half of the 14C were Jaume, Joan and Pere Serra, who are represented here most notably by Pere Serra's Virgin of Tortosa. The decorative style of c 1400 known as the International Gothic—a mingling of Italian, French and Flemish influences—had as its chief Catalan exponents Lluís Borrassà (the semicircular Retable of Guardiola of 1404) and Bernat Martorell (the Retable of St. Vincent), the latter being an artist who was known until recently as the Master of St. George from a famous work in the Art Museum of Chicago.

Flemish influence, in painting, sculpture, music and architecture, came to predominate throughout Spain from c 1440 onwards. One of the earliest Catalan associates of the so-called Hispano-Flemish School, and the one most faithful to Flemish models, was Lluís Dalmau, who appears to have met Jan van Eyck when the latter was accompanying a diplomatic mission to Spain and Portugal in 1427–28. The direct influence of Van Eyck is at any rate apparent in Dalmau's masterpiece, the Virgin of the Councillors, which was painted in 1445 for the chapel of Barcelona's Town Hall, and portrays the Virgin and Child flanked by the city councillors, and SS. Eulàlia and Andrew; the figures are depicted with extreme naturalism within a minutely detailed Gothic interior. The Catalan contemporaries of Dalmau were generally more conservative artists than he was, as is exemplified in their continuing use of gold backgrounds right up to the end of the 15C. The most prolific and important of these artists was Jaume Huguet, whose work combines naturalistic detail, with decoratively embossed gold backgrounds, and a late medieval love of chivalry: his major work in the museum is the central panel of the Triptych of St. George, the wings of which are in Berlin. The museum's culminating works of Flemish-inspired realism are by two late 15C artists who settled in Catalonia. One is the gruesome Beheading of St. Cugat by the northern-born Anye Bru, a work of coarsely expressive brutality recalling German paintings of this period. The other is the Descent into Limbo by the remarkably original Cordoban-born artist Bartolomé Bermejo, whose Pietà in Barcelona Cathedral (see p. 60) has much of the pathos and grandeur characteristic of the art of Van der Weyden. The Descent into Limbo shows the naked and realistically observed figure of Christ struggling against a chiaroscuro background of agitated bodies.

Catalan art entered a sharp decline from c 1500 onwards, and the museum's relatively scant holdings of Catalan artists from the Renaissance up to the neo-classical period contains little of interest, the most important works being a series of 20 large canvases of the Life of St. Francis (from the destroyed Barcelona Monastery of San Francisco) by the leading Catalan painter of the Baroque period, Antoni Viladomat (1698–1755). The 16–18C paintings by non-Catalan artists are mainly minor or school works and include canvases by El Greco, Ribera, Zurburan, Carreño and Vicente López, and drawings by Raphael, Guido Reni and Van Dyck. The new Museu d'Art de Catalunya will also feature the early 19C Catalan works that have hitherto been displayed in the Museu d'Art Modern in the Ciutadella (see p. 117); among these works are paintings by the so-called Catalan Nazarenes, a Rome-based group active in the mid-1830s who—taking their lead from the German Nazarenes—attempted to emulate the simple forms, colouring and draughtsmanship of religious art before Raphael. The large collections of ceramics which were previously on show in the Palau Nacional have now been moved definitively to the Palau Reial at Pedralbes (see p. 142).

A steeply ascending path, flanked by recently installed escalators, lead from behind the Palau Nacional up to the main sports area of the Olympic Games (the so-called *Anella Olímpica or Olympic Ring), an area linked to the Avinguda del Marquès de Comillas by the AVINGUDA DE L'ESTADI. The exciting new architecture to be seen here includes the building of the

The original 1928 façade of the Olympic Stadium

*INEFC (National Institute of Physical Education of Catalonia), which you will find by turning right once you reach the Avinguda de l'Estadi from the Palau Nacional. This chillingly austere example of Post-Modernism—which will serve as the press centre during the Olympic Games, as well as hosting a variety of sports events—was built in 1984–90 by Ricardo Bofill and his studio. The first major building commissioned in Barcelona from this internationally-renowned native-born architect (who established his reputation largely in and around Paris), the INEFC features a pedimented frontispiece set in between two vast blocks inspired by classical courtyards, the whole articulated by Doric arcading, and built out of ochre-coloured pre-cast concrete, aluminium and tinted glass; though the materials are modern, the building recalls the totalitarian architecture of Hitler, Mussolini and Franco, similarities that are reinforced by the singular officiousness of the security guards who work here. As you head north from here along the Avinguda de l'Estadi, you will pass the Complex Esportiu Bernat Picornell (sports complex) before reaching the enormous square overlooked by the two main stadiums of the Olympic Games. The smaller of the two is the **Sant Jordi Sports Pavilion**, a most elegant covered structure built in 1984–90 by the Japanese architect Arata Isozaki. This stadium can also be adapted for concerts and other such activities; the opera singer Luciano Pavarotti gave a recital here eight days after the inauguration of the building in September 1990, and the Rolling Stones performed here in June 1991, attracting an audience of 78,000, which was apparently a record for an indoor rock concert. The **Olympic Stadium**, which rises above the Sant Jordi Pavilion, is a remodelling of 1986–89 of a magnificent eclectic structure built by Pere Domènech i Roura for the sports events of the International Exhibition of 1929; a triumphant equestrian bronze by Pau Gargallo has recently been returned here after having been kept for many years in the Palau de la Virreina.

The Anella Olímpica occupies high and exposed ground commanding extensive views to the south and west of a great gaunt expanse featuring a scorched semi-wasteland, distant housing developments and the city's main cemetery. Descending the hill and heading in a westerly direction along the Carretera dels Mondials you would come eventually (after a good 20-minute walk) to the commemorative park known as the *Fossar de la Pedrera: designed in 1983 by Beth Galí i Camprubí, and containing a pond and monumental geometric forms, it was intended as a memorial to the executed first president of the Catalan Republic, Lluís Companys. Remaining instead in the Park of Montjuïc, you should continue walking east along the Avinguda de l'Estadi until you reach—just beyond the turning to your left which descends towards the Museu Etnologic (see below)—the white and cheerful open-plan building containing the **Fundació Miró**.

The Miró Foundation was built in 1972–74 to house a large group of works donated by Joan Miró to his native city; in addition the Foundation was intended as a centre for the study and promotion of modern art, complete with a library, exhibition spaces, auditoria, a bookshop and other such facilities. The building was one of only two buildings executed in Barcelona after the Civil War by the outstanding locally-born architect Josep Maria Sert, a close friend of Miró's who had previously designed the artist's studio in Majorca. Sert was an architect who believed passionately in the integration of a building with the landscape, and in the close collaboration between architects, sculptors and painters. These principles were the hallmark of his remarkable Maeght Foundation in St. Paul-de-Vence, which provided the model for the Miró Foundation, and for which Miró had created numerous sculptures, mosaics and other works.

The Miró Foundation is beautifully set within the luxuriant shrubbery of the Montjuïc Park, and centred around a patio commanding magnificent views over Barcelona. Sculptures by Miró adorn the terraces, and the building and its grounds also incorporate works by other artists, most notably garden sculptures by Calder and Chillida. As with the Maeght Foundation, lighting for the rooms is supplied by overhead windows cut out of cylindrical forms attached to the roof; a comparable lighting system had been used by Le Corbusier, who in turn had derived the idea from industrial architecture. The architecture and setting of the Miró Foundation are in many ways much more exciting than the works it exhibits, which date mainly from the latter years of the artist's life, and include numerous paintings and tapestries in the brash decorative style which the artist employed for his designs both for the Caixa de Catalunya and the Spanish National Tourist Office; the sculptures of these years are at least less repetitive and more entertaining, revealing as they do the artist's inventiveness and delightful sense of humour. The photographs on the ground floor of representative paintings from all periods of the artist's life highlight the limitations of the Foundation's holdings, limitations only partially compensated for by the later donation of the Pilar Juncosa Collection, which includes some of the powerful and disturbing Surrealist works of the 1930s and 1940s. Miró's graphic work is the aspect of his art best represented by the Foundation, and features no less than 5000 drawings from his student years onwards, and a complete set of his prints (among which are a series of impressive black and white lithographs of 1939–45 commenting on the Spanish Civil War). In addition the museum has a collection of works in hommage to Miró donated by friends and admirers such as Léger, Motherwell, Ernst, Saura, Sam Francis, Rauschenberg, Moore, Duchamp, Millares, Penrose and Balthus; of particular interest is a fountain by Calder which was built by the artist for the Spanish Republican Government's Pavilion at the Paris Universal Exhibition of 1936 (the same pavilion for which Picasso had painted his Guernica). Finally, for those who do not want to pay to see the Foundation's collections, you can always come here simply to browse in the building's excellent bookshop of modern art, or else to sit in the cheerful and tasteful café, which has tables placed within the luxuriant central courtyard.

Continuing east from the Foundation along the AVINGUDA DE MIRAMAR (the eastern continuation of the Avinguda de l'Estadi), you will come shortly to the funicular station, from where you can take a funicular either down to the Plaça Raquel Meller (see p. 95), or else up to the castle which stands at the very top of the steep Montjuïc hill (the latter service, which has been closed for many years for repairs, is expected to re-open in 1992). An alternative ascent to the castle is by chair-lift from a station which adjoins that of the funicular; the chair-lift makes the ascent in two stages and, half-way up, you can get out to visit Montjuïc's vertiginously placed Parc d'Attraccions (fun fair). The castle or *Castell de Montjuïc is situated on what was probably a Jewish burial-ground, as the name Montjuïc is derived from the words 'Mont jeu' or Jewish Mountain. Presumably there must have been some watch-tower here in ancient times, but the first documented fortification on the hill was built as late as 1640, at the time of the War of the Harvesters. The original structure, enlarged during the war with France, was completely rebuilt by Juan M. Cermeño between 1751 and 1759, and given its present star-shaped pentagonal plan based on French neo-classical models. During the Civil War the castle served as a military prison, and it was here, on 15 October 1940, that the Catalan President Lluís Companys was executed. The army abandoned the building in 1960, since when it has served as the *Museu del Exercit, a military museum of exceptional tedium worth visiting principally for the spectacular views.

Back at the funicular station on the Avinguda de Miramar you could continue walking east until the PLAÇA DE CARLES IBÊÑEZ, immediately beyond which is the cable-car service leading over the port and down to Barceloneta (see p. 111). Alternatively you could retrace your steps back to the Miró Foundation and keep walking west until you reach the PASSEIG DE SANTA MADRONA, which winds its way around some of the more attractive stretches of the Montjuïc parkland, where you will find to your right shaded alleys, fountains, cascades, terraces, an amphitheatre inspired by that of Epidaurus and an abundance of pines, cedars, eucalypti, palms, citrus trees and other luxuriant and exotic vegetation (from the Miró Foundation there are paths leading directly down the hill almost all the way to the Museu Arqueològic). Half-way down the Passeig de Santa Madrona is the *Museu Etnològic, which is housed in an uninspiring modern building of 1973, the walls of which are decorated with reliefs by Eudald Serra i Guëll of anthropological scenes. The well if unimaginatively displayed collections include especially large and interesting groups of objects from Latin America and Morocco. The **Museu Arqueològic**, at the bottom of the Passeig de Santa Madrona, occupies an arcaded pavilion built by Pelagi Martínez in 1927–29 to house the section of the International Exhibition devoted to the Graphic Arts. As with the former Palau de Agricultura, on the other side of the street, the building was inspired by the architecture of the Italian Renaissance, a source of inspiration particularly appropriate to the outstanding collections of ancient art on display here. The museum, wonderfully modernised in 1986–89 by Josep Llinàs, is centred around a white hexagonal-shaped hall, and includes an excellent group of Roman mosaics, numerous finds from the Greek settlement of Emporion (the Catalan town of Empúries), and a superb room devoted to Carthaginian finds from Ibiza, among which is the celebrated *Dama de Ibiza, a bust richly studded with jewellery. The former Palau de l'Agricultura, at the junction of the Passeig de Santa Madrona with the CARRER DE LLEIDA, was built by Manuel M. Mayol i Ferrer in 1927–29; in 1984–85, it was converted into the theatre known as the *Mercat dels Flors, a venue for such experimental groups as the Furia dels Baus. From here you can continue walking down the Carrer de Lleida until you reach the Avinguda del Paral-lel, at a point just to the east of the Plaça d'Espanya.

2   THE EIXAMPLE

By the early 19C Barcelona was almost literally suffocating within its medieval enclosure and various attempts were made to take this down so as to allow the city to expand freely towards the mountains. Finally, in 1846, the municipal government put forward a draft plan for demolishing the walls and creating what was to be known as the 'Enlargement' or Eixample (Ensanche in Spanish). The Spanish Government hesitated for many years over whether to give permission for such a plan, and it was not until the late 1850s that a municipal competition was held to decide on the architect who would draw up the final project. The competition was won by Antoni Rovira, who produced a radial plan which not only had a visionary grandeur but also drew together the old and new towns of Barcelona in a way which the plan eventually realised would never do. Unfortunately, the choice of the municipality was rejected by the Spanish Ministry of Works, who approved instead a strictly rectangular grid-plan devized by Ildefons Cerdà; the rejection of the Rovira plan by the Madrid authorities is frequently taken as yet another example of the way in which Catalan individuality has been squashed by Spanish centralism. Cerdà's plan, which was comparable to the contemporary plan for the expansion of Madrid, featured regular blocks of 114 square metres, and streets that were 20 metres wide, the whole criss-crossed by vast avenues and scattered with gardens. In the end the gardens were never built, the spaces that had been reserved for them falling victim to the ruthless property specualtion which ensued imediately after work on the Eixample had begun in 1860. An exciting and cruelly satirical account of the planning and creation of the Eixample is to be found in Eduardo Mendoza's novel, *The City of Marvels* (English translation, 1989).

Many of Barcelona's inhabitants feel that the spacious and elegant Eixample constitutes the city's main attraction, and this feeling is likely to be shared by anyone with a passionate interest in Gaudí and Moderniste architecture. For the general sightseer, however, the Eixample can be a daunting prospect owing to the sheer monotony of the layout and the great distances separating its innumerable monuments of interest. Most tourists tend to limit their visit to the Eixample to a walk along the Passeig de Gràcia, and a journey by bus, metro or taxi to the outlying Sagrada Família. Any fuller tour of the district, such as the one outlined below, requires considerable energy and dedication, particularly if undertaken entirely on foot.

However much time you decide to devote to the Eixample, your starting-point is likely to be the vast **PLAÇA DE CATALUNYA**, which has its origins in a field lying between the northern entrance to La Rambla (see p. 42) and the future Passeig de Gràcia. Rovira planned a monumental esplanade for here—800 metres long and 200 metres wide—to which he gave the impressive name of 'Forum de Isabel II'; this space would have been at the very centre of his radial plan of Barcelona and provided a suitably grand approach to the medieval cathedral. Cerdà had more modest plans for this space, and simply intended to extend the Rambla northwards and link it to a square attached to the southern end of his projected Passeig de Gràcia. General resistance to the Cerdà plan, combined with lingering nostalgia for the rejected project of Rovira, led eventually to a compromise solution being adopted, the execution of which was delayed for many years and necessitated the demolition of various structures that had been put up here in the interim by private developers. The definitive project, based on designs put forward by Puig i Cadalfach between 1915 and 1922, was drawn up in 1925 by Fransesc de P. Nebot, Pere Domènech, Antoni Darder, Fèlix d'Azua and Enric Català. The square, which was inaugurated on 2 November 1927, is surrounded by pompous and uninspiring buildings, and is centred around a circular garden with fountains, rings of trees, statuary and an overall desultory character. Among the sculptures are Pau Gargallo's Shepherd with a Flute (on the square's northern side) and, on the south-western corner, a kneeling female nude by Josep Clara entitled Goddess, the original of which is now in the courtyard of the Town Hall (see p. 69). None of the buildings that surround the square—most of which are the headquarters of banks—are of especial architectural interest, though readers of Orwell's *Homage to Catalonia* should cast a glance at the *Banco Español de Credito on the square's northern side: formerly the Hotel Colon, it served during the Civil War as the headquarters of the socialist group known as PSUC, and its façade—as Orwell describes—was covered with portraits of Marx, Lenin and Stalin. An uninspired 1960s block on the square's eastern side houses the department store, *El Corte Inglés, where a popular roof-top cafeteria provides a good vantage-point to observe the hectic life of the Plaça de Catalunya, a vista best appreciated at night-time. Underneath the square you will find train and metro stations, as well as a labyrinthine complex of passages and shopping arcades.

Running north from the corner of the Plaça de Catalunya is the RAMBLA DE CATALUNYA, which, beyond the Gran Via de les Corts Catalanes, has a pedestrian central alley lined with rows of lime trees; markets are occasionally held here, most notably a poultry market at Christmas-time and a market selling palm branches three days before Palm Sunday. Parallel to the east, and beginning at the north-eastern corner of the Plaça de Catalunya, is the city's most elegant thoroughfare, the famous **PASSEIG DE GRÀCIA**.

The Passeig de Gràcia has its origins in the road leading from Barcelona to the former village of Gràcia (see Rte 3B). In 1827 it was converted into a wide tree-lined promenade, which was illuminated by gas lamps after 1853, and provided with horse-drawn trams after 1871. With the development of the Eixample, the Passeig de Gràcia replaced La Rambla as the fashionable promenade for the city's aristocracy and upper-middle classes. It became also the central artery of the luxury district of the Eixample which came to be known as the *Quadrat d'Or or 'Golden Quadrangle', a district formed by the hundred or so blocks contained within the area bordered respectively to the west and east by the Carrer de Aribau and the Passeig de Sant Joan, and to the north and south by the Avinguda Diagonal and the 'Rondes'. The earliest buildings here were two- or three-storey one-family dwellings with gardens, but from the 1890s onwards these came to be replaced by apartment blocks for the wealthy middle classes, the whole area becoming eventually transformed into a densely populated residential and commercial district. From about 1925 the ground floors of many of the buildings along the Passeig de Gràcia were let out to retailers, and the street soon emerged as the foremost shopping thoroughfare of the city, with numerous international fashion houses being represented here; the upper floors of most of the former residential buildings along this street have now been taken over by offices.

The Quadrat d'Or has the reputation of having the largest concentration of Art Nouveau buildings in the world, among which are several of the most famous masterpieces of this style. A comprehensive listing of all these buildings is beyond the scope of a guide book, but the tourist with a specialist interest in Art Nouveau should acquire the excellent pamphlet on the Quadrat d'Or distributed free by the Tourist Office of Barcelona and containing details of no fewer than 150 buildings of this period.

A tour of this district should begin by walking the whole length of the Passeig de Gràcia, the entrance to which from the Plaça de Catalunya is marked by the neo-Gothic corner tower of the *Casa Pascual i Pons (Nos 2–4), which was built by Enric Sagnier Villavecchia in 1890–91. Next along the street, also on the right-hand side (at Nos 6–14), come the group of buildings known as the *Cases Rocamora, an imposing and elaborate Moderniste ensemble of 1914–20, designed by Joaquim and Bonaventura Bassegoda Amigó and featuring elements derived from French Gothic architecture. Further up, at No. 11 (at the corner with the Gran Via de les Corts Catalanes), rises Lluós Bonet's *Banc Vitalici d'Espanya of 1942–50, an American-style skyscraper with conventionally classical decorative detailing. The building typifies the reaction which had set in after the Civil War to the progressive Modernism of the 1930s, an excellent example of which can be seen on the other side of the Passeig de Gràcia, at No. 18. This, the jewellery shop known as the *Joieria Roca*, is a Functionalist work of 1934 by Josep Lluís Sert. The flat continuous façade in glass and finely polished stone, smoothly rounded at the corner with the Gran Via, has been excellently preserved even down to its Art Deco lettering, but the interior was much altered after the shop was extended in 1964 by Marcelo Leonori.

Continuing up the Passeig de Gràcia you will pass to your left (at No. 21) the pompous French-style corner building designed by Eusebi Bona i Puig in 1927 as the headquarters of the insurance company of La Unión y el Fénix Español; the building is closely similar to this company's former headquarters in Madrid, which forms one of the most prominent landmarks of the Gran Via. One block further up you come to the junction of the CARRER DE CONSELL DE CENT, where, on turning right, you will come to the earliest buildings to have been constructed in the Eixample. These buildings of neo-classical simplicity are diagonally placed at the corners of the intersection of the street with the Carrer de Roger de Llúria; built by Antoni Valls i Galí in 1862–64, they were put up on a site owned by the designer of the Eixample, Josep Cerdà. Another survival from the early days of the Eixample is the *PASSATGE PERMANYER, a passage dividing in two one of the blocks lying immediately to the south of the Cerdà buildings (the alley can be entered either from the Carrer Roger de Llúria or the parallel Carrer de Pau Claris). This and the handful of other remaining *Passatges* in the Eixample mark the spaces that Cerdà had originally intended as gardens, but that soon came to be covered with terraces of one-family houses. The Passatge Permanyer is flanked by two particularly harmonious rows of terraces, built by Jeroni Granell i Barrera in 1864 in what was described at the time as '*a l'Anglesa*' (in an English style), each of the two-storey houses having its own front garden with railings. It is worth continuing two blocks further east down the Carrer del Consell de Cent to see at No. 372 (at the corner with the Carrer de Girona) the charming Moderniste baker's and pastry shop known as the *Horno Sarret*, which dates back to 1906 and features particularly splendid façades created out of expressively undulating wooden forms.

Returning to the Passeig de Gràcia and continuing north, you will pass immediately to your left a block comprising the most famous ensemble of Moderniste buildings in Barcelona. The block is known by the punning name of **MANZANA DE LA DISCORDIA**, '*manzana*' being the Spanish name for both 'block' and 'apple'; the '*discordia*' (discord) is a reference to the disparate and clashing Moderniste styles represented by this group of buildings. The first of the buildings, at No. 35 (at the corner with the Carrer de Consell de Cent), is the **Casa Lleó Morera**, which dates back to a house of 1864, one of the earliest to have been erected on the Passeig de Gràcia. Completely remodelled between 1902 and 1906 by Domènech i Montaner, the present building is generally regarded as one of the latter's greatest residential works, and certainly an example of Modernisme at its most florid, with a profusion of floral decorative motifs and an overall *horror vacui*. The building remained in the possession of the Lleó Morera family until 1943, when its upper floors were sold off as offices, and its ground floor acquired as a shop for the luxury retailers Loewe; in the creation of this tastelessly decorated shop, the ground floor of the building was entirely mutilated, thus depriving the façade of one of its richest layers of ornamentation. The main floor of the building is now in the safe hands of the Barcelona Patronat de Turisme, which has brought to completion a restoration campaign initiated in 1988 by the Mutualidad General de la Abogacía. Though the rooms of this main floor are used as the offices of the Patronat de Turisme, they can usually be visited during office hours by asking the secretary in the entrance lobby. Every attempt should be made to visit these rooms, for they constitute a magnificent decorative ensemble which entailed the collaboration of the sculptors Eusebi Arnau and Joan Carreras, the painter Josep Pey, the mosaic artists Mario Maragliano and Lluís Bru Salelles, the stained-glass specialists Joan Rigalt and Jeroni Granell and the ceramicist Antoni Serra Fiter. Particularly colourful is the former dining-room (now used as a boardroom), which has a rounded bay window covered entirely with a stained-glass decoration of birds and flowers. Within the same room are delightful genre scenes featuring members of the Lleó Morera family dressed in contemporary costume, and engaged in such activities as picnicking; these scenes, designed by Josep Pey, are executed in mosaic with the faces highlighted in ceramic relief. The furniture created by Gaspar Homar for this room can now be seen in the Museu d'Art Modern (see p. 104).

Adjoining the Casa Lleó Morera, at 37 Passeig de Gràcia, is the *Casa Mulleras, a relatively austere structure built in 1906 by Enric Sagnier Villavecchia and decorated with a combination of classical and discreetly rococo elements. Yet more severe and conventional is the next building, the *Casa Bonet, which dates back to 1871 but was remodelled in 1915. With the **Casa Amatller** (No. 41), the Manzana de la Discordia once more regains its architectural distinction. A remodelling of an earlier structure, this was carried out by Puig i Cadafalch in 1898–1900 for the chocolate manufacturer Antoni Amatller; it was the first of the buildings constituting the Manzana de la Discordia to be completed. The eclectic façade, so characteristic of this architect who was also a historian, archaeologist and politician, brings together elements from secular and religious buildings, as well as from the Catalan Gothic and Northern architecture, the latter influence being particularly apparent in the enormous stepped gable, which seems derived from some fantastical vision of Holland. The building has been dubbed by the architectural historian Cirici Pellicer as the 'apotheosis of the Decorative Arts', and the façade is certainly remarkable for its decorative richness, with star-like ceramic plaques studding the gable, geometrical sgraffito decoration above the upper gallery, elaborate wrought-iron balconies, stained glass, ceramic tiles by Manuel Ballarín and intricate and deeply modelled statuary by Eusebi Arnau and Alfons Juyol. The interior, which houses the Institut Amatller d'Art Hispànic (an institution founded in 1942 by Antoni Amatller's daughter Teresa), features further statuary by Arnau and a heavy, Nordic-style hall by Gaspar Homar.

The neighbouring **Casa Batlló**, at 43 Passeig de Gràcia, completes the Manzana de la Discordia, and brings the row to a suitably fantastical climax. As with the other structures on the block, this was a remodelling and extension of a previous structure, the architect's brief being in this case to add two floors, produce new front and back façades, and create an entirely new main floor. The architect was Antoní Gaudí, who carried out the work between 1904 and 1906. The front façade, exemplifying Gaudí's love of melting amorphous forms, is encrusted all over with blue ceramic decorations—resembling strange subaqueous forms—by his usual collaborator Josep Maria Jujol. Its most striking feature is its undulating, ceramic-tiled roof, the design of which took into account the steep gable of the adjoining Casa Amatller, while revealing to the full the greater dynamism of Gaudí's architecture in relation to that of Puig i Cadafalch. The actual shape of the roof was almost certainly intended to suggest the figures of St. George and the Dragon, the saint being represented by the turret crowned by a cross, and the dragon wittily evoked through ceramic tiles and ribs that appear respectively to be the animal's scales and bones. The back façade, which can be seen from an alley leading off the adjacent CARRER D'ARAGÓ, much more sober, though has a colourful upper level resplendent with ceramic floral decorations. The interior decoration of the main floor rooms has been excellently preserved, but these rooms can only be visited from 08.00–10.00 having made previous arrangements with the Cátedra Gaudí (which is open from 08.00–14.00; tel: 2045250). At any rate you can always freely walk into the small entrance lobby to admire the curious staircase well, which was designed to create an illusion of deep recession, an effect achieved through tapering walls, and blue ceramics that become increasinly pale in hue the nearer they reach the skylight.

From the Casa Batlló you should turn left on to the Carrer d'Aragó to visit, at No. 255, the former **Editorial Montaner i Simon**, which was designed by Domènech i Montaner in 1879 as the commercial premises of his brother, a partner in the publishing company, Montaner i Simon. Regarded as a key work in the early history of Modernisme, the building expressed Domènech's belief in a rational architecture involving the latest technologies, and was the first building in Barcelona other than a market or railway station to take the form of an ironwork structure clad in brick. The element of fantasy, so necessary as well to Modernisme, was provided by the actual brickwork, which was inspired by the techniques of the Mudéjars. In 1987, under the architectural direction of Roser Amadó and the appropriately named Lluís Domènech, work was begun on the transformation of the building as the seat of the *Tàpies Foundation, which was opened in 1990, and is now one of the more popular of the city's recent attractions. Antoni Tàpies himself boldly embellished the façade with a crowning sculpture entitled Chair and Cloud, an expressively untidy aluminium mesh resembling a large piece of steel wool which has been torn at by a madman. The interior, with its original ironwork columns and beams, has been strikingly modernised, the upper part being used as a specialist library of modern art, and the rest functioning as an art gallery hosting selections of the foundation's large bequest of Tàpies' paintings, sculptures and graphic work (the latter being always exhibited in the darkened basement). The main works owned by the foundation, however, as with those by Miró in the latter's foundation on Montjuïc (see p. 121), date from the artist's more recent years, and do not represent perhaps the best of his art.

Back on the Passeig de Gràcia and continuing north you will reach after two more blocks the CARRER DE MALLORCA, where you should turn right. At No. 278 of this street (at the corner with the Carrer de Roger de Llúria), you will find the **Casa Montaner**, another building associated with the Montaner family of the Editorial Montaner i Simon. This family home was begun in 1885 by Josep Domènech i Estapà, who had previously built a nearby (and no longer extant) palace for the Montaners' partners, the Simons. For reasons that are not known the architect was replaced in 1891 by the owner's cousin, Lluís Domènech i Montaner, who completed the building in 1896. Since 1980 the palace has housed the Delegaciè del Govern a Catalunya, and can be visited on Saturday mornings 10.00–13.00. The first two floors of the exterior are by Josep Domènech and in their sober eclecticism differ markedly from the crowning floor added by Lluís Domènech, a work of great ornamental richness featuring mosaic decorations designed by Gaspar Homar. Lluís, aided by two other of his usual collaborators, the sculptor Eusebi Arnau and the stained-glass artist Rigalt, was responsible as well for the magnificent vestibule, with its brilliantly coloured stained-glass skylight and its grand staircase profusely carved with motifs of baroque and plateresque inspiration. The rooms contain several works on loan from the Museu d'Art Modern (see p. 104), including paintings by Brull and Eliseu Meifrèn.

Further east the Carre de Mallorca, on the opposite side of the street, is yet another work by Lluís Domènech i Montaner, the *Casa Thomas (Nos 291–93), which was built in 1895–98 as a two-storeyed building to be used both as a home and workshop for the Thomas engravers, further relatives of Domènech; in 1912 it was given an additional three floors by Domènech's son-in-law, Francesc Guàrdia Vial, who respected the intricately ornamental nature of the original façade, and probably worked in collaboration with his father-in-law. The entrance at No. 293, which leads today to a lawyer's office (occupying the upper part of the building), will take you into a beautiful small vestibule decorated with ceramic tiles, stained-glass windows and elaborate carvings. The ground floor and basement (entered through the door at No. 29) comprise what was originally the Thomas's workshop and were sensitively transformed in 1979 as the show-room of the leading Barcelona design firm B.D. Ediciones de Diseño. B.D. was founded in 1972 by Oscar Tusquets, Lluís Clotet, Pep Bonet and Cristià Cirici, all of whom had studied architecture together at the Escuela Técnica y Superior de Arquitectura de Barcelona; on graduating from this institution in 1965 they had set up the architectural firm of Studio Per. The design critic Alexandre Circi, in an article on Studio Per written in 1969, identified this group with the youth generation of the 1960s who 'are incorporating themselves into active life at the moment of the consumer boom, of the sexual revolution and the youth movements of Paris, Amsterdam and Berkeley.'

Returning to the Passeig de Gràcia, the next major building which you will see as you head north is Antoní Gaudí's secular masterpiece, the **CASA MILÀ** (at No. 92), the massive curved façade of which spreads around into the adjacent Carrer de Provença. Built in 1905–10, when Gaudí was at the height of his fame and at work both on the Sagrada Família (see below) and the Park Güell (see p. 149), the Casa Milà was a residential and commercial block commissioned by the local businessman Pere Milà i Camps. The building, with its sinuous façade centred around the corner of two streets, breaks away from the rigid geometry of Cerdà's Eixample, and can almost be regarded as a work of sculpture; revealingly, shortly after work on the building had begun, Gaudí adapted his original plans as a result of a scale plaster model commissioned from Beltran. The stone façade, which appears to have been modelled rather than designed, has been frequently likened to an abandoned quarry-face, thus giving rise to the building's nickname of *'La Pedrera'* or 'Quarry'; the rippling and smoothly eroded forms are also reminiscent of waves, an image reinforced by the extraordinary ironwork balconies by Josep Maria Juyol, which give the impression that the building has been covered in seaweed. The originality of the building is not simply limited to the exterior but also to the complex arrangement of the interior, which is centred around two undulating and irregular courtyards adorned with ceramics and traces of murals. Gaudí was also responsible for the interior decoration of the first-floor rooms where Milà and his family lived, but this was stripped shortly after Milà's death by his wife Roser Segímon i Artell. The building was acquired in 1986 by the Caixa de Catalunya, which embarked on a thorough restoration campaign, which included the cleaning of the façade and the removal of later structural alterations on the upper floor. The Caixa arrange daily guided tours of the building in various languages and at hourly intervals. The restored upper rooms (the parabolic arches of which had been covered by brickwork) will eventually contain photographic exhibits relating to Gaudí's work. The highpoint of the tour, however, is undoubtedly the visit to the fantastical rooftop, with its strange twisted chimneys and ventilation shafts, which are coated with fragments of pottery, marble and glass. The straight and undecorated chimneys were later additions, as were the safety railings: Gaudí was reluctant to install railings, believing that these detracted from the wild mountain-top character of the roofline. To this surrealistic landscape, Gaudí had originally indended to add a sculptural group over 4 metres high representing either the Virgin of La Gràcia (the name of the former township which began at the Carrer de Provença) or the Virgin of Roser (in honour of his patron's wife); however, Milà, in view of the anarchist disturbances of the time, thought it unwise to crown the building with such a prominent Catholic symbol, and Gaudí had to content himself with the cross-like shape of the central chimney. From the roof an excellent view can be had of the Sagrada Família, and at one time you could also see both the Casa Battló and the Park Güell, but these have now been hidden by recent development.

Almost adjoining the Casa Milà, at 96 Passeig de Gràcia is the palatial *Casa Casas, which was built by Antoni Rovira i Rabassa in 1898–99 as the residence of the painter Ramon Casas; for many years Casas' friend and colleague Salvador Rusiñol had an apartment on the third floor. Elements of the original interior decoration by Josep Pascó i Mensas have survived, including—on the main floor—a magnificently elaborate fireplace. The building is now occupied by Barcelona's most progressive and influential department store, **Vinçon**.

Founded on the present premises in 1940 by Jacinto Amat, Vinçon was originally a shop specialising in the import and sale of German porcelain. In the 1960s, under the direction of Jacinto's son Fernando (born 1941), the shop expanded into gifts and office and shop equipment, soon achieving a reputation as Spain's leading showcase of modern furniture. Fernando Amat was influenced to a certain extent by the British store Habitat, but, unlike the latter's founder Terence Conran (whom he met in 1974), he resisted the temptation to develop his shop into a large chain, and was thus able to keep a much closer eye on the quality of the goods and design. By giving priority to objects that he preferred rather than to what the market wanted, Amat's store took on an increasingly avant-garde character, as was exemplified in the activities of its special exhibition hall, the Sala Vinçon. This hall, which continues to function today, has been the setting of performance art, installations, lectures on everyday objects, conceptual art and exhibitions of avant-garde furniture and design, its first major show (in 1973) being of the Post-Modern tables of Bigas Luna. Amat's best known discovery was the designer of the Olympic logo, Javier Mariscal (see p. 151), who has been closely associated both with the store and the Sala Vinçon since his student days in the early 1970s.

Turning left off the Passeig de Gràcia along the CARRER DE PROVENÇA you will reach, at the corner with the Rambla de Catalunya, the charming basement bar known as the *Bodigueta* (100 Rambla de Catalunya). This narrow and intimate bar, which is very popular with those frequenting the many surrounding cinemas, is one of the Eixample's rare survivals from the 1940s, its decoration of marble tables, wooden panelling and packed shelves of bottles having changed little since the time the place opened in 1949; its speciality are its excellent wines, served with *bocatas*, or small sandwiches (the cheese ones are particularly good). Another traditional Eixample establishment is the adjoining *Saló de Te Mauri* (at 102 Rambla de Catalunya), a lavishly decorated confectioner's and tea-room (with a pseudo-baroque ceiling painting and an elaborately carved wooden counter), frequented by Barcelona's old families and those recuperating from an afternoon's shopping. You can return to the Passeig de Gràcia along the PASSATGE DE LA CONCEPCIÓ, which runs parallel to the Carrer de Provença, and is another of the Eixample's surviving passages lined with one-family housing of the late 19C. At No. 5 is the smart and fashionable restaurant called *El Tragaluz* (opened in 1990), which has an interior decoration by Sandra Taruella and Pepe Cortés, and graphic designs by Mariscal; there is a reasonably priced downstairs restaurant, but the most exciting interior feature of the place is the expensive upstairs restaurant, which is situated in what appears to be a large conservatory. The owners of the restaurant had made their name with the nearby *Mordisco* restaurant (at 265 Carrer del Rosselló, the street parallel to the north), a small and self-consciously informal establishment also designed by Sandra Taruella, and popularised by the famous, including artists such as Mariscal and the painter Miquel Barceló. Also on the CARRER DEL ROSSELLÓ (at No. 208) is the first of Barcelona's designer bars to achieve a truly popular success, *Nick Havanna*, the name of which is derived from a fictious cowboy hero of the West. The competition to design this place was won in 1985 by Eduard Samsó, who created within the bar a great variety of spaces, each of which was intended to appeal to a particular clientele; thus you can wander from a standing area overlooked by a wall of videos to a sumptous seating area with armchairs designed by the fashionable French artist Philippe Starck. A giant pendulum provides another of the many distractions, but the real surprises are to be found in the toilets, which were among the first in Barcelona to be designed with a view to being an important space in their own right: in these particular ones the basins are treated almost as shrines, and the urinals as a cascading, mirrored waterfall.

One block to the north of the Carrer del Rosselló, the Passeig de Gràcia crosses the wide AVINGUDA DIAGONAL before coming to an end in a small stretch enclosing a verdant garden. One of the buildings at this northern extremity of the street is Lluís Domènech i Montaner's *Casa Fuster (at No. 132), a structure of 1908–10 featuring one of this architect's charateristically varied and richly ornamented façades, in this case mingling classical elements with others inspired by both the Venetian and Catalan Gothic.

After returning to the junction of the Passeig de Gràcia with the Avinguda

Diagonal, you should turn left, heading down the latter avenue in an easterly direction. Almost immediately to your left, at No. 442, is the *Casa Comalat, a fine Moderniste structure built in 1909–11 by Salvador Valeri Pupurull, and featuring an expressively undulating crowning-piece; installed within the ground floor is what is now one of the more sedate of Barcelona's designer bars, *Sí Sí Sí*, which was designed in 1985 by Gabriel Ordeig. On the other side of the street, at No. 373 (at the corner with the Carrer del Roselló), is the **Palau Quadras**, a former residential block which was transformed by Puig i Cadafalch in 1902–04 as a palace for the Baron of Quadras. The main façade is distinguished by a projecting gallery with exquisitely elaborate carvings of Gothic Plateresque derivation, executed by Alfons Juyol to the designs of Eusebi Arnau; the vestibule and main rooms have been well preserved, and include stained-glass windows, ceramic decorations and an intricately carved fireplace. The whole interior makes a delightful and intimate setting for the tastefully displayed *Museu de la Música, which has been housed here since 1980, and features a large collection of old instruments, as well as numerous personal mementoes of Pau Casals, Albeniz and Granados. As you continue down the Avinguda Diagonal, you will see rising up on the left-hand side of the street (at No. 416–20) Puig Cadafalch's best known building, the *Casa Terrades of 1903–05; this large residential block, resembling a fantastical Gothic fortress, is generally known as the Casa de les Punxes from the 'witch's hat' spires which crown its turrets. Two blocks further on you will cross the CARRER DE BAILÈN, where on turning right you will come, at No. 113, to a white residential block situated at the intersection with the CARRER DE VALÈNCIA. Known as the *Casa Llopis Bofill, this was built in 1902 by Antoni M. Gallissà i Soqué, an architect who had worked with Domènech i Montaner, and had been in charge of the crafts workshop which the latter had instigated in the café/restaurant of the World Exhibition (see p. 110). Gallissà's close collaboration with craftsmen such as stuccoists and ceramicists is evident in his few known buildings, of which the most important was the Casa Llopis Bofill, a sensual neo-Moorish structure clearly inspired by the Alhambra in Granada. One block further along the Carrer de València is a former *Salesian Monastery and church, an elaborate neo-Gothic complex built in 1882–85 by Joan Martorell i Montells, who was very much influenced at the time by the ideas of Ruskin and Viollet-le-Duc. The church, now the parish church of Sant Francesc de Sales, has elaborate sculptural decoration in the presbytery by Enric Monserdà.

From the church you can return to the Avinguda Diagonal by walking one block to the north along the broad PASSEIG DE SANT JOAN. On the other side of the Diagonal, the Passeig de Sant Joan is adorned in its centre with bosky gardens, overlooking which, at No. 108, is Puig i Cadafalch's *Casa Macaya of 1901. The white stuccoed façade of this building features detailing of late Gothic inspiration, the intricate carving being the work of Eusebi Arnau; inside is a fine Gothic-inspired courtyard complete with gargoyles and an open staircase, but the rest of the interior has lost its original appearance, and has recently been transformed into a cultural centre run by the Caixa de Pensions. Continuing down the Avinguda Diagonal, the next building of note is the *Casa Planells, at No. 332 (at the junction with the CARRER DE SICÍLIA; built in 1923–24, this curiously undulating structure is the work of Josep Maria Jujol, Gaudí's most faithful collaborator. Turning left here along the Carrer de Sicília, you will find yourself in front of the most important and notorious work of Gaudí himself, the **TEMPLE DE LA SAGRADA FAMÍLIA**.

Contrary to what is often believed, the Sagrada Família was never intended as Barcelona's new cathedral, but was originally planned instead as a church to house a copy of the Holy House of Loreto. The idea for such a building had been formed during a visit made in 1869 to the Italian town of Loreto by Josep M. Bocabella, the founder of a religious society which was devoted to the cult of St. Joseph, and had as one of its main aims the bridging of the ever widening gulf between workers and employers. A suitable site for the church was acquired by the society, and work on the building was begun in 1882, under the direction of Francesc de P. de Villar. Villar planned a structure inspired by a Gothic cathedral, but disagreements with Bocabella led to his dismissal after only a small section of the crypt had been completed. On 3 October 1883, the task of completing the building was entrusted—on the advice of the architect Joan Martorell—to the 31-year-old Antoní Gaudí. Using as his starting-point Villar's original plan, Gaudí evolved a project of ever increasing originality, ambitiousness and scale. While respecting the Gothic cathedral plan of ambulatory, transepts and five aisles, he intended the building to be 60 metres wide at the crossing and to have a central nave which would be 95 metres long; the massive transept façades were to have four towers of an average height of 100 metres, while four more towers would surround a crossing tower no less than 170 metres high. The originality of Gaudí's projected church lay not simply in its remarkable size and the bizarreness of the forms, but in such novel features as an exterior ambulatory which was to have surrounded the whole building and to which Gaudí gave the misleading name of *claustre*. Gaudí was to be involved in the construction of the building for the rest of his life, refusing to take on any other architectural commissions after the death in 1914 of his close friend and collaborator, Francesc Berenguer i Mestres. Those who worked on the building were paid the most meagre of wages, including Gaudí himself, who in the end was able to renounce all payment thanks to the money that he had made on other works. Suffering from poor health from 1910 onwards, Gaudí spent his last years living unwashed and unkempt in a worker's shack on the site.

At the time of Gaudí's death in 1926, all that had been completed of the building was the crypt, the apse and part of the transept façade of the Nativity; the latter façade was still missing three of its four projected towers, but these were erected soon afterwards by Domènech Sugrañes. George Orwell, describing the church during the Civil War, at a time when both Gaudí and Modernisme in general had reached the nadir of their popularity, greatly regretted that the main body of the building had escaped the attentions of the anarchists, thinking it 'one of the most hideous buildings in the world... [with] four crenellated spires exactly the shape of hock bottles'. Work on the building was renewed in 1952 and has been continuing since then (most recently under the direction of Jordi Bonet). Using modern production methods, it might be possible to complete the building by 2020, though there are many people who believe that the place should have been left as a monumental shell commemorating Gaudí's visionary but wayward genius. The absence of any detailed plans indicating exactly what Gaudí had intended, combined with Gaudí's tendency constantly to alter his ideas at construction stage, certainly provide insuperable obstacles for those attempting to complete the building in as faithful a way as possible. Funds for the completion of the church continue none the less to pour in, and, as with 'Mad Ludwig' of Bavaria's Neuschwanstein, the enormous investment which has been put into the building will almost certainly be recouped hundreds of times over through the place's sheer importance as a tourist attraction.

The architectural magnificence of the Sagrada Família in its present state is due entirely to the dynamic and sculpturally-conceived south transept façade, which overlooks the Plaça de Gaudí. Dedicated to the Nativity of Christ and executed between 1893 and 1904, it features three portals in the shape of Gaudí's adored parabolic arches. The portals, representing (from left to right) Hope, Charity and Faith are encrusted with a struggling mass of naturalistic statuary, some of the figures being made from life casts. The strange oozing forms surrounding the figures give a grotto-like character to the portals, a character which accords well with the tapering crenellated-towers above, the shape of which was inspired by the curiously eroded peaks lying behind the monastery at Montserrat; the expressively twisted tops of these towers are decorated with polychromed mosaics. You can climb by lift to the base of the towers, and from there wind your way up each of the openwork spires, a disorientating experience likely to induce claustrophobia, agoraphobia and vertigo, all at the same time.

Entering the main body of the building through the Nativity transept, you will see to your right the wall of the apse, which was one of the earliest parts of the church to be completed, and also the dullest, being an unremarkable neo-Gothic work. The transept in front of you was built entirely after 1952 and has a façade which acts as a grey, concrete travesty of that of the Nativity transept; its sculptural decoration—representing, as Gaudí had intended, the Passion and Death of Christ—was executed by Josep Maria Subirachs. The building's west façade, which is to be dedicated to the Celestial Glory, is currently being constructed. A small and gloomily old-fashioned museum relating to the history of the building is to be found in the crypt, which was restored by F. Quintana i Vidal in 1939–50, following extensive damage caused during the Civil War; the main interest of a visit here is to pay hommage to Gaudí's tomb.

Just outside the site, at 253 Carrer de Marina (on the north-western corner of the Plaça de Gaudí) is the parish school known as the *Escuelas de la Sagrada Família, a modestly sized and simply decorated structure built by Gaudí in 1909–10; its undulating façade is hidden by a wall from the street.

Directly in front of the Nativity façade begins the recently remodelled *AVINGUDA DE GAUDÍ, an elegant sloping thoroughfare covered in café tables, and decorated near its centre with ironwork street-lamps by Pere Falquès of c 1900. Whereas the Sagrada Família, at the lower end of the street, provides an outstanding vista looking towards the sea, a scarcely less remarkable vista to the north is supplied by the **Hospital de la Santa Creu i de Sant Pau**, the most ambitious undertaking of Domènech i Montaner.

Pau Gil i Serra, a Catalan banker resident in Paris, bequeathed in his will a large sum of money for the setting up in Barcelona of a model hospital complex, designed on the lines of the then fashionable garden cities, and with the hospital's functions divided for sanitary reasons between different pavilions, some of which were to be joined by underground galleries. In 1891 the executors of the will acquired 30,000 square metres of land for this purpose, and entrusted the overall design of the complex to Domènech i Montaner. The foundation stone of this hospital—which by the terms of the will had to bear the name of Gil's patron saint, Paul—was laid on 15 January 1902, but by 1911, when funds had run out, only eight of Domènech's projected 46 pavilions had been erected, and none of these was as yet in a suitable state to be used. The executors were forced to enter into negotiations with the administrators of the Hospital de la Santa Creu in the Raval (seep. 90), an institution which at that time was greatly in need of space to enlarge and modernise its premises. Eventually it was agreed that the two institutions would be joined together, the Hospital de la Santa Creu being transferred to the site of the Hospital de Sant Pau. New funds for the completion of the complex subsequently became available, and the land on which to build was extended to a total of 145,470 metres; Lluís Domènech's son, Pere Domènech i Roura, came to the assistance of his father, and was responsible for the design of many of the later pavilions. The complex was finally completed by the beginning of 1930, and officially opened on 16 January of that year by Alfonso XIII. Insensitive modernisations were carried out in later years and, though the complex continues to function as a hospital, a large section of it has been left to ruin.

The Hospital de la Santa Creu i de Sant Pau, Barcelona's most extensive Moderniste complex, is a fascinating if melancholy place to visit, with a haunting, dream-like atmosphere, particularly if seen on a winter's evening. The brick pavilions, with their medieval and Byzantine overtones and colourful ceramic-tiled roofs, are remarkable for their variety and overall fantasy, the ones that have been abandoned providing an element of the macabre. Essentially this is a place simply for wandering around, but one building in particular deserves special attention, the **Adminstrative Pavilion**, which was built by Lluís Domènech in 1905–10, and stands at the entrance to the complex, directly facing the northern end of the Avinguda Gaudí. The brick and stone façade, which brings together elements from Byzantine architecture and the Catalan Gothic, has a steepled frontispiece rising up on steps, and is adorned with statuary by Pau Gargallo and his studio. As in all his buildings Domènech worked closely here with a great number of craftsmen, and the interior is of particular ornamental richness, aglow with ceramic decorations and stained glass, hung with elaborate ironwork lamps, and richly carved throughout. As you walk up one of the grand flights of steps which lead off from the large vestibule, the overall effect is particularly dramatic, with star-shaped vaulting coming suddenly into view above you, giving you the impression that you are entering some fantastical cathedral-like structure. From the windows of the upper hall, there are outstanding views looking all the way down the Avinguda de Gaudí to the Sagrada Família.

Returning to the Plaça de Gaudí, and heading south down the CARRER DE MARINA, you will cross the Avinguda Diagonal before reaching, one block further down, the *PLAÇA DE TOROS MONUMENTAL. Built in 1916 by Ignasi Mas Morell and Domènec Sugrañes Gras, this is claimed to be the only Moderniste bull-ring in the world, and is certainly a most curious building, with huge ceramic-coated eggs crowning brick towers perforated by parabolic arches. The only one of Barcelona's two bull-rings still to be used for bull-fights, this features a small *Museu Tauri, which includes documentation relating to the career of the legendary bull-fighter Manolete, who was killed in the ring of the Catalan town of Lérida in 1947. The southern side of the building overlooks the wide GRAN VIA DE LES CORTS CATALANES, where you should turn right and head west towards the Plaça de Tetuan. In the middle of the round garden at the centre of this busy intersection there now stands the **Monument al Doctor Robert**, which was originally situated in the Plaça de la Universitat, but was dismantled in the Civil War in the belief that it would be a rallying point for nationalist Catalan rebels; it was erected on its present site in 1979. Commemorating the popular mayor of Barcelona, Dr Bartolomeu Robert (1842–1902), it was sculpted by Josep Llimona in 1910, and is the most remarkable Moderniste commemorative monument in the city. A stone bust of Dr Robert being kissed by a woman representing Fame surmounts a tapering stone base adorned with seven allegorical and realistically modelled figures in bronze, much of the pictorial power of this monument being derived from the contrast between bronze and stone. The undulating base, which seems to have been removed from the façade of the Casa Milà, has often been attributed to Gaudí, who was a close friend of Llimona's.

Gaudí was fatally injured one block to the west of the Plaça de Tetuan, at the intersection of the Gran Via de les Corts Catalanes and the Carrer de Bailèn. It was here, on 7 June 1926 that he was run over by a tram, his body being subsequently mistaken for that of a tramp; he died three days later in the Hopital de la Santa Creu i de Sant Pau, and was buried in the crypt of the Sagrada Família.

One block to the south of the Plaça de Tetuan is the CARRER DE CASP, which runs parallel to the Gran Via de les Corts Catalanes. Heading west

west along this street, you will pass to your left, at No. 48, the **Casa Calvet**, the most restrained of the three residences created by Gaudí for the Eixample. Built in 1898–99 as a store and residence for a textile merchant family, the Calvets, it features a flat, rusticated façade crowned by two undulating pediments, the whole revealing the strong influence of the Catalan baroque. The tiny vestibule is worth visiting for its ceramics and Gaudí-designed lift, but the porter stationed here does not encourage lingering. The furniture which Gaudí created for the Calvet store and office was his first to reveal strong naturalistic inspiration; it can now be seen in the Museu d'Art Modern in the Ciutadella (see p. 104). Further along the Carrer de Casp (at Nos 24–26, at the corner with the Carrer de Pau Claris), is the *Casal de Sant Jordi, a former commercial and residential block built in 1929–31 by Francesc Folguera i Grassi; a three-sided block of great simplicity, this is generally regarded as one of the finest examples of the progressive, rationalist tendencies within the architecture of the Noucentisme movement.

Continuing along the Carre de Casp you will pass to your left (at No. 6) the *Teatre Tívoli (a grand cinema built by Miquel Madorell i Rius in 1917–19), before coming out again at the lower end of the Passeig de Gràcia. From here you should continue west along the GRAN VIA DE LES CARTS CATALANES, where you will find, shortly to your right, the imposing *Cine Coliseum, an example of Noucentiste architecture at its most pretentious, in this case taking its inspiration from Charles Garnier's Opera House in Paris; it was built in 1923 by Francesc de P. Nebot i Torrens. One block further on is the *Edifici de la Universitat, the main building of Barcelona University. The origins of the university are in the Estudis Generals, a college situated at the lower end of the Rambla; after this was suppressed in 1717, the role of a centre of Catalan higher education was taken over by the University of Cervera, which was transferred to Barcelona in 1842, and temporarily housed in the former Carmelite convent on the Carrer del Carme. The present building was built by Elies Rogent in 1859–62, and takes the form of a vast neo-Romanesque block inspired by the monastery of the Catalan village of Poblet; inside the building neo-Romanesque elements are contrasted with detailing of Byzantine and Islamic inspiration, as is particularly evident in the splendid Assembly Hall. With the expansion of Barcelona University in recent times, most of the faculties were moved to the south-western end of the Avinguda de Diagonal.

Immediately beyond the university block, you will pass to your right the entrance to the CARRER DE ARIBAU, where you will find at No. 27 the night-time bar called *Satanassa*, which was created in the late 1980s as a reaction to the tasteful designer bars of the time, and is loud, camp and kitsch, with an overall erotic decoration of painted naked figures and absurd sculptures; this example of so-called 'anti-design' was designed by Rafa.

The remaining attractions of the Eixample are more scattered, and include, six blocks further west down the Gran Via de les Corts Catalanes, the fascinating Moderniste house known as the *Casa Golferichs. One of the first and most important buildings of Gaudí's assistant Joan Rubió i Bellvé, this was built in 1900–01 near the edge of the Eixample, at a time when there was still room for houses to have small gardens. A brick structure combining influences from William Morris and Islamic architecture, the house features exceptionally wide wooden eaves, and a neo-Gothic corner room, behind which members of the family used to sit and watch the parading carriages in the street. In a ruinous state by the mid 1980s, the house was almost pulled down by the notorious property speculator Nuñez y Navarro, but was saved and restored by the Town Hall, who keep here a small cultural centre specialising in exhibitions of anthropology. Some of the original interior has survived, most notably around the large and impressive staircase well, which is decorated all over with green

The mysterious and ungainly look-out towers bordering the Parc de l'Espanya Industrial

embossed patterns. A few doors further down, at Nos 475–77, is the *Casa de Lactància, which was built in 1908–13 by Pere Falqués and Antoni de Falguerra Sivilla. The façade, of late Gothic inspiration, is crowned by an elaborate parapet containing a large central relief sculpted by Eusebi Arnau. The relatively sober exterior contrasts with the covered patio inside, a light and colourful space glazed with stained glass, and featuring bricks painted a pale blue and a first-floor gallery adorned with green ceramics; the building is now an old people's home, and visitors provide a welcome distraction for the residents.

The western boundary of the Eixample is marked by the *Estació Barcelona Central-Sants**, which is best reached from the *Casa de Lactància by taking the metro from the nearby Rocafort station. Sants is the main and most modern railway station of Barcelona, and its interest for the sightseer lies essentially in the surrounding urban spaces comprising the *PLAÇA DELS PAÏSOS CATALANS and the *Parc de l'Espanya Industrial . The former, built in 1981–83 by Helio Piñón Pallarés and Albert Viaplana i Vea, was the prototype for the many bleak squares that have mushroomed in Barcelona in recent years. Intended to tidy up what had previously been a chaotic intersection, the square was created on a space—above the station's sunken tracks—which could not support the weight of any buildings, soil or trees. The architects conceived the square as a vast sculpture, the bare expanses of pavement being articulated at wide intervals by canopies, poles and other apparently abstract forms that are meant to be full of playful figurative references: thus a long canopy with a wavy roof is said to suggest the smoke of a moving train. The average visitor is unlikely to appreciate these subtleties, or to comprehend the design historian Guy Julier's description of the place as a 'lyrical Minimalist essay which ensured its revival as a viable aesthetic beyond Postmodernism.' Far more entertaining, if similarly ugly, is the Parc de l'Espanya Industrial, which has been extravagantly described as a 'mixture of Disney and Gaudí'. Built in 1984–86 by the Santander architect Luis Peña Ganchegui, it has the conventional attractions of trees, fountains and a large lake, but is likely to be remembered not for these but for a row of large lookout towers that resemble lighthouses but serve no apparent function. Various sculptures adorn the park, the most memorable—for children at least—being Andres Nagel's enormous work in coloured metal representing St. George and the Dragon (1985), which doubles as a slide.

Heading north east from the Plaça Països Catalans along the Carrer de Josep Tarradellas, and taking the first turning to the right you will enter the CARRER DEL ROSELLÓ, on which is situated—five blocks along—the main entrance to the complex comprising the *Universitat Industrial de Barcelona. This technical college, dating back to 1908, was created on a site previously occupied by the Batlló textile mills, of which a tall brick chimney of 1868 survives. The main buildings of the college were built in 1927–31 by Joan Rubió i Bellvé, and include a large residential block to which is attached a fascinating chapel supported inside by giant parabolic arches. Skirting the northern side of the college is the CARRER DE PARÍS, along which you should walk east, turning left after two blocks into the CARRER DE CASANOVA. Near the junction of the latter street with the Avinguda Diagonal is the charming **Casa Companys** (at No. 203), a white chalet-like structure built by Puig i Cadafalch in 1911 for Pere Companys. The building belongs to the so-called 'white period' of Puig i Cadafalch, and its cheerful simplicity is often interpreted as symptomatic of the transition between

Modernisme and Noucentisme. Under the eaves of its steeply-pitched roof is to be found a sgraffitoed decoration of the Assumption of the Virgin. The bright interior, adapted in 1940 as a surgery for Dr Melcior Colet, retains elements of the original ground-floor decoration, including some fine stained-glass windows in the hall. The building has recently been restored to house the *Museu i Centre d'Estudis de l'Esport Dr Melcior Colet, an undeservedly little visited museum hosting simply displayed exhibitions relating to the history of sport in Catalonia.

Walking north-east from here down the Avinguda Diagonal, you will pass to your right, at Nos 423–25, the *Casa Sayrach, a large residential block built by Enric Granados in 1915–18; the sinuous roof-line clearly reflects the influence of Gaudí's Casa Milà. One block further down is the entrance to the Carrer de Balmes, where you will find, at No. 161, one of Barcelona's most extravagant designer bars, *Velvet*. Designed by Alfredo Arribas in 1987, this disco-bar represented a reaction against the chic sobriety of previous establishments such as *Network* (see Bars and Restaurants). Inspired in its lurid sensuality by David Lynch's film *Blue Velvet* (1987), it features a great ramp which takes you down into a world described as a 'delirium of total design', created out of brick, steel, glass, slate, velvet, wood, stone, and a myriad of sensuous forms and lush, decadent colours.

Continuing down the Avinguda Diagonal, you will see shortly to the right, at the western end of the Rambla de Catalunya, Puig i Cadafalch's *Casa Serra, a structure of 1903–08 resembling a fantastical late Gothic palace; the building, recently restored to house the main seat of the Diputació de Catalunya, is adorned outside with elaborate sculptures by the ubiquitous Eusebi Arnau. Immediately beyond the building, you will come back to the upper end of the Passeig de Gràcia.

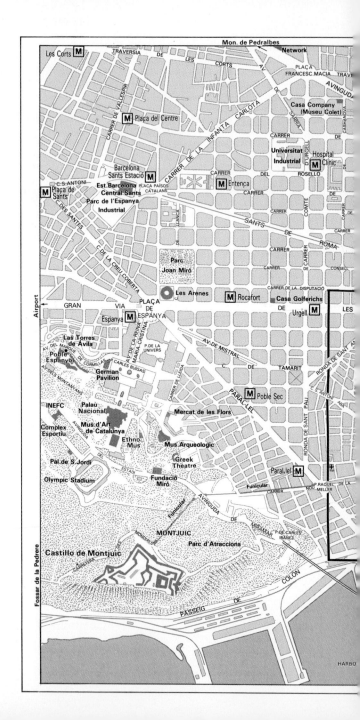

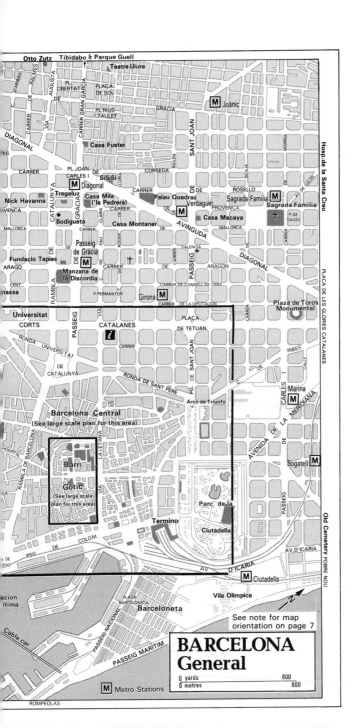

Otto Zutz   Tibidabo & Parque Guell

Teatre Lliure

PLAÇA
DE SOL

PLT.
LIBERTAD

PL. RIUS
I TAULET

GRACIA

M Joanic

DIAGONAL

Casa Fuster

SANT JOAN

Hosp. de la Santa Creu

CARRER

PL. JOAN DE CARLES I

M Diagonal

SISISI

CORSEGA

ROSELLO

Sagrada Familia   M

Nick Havanna

Tragaluz

Casa Mila ('la Pedrera')

Palau Quadras   Verdaguer

PROVENCA

Sagrada Familia

Bodigueta

Casa Montaner

M   Casa Macaya

P. DE GAUDI

MALLORCA

CARRER

Passeig de Gràcia

M

AVINGUDA

MALLORCA

DIAGONAL

Fundacio Tapies

CARRER

VALENCIA

Manzana de la Discordia

PASSEIG

ARAGÓN

nassa

RAMBLA

P. PERMANYOR

CARRER DE CONSELL DE CENT

Girona   M

Plaza de Toros Monumental

CARRER   DE LA DIPUTACION

Universitat

CORTS

PASSEIG

PLAÇA

DE TETUAN

CATALANES

i

RONDA UNIVERSITAT

CARRER

DE

CATALUNYA

RONDA DE SANT PERE

RIBES

CALLE

DE SANT JOAN

PG.

Marina   M

Arco de Triunfo

Barcelona Central
(See large scale plan for this area)

CARRER

AVENIDA   DE   LA   MERIDIANA

Barri

Bogatell   M

Gotic
(See large scale plan for this area)

Parc de la

PASSEIG

Termino

Ciutadella

AV. D'ICARIA

COLOM

AV   D'ICARIA

PSG   DE PAZ

M Ciutadella

Old Cemetery POBRE NOU

acion itima

PLAÇA BARCELONETA

Barceloneta

Vila Olimpica

Cable car

PASSEIG NACIONAL

See note for map orientation on page 7

PASSEIG MARITIM

BARCELONA
General

0 yards   800
0 metres   800

M   Metro Stations

ROMPEOLAS

3 GREATER BARCELONA

A. Pedralbes and Diagonal

Of the once separate townships that make up Greater Barcelona, **Pedralbes**, together with the adjoining district of Sarrià (see also p. 148), is today one of the smartest, with an abundance of wealthy villas and residential blocks set among the exotic vegetation which covers the lower slopes of the Tibidabo range. Beginning a tour of Pedralbes at the Palau Reial metro station, you will find yourself in the so-called *Barrio Bajo or Lower District of Pedralbes, which extends north of the verdant western end of the Avinguda de la Diagonal. The *Palau Reial de Pedralbes—the entrance gates to which adjoin the metro station—occupies land which was presented to the Spanish royal family by Gaudí's patron, Count Güell. The former Güell residence within the estate was transformed after 1919 into an imposing palace for Alfonso XIII. The king slept in the palace in 1926, but the building was not finally completed until the inauguration of the International Exhibition of 1929. With the downfall of the king in 1931, the palace was handed over to the Barcelona Town Hall, which installed a Museum of Decorative Arts here; in 1936 it was taken over by the President of the Republic and later became the Barcelona residence of Franco. Opened again to the public in 1960, it currently houses the excellent **Museu de Ceràmica**, which has a representative selection of Spanish ceramics from ancient times up to recent artists such as Miró and Picasso; the Museu d'Arts Decoratives will shortly be returned here, and the building will also house part of the Cambó Collection, a bequest of old master paintings (ranging from Botticelli to Fragonard) which is divided between Barcelona and the Prado Museum in Madrid. The building itself, designed by Eusebi Bona and Francesc de P. Nebot, is a pompous classical structure with a lavishly marbled interior and fresco decorations taken from local 18C palaces. The lush surrounding gardens, which were relaid in 1925 by Nicolau M. Rubió i Tudurí, are shaded by old trees and feature a wooden crucifix donated by Romania. You will also find here a small museum of old carriages (*Museu de Carruatges), and a fountain which was designed by Gaudí for the Güell estate in 1884, and discovered in 1983 after having been hidden for many years under ivy.

The finest survival of Gaudí's work for the Güell Estate are the **Main Gate and Entrance Pavilions**, which are situated just to the north of the Palau Reial and can be reached from the Avinguda de la Diagonal by walking north along the Avinguda de Pedralbes until you come to the Passeig de Manuel Girona; they will be seen immediately to your left at the intersection of the two streets. Designed by Gaudí in 1887, at a time when he was heavily under the influence of Islamic architecture, the fantastically turretted and irregularly-shaped pavilions combine elaborate brickwork with coloured ceramics, white-washed walls and painted decoration; the longer of the two pavilions, which was originally a stable block, is now the seat of the centre of Gaudí studies known as the *Cátedra Gaudí. The main gate features some of the most extraordinary ironwork in Gaudí's whole career, the iron being expressively twisted to form what is known as the Drac de Predalbes, or Dragon of Pedralbes.

Continuing to climb north up the shaded Avinguda de Pedralbes, you will pass to your left the Carrer de Sor Eulàlia d'Anzizu, where you will find at

No. 46 *Les Escales Park, a luxury residential development designed in 1967 by Josep Lluís Sert while still in exile in America; despite its concessions to local building traditions such as the use of ceramics and wooden shutters, the complex remains essentially American in character, and as such did not meet with much success in Catalonia, where Sert was criticised for having lost touch with his architectural roots. At the top of the Avinguda de Pedralbes is a village-like square with steps leading up to the main entrance of the **MONESTIR DE SANTA MARÍA DE PEDRALBES**, the best preserved monastic complex to survive in Barcelona.

The Monestir de Santa María de Pedralbes was founded as a Clarissine Convent in 1326 by Elisenda de Montcada i de Pinós, the fourth and last wife of Jaume II the Just. The church was constructed at great speed, being consecrated only one year after the convent's foundation. The enormous main cloister was completed shortly afterwards, though a third storey was added to it in the early 15C. A closed order of Clarissine nuns continues to live in the convent, but they now occupy new quarters built for them in 1976–83 by the Barcelona Town Hall so as to facilitate access to the building for tourists. The main entrance to the convent is on the charming Plaça del Monestir, which is surrounded by fragrant gardens. The entrance portal is attached to the lateral façade of the church, a structure of great unity and simplicity dominated on the exterior by an octagonal bell-tower which was admired by Le Corbusier for its geometrical regularity.

The interior of the single-aisled church—a visit to which is separate from that of the rest of the convent—features, in a vaulted niche immediately to the right of the high altar, the fine if highly restored *Tomb of Queen Elisenda, which was completed shortly before her death in 1364, and shows the recumbent queen mourned by angels. Entering the convent through the door just to the left of the church, you will find yourself in the **main cloister**, which is composed of two superimposed Gothic arcades of exceptional elegance, and a low upper gallery; the luxuriant cypress-shaded garden in the middle has a classical Plateresque wellhead commissioned during the rule as abbess of Teresa Enriquez (1495–1507). Walking around the cloister in an anti-clockwise direction, you will come immediately to your right to the artistic highpoint of the convent, the **CHAPEL OF ST. MICHAEL**, which is decorated with the finest surviviving mural cycle from 14C Catalonia. The murals, redolent of the art of Trecento Italy, were commissioned from Ferrer Bassa in 1343, and completed in 1346, two years before the artist's death from the plague which devastated Barcelona in 1348. Featuring an upper and lower level depicting respectively the Passion of Christ and the Life of the Virgin, the murals were executed in a mixture of oil and tempera; the wall facing the chapel's entrance contains representations of saints. Elsewhere around the cloister you will find two cells containing biblical dioramas in questionable taste, a reconstruction of the original infirmary and a refectory restored in 1894 by Joan Martorell. At present a large part of the convent is being transformed to house part of the impressive bequest of paintings donated to Spain by Baron Thyssen-Bornemisza (the greater part of the collection will be shown in the Palacio Villanueva in Madrid).

Rising to the west of the convent is the *Nou Monestir Benedictí de la Mare de Déu de Montserrat (101 Carretera d'Esplugues), which was designed by Nicolau M. Rubiá i Tudurí in 1922, and completed in 1940 by Raimon Duran i Reynals, following Rubiá's exile after the Civil War. The monks of Montserrat who commissioned the building wanted a neo-medieval structure, but those who financed the construction insisted on a monastery imbued with the Renaissance spirit of Noucentisme; the end result was a pastiche of Brunelleschi, Bramante and Michelangelo.

Heading east of the Monestir de Pedralbes along the Carrer del Monestir, and continuing east along the Paseig Reina de Montcada, you will be following an attractive garden-lined route commanding extensive views; eventually you will reach the neo-classical *parish church of Sarrià, from where you could continue east to the Museu Clarà (see p. 148).

Returning instead down the Avinguda de Pedralbes to the lower part of Pedralbes, you could make your way back to the centre of Barcelona along the Avinguda de la Diagonal. This western extension of the Diagonal was built in the 1920s to connect the city with the Palau Reial, and, 30 years later, came to serve the Ciudad Universitaria. One of the finest of the university buildings, the *Facultat de Dret (Law Faculty), stands in gardens adjoining the eastern side of the Palau Reial, at No. 684 Avinguda de la Diagonal; built in 1958 by Guillermo Giráldez Dávila, Pedro López Iñigo and Xavier Subias i Fages, this light and cheerful Functionalist block is one of the finest Catalan examples of the so-called International Style, and brought to Catalan architecture of its day a welcome breath of fresh air after the pompous heaviness and severity of so many of the buildings of the post-Civil War period. Fascist planning and architectural ideals characterise the bulk of the University City, which was begun in 1955, but according to models formulated in the 1940s. Both the overall design of the city, and its location in an area which had not only been set apart for residential purposes but also was divided in two by the Diagonal, were heavily criticised by the city's young progressive architects associated with Grup R, but to little avail. Most of the buildings are spaciously arranged on the southern side of the Diagonal, on land which has been designated as one of the city's Olympic areas, on account of the important sports facilities that are to be found in its southern half. As you head south from the the the Diagonal down the Avinguda de Joan XXIII (the southern continuation of the Avinguda de Pedralbes), the vista is dominated by the *Camp del Futbol Club Barcelona, a vast stadium which was built in 1954–57 (by Lorenzo García Borbán, Francesc Mitjans i Miró and Josep Soteras i Mauri), and enlarged to hold 120,000 spectators on the occasion of the 1982 World Cup. Within the stadium is a museum relating to Barcelona FC (better known as Barça), the world's wealthiest football club; apart from seeing trophies, photographs, old programmes, and an audio-visual presentation (in Spanish and Catalan only), a tour of the museum includes a visit to the marble Royal Box, which offers a magnificent view of the stadium. Incongruously situated in front of the building, and serving as the Football Club's offices, is one of Barcelona's surviving rural mansions known in Catalan as *Masías*, this particular one being a simple stone structure of 1702. Another such structure, dating back to 1602, is to be found off the northern end of the Avinguda de Joan XXIII (on the intersecting Carrer Salvador Cardenal), this one serving as an annexe to one of Barcelona's most luxurious hotels, the Princesa Sofia.

Heading east from the Princesa Sofia down the Diagonal you will pass to your right (at the intersection with the Gran Via de Carles III), the impressive *Torres d'oficines Trade; built in 1966–69 by José Antonio Coderch de Sentmenat and Manuel Valls i Vergés, this complex comprises four tall towers made out of undulating curtain walls of tinted glass. Further east, at the junction with the Avinguda de Sarrià, is the *Edifici 'Talaia de Barcelona', one of Barcelona's tallest skyscrapers, built in 1966–70 by Federico Correa i Ruiz, Alfonso Milà i Sagnier and José Luis Sanz Magallán.

On the other side of the Diagonal, at No. 616, is the leading 'designer-bar' known as *Network*. Created in 1987 by Eduardo Samsó and Alfredo Arribas, this is a high-tech bar with a selfconsciously post-nuclear character. The decoration, inspired by futuristic films such as Terry Gilliam's *Brazil* and Ridley Scott's *Blade Runner*, conjures up a future set in a bunker, with television screens peering out of bare concrete walls and exposed wires dangling from the ceiling. The restaurant section, which remains highly fashionable despite the awfulness of the food, was designed to encourage social mixing, with furniture and television screens arranged in a way which makes it impossible to avoid eye contact with your neighbours. A number of interesting modern buildings are situated on the streets to the north west of *Network*, in particular on the Carrer de Johann Sebastian Bach, where you will find at No. 7 *bis* a shuttered residential block of 1957–61 by José Antonio Coderch de Sentmenat, and, at No. 28, an influential early work by Ricardo Bofill—a block of luxury flats centred around an unusually shaped courtyard. East from here is the long Carrer de Muntaner, which runs from the Diagonal all the way north to the Plaça de la Bonanova (see p. 147). At No. 314 is the *Clinica Barraquer*, which was built by Joaquim Lloret i Homs in 1934–40, and has a wonderful Art Deco interior with classical decorative elements. The architecture of this clinic differs markedly from the Le Corbusier-inspired Functionalism associated with the avant-garde group of the 1930s known as GATCPAC. One of the finest examples of the latter style of architecture is to be seen slightly further up the Carrer de Muntaner, at Nos 342–348. This, a block of *Duplex Flats* dating from 1930–31, was the first important work by GATCPAC's most influential architect, Josep Lluís Sert. West from the Carrer de Muntaner you will reach the borders of the district of Gràcia (see Rte 3B).

B. Gràcia and Tibidabo

The former township of Gràcia, which extends from the northern end of the Passeig de Gràcia up to the Plaça de Lesseps, was named after the 15C Monastery of Santa María de Jesús de Gràcia, which was destroyed during the War of Succession. An industrial township in the 19C, with strong liberal and revolutionary traditions, Gràcia became from the 1960s onwards one of Barcelona's most fashionable residential districts for young middle-class intellectuals. Within its network of narrow streets crammed with modest 19C blocks and houses, there grew up numerous lively bars, bistro-like restaurants and 'Off-Barcelona' theatres. Many of these establishments still survive, but the overall character of the area has become rather more sedate in recent years, largely due to the once radical but now wealthy residents complaining about the night-time level of noise.

Immediately to the east of the railway station of Gràcia, on the Plaça de Llibertat, is one of the finest survivals of 19C Gràcia, the *Mercat de la Llibertat, an ironwork structure built by Francesc Berenguer in 1893. Just to the south of this runs Gràcia's main east-west artery, the Travessera de Gràcia, half-way along which, to the south and north respectively, are the districts' two principal squares, the small and charming Plaças Rius i Taulet and Sol. The former is popularly known as the 'Square of the Clock' (Plaça del Reloj) from its tall, free-standing clock-tower of 1862, which is decorated with terracotta reliefs representing the Zodiac; a rallying-point for revolutionaries in uprisings that took place in 1870, 1873 and 1874, the tower became a famous symbol of Liberty and was reproduced on the cover of the 19C Liberal newspapers, *L'Esquella de la Torratxa* and *La Campana de Gràcia*. The Plaça del Sol, which was sensitively remodelled in 1983–85 by Jaume Bach and Gabriel Mora, is today the livelier of the two squares, with open-air cafés and regular *Sardana* dancing. Two blocks to the north of the Plaça Sol, at 47 Carrer de Montseny, is the *Teatre Lliure, which, since its foundation in 1976, has been one of the most important and progressive of Barcelona's small theatres. The main force behind this theatre was the recently deceased director and stage-designer Fabià Puigserver (1938–91), who was responsible for the award-winning interior design of the building; in the theatre's early years, another associate of the place was the leading Spanish theatre director of today, Lluís Pasqual.

At its western end, the Carrer del Montseny joins the Gràcia's main east-west artery, the Carrer Gran de Gràcia, which runs the whole length of the district. Walking north up this you should turn left into the Carrer Les Carolines to see (from the outside only) Gaudí's **Casa Vicens**, at Nos. 18–24. Built in 1883–88 as a summer house for Manuel Vicens Montaner, this extraordinary building, lavishly coated in ceramics, is one of the most oriental-inspired of Gaudí's structures; a section of the fantastical ironwork railings has now been incorporated into the main entrance gate of the Park Güell (see p. 149). Walking to the western end of the Carrer Les Carolines, and crossing the Avinguda del Princep d'Astúries, you will find one block further west the Carrer de Saragossa, where, at No. 57 is the *house and studio built in 1960–63 by José Antonio Coderch de Sentmenat for the painter Antoni Tàpies; from the street the house appears entirely hidden behind louvred metal shutters.

To begin the ascent from here to Tibidabo, you should return to the Gràcia station and from there take the underground train to the Avinguda del Tibidabo. From the latter station you could continue the climb by walking up the long and steep avenue of that name, an avenue lined with imposing turn-of-the-century villas and gardens. The avenue is also served by Barcelona's last surviving tram (the others ceased functioning in the 1960s), the picturesque Tramvia Blau (Blue Tram), which dates back to the beginning of the century. Half-way up the avenue, at No. 31, is an outstanding Moderniste house built in 1903–13 by Joan Rubió for the Roviralta family and popularly known as 'El Frare Blanc' or 'White Friar', not because of its white coat of plaster but because it occupies a site which had previously belonged to a Dominican convent. The exterior comprises a fantastical interpretation of the Catalan Gothic style, with widely projecting eaves; the white-washed and recently revamped interior now provides the setting for the fashionable restaurant, the *El Asador de Aranda*, which achieved notoriety in the summer of 1990 as the place where a male striptease was put on for the benefit of the American rock singer, Madonna. The quiet residential street by the side of the building, the Carrer Teodor Roviralta, will take you to the excellent **Museu de la Ciència** (Science Museum), which occupies a turn-of-the-century building by Domènec Estapà which was beautifully remodelled and enlarged in 1980. The museum, which is run by the Caixa de Pensions, presents science in a genuinely imaginative and accessible way through the use of hundreds of different exhibits that can be activated by the spectator; there is also a planetarium and a special section for children.

At the top of the Avinguda del Tibidabo, where the Blue Tram terminates, is a charming small square featuring an old funicular station, and an adjoining palm-lined terrace containing the restaurant *La Venta*, a cheerful olive green establishment characterised by its informal chic, *nouvelle cuisine* and famous clients such as the designer Mariscal. The restaurant's owner, Paco d'Ors, also runs the intimate adjoining bar, *Merbeyé*, which was opened in 1978 and features one of the first interiors to be associated with Mariscal, containing not only graphic designs by him, but also such whimsical features as its two large fans, one of which appears to have carved a dent through one of the bar's columns, the other to have cut through a column completely. On the other side of the square, overhanging the steep slopes of the hill, is *Mirablau*, an elegant bar which was opened in 1989 and offers a spectacular view of Barcelona, a view which is particularly magical at night; the bar stools have been placed the whole length of the bar's panoramic window.

The last stage of the ascent up to the summit of **Tibidabo** (542 metres) is done usually by funicular, which climbs through a dense forest of pines and passes near the Fabra Observatory, a turn-of-the-century structure by Domènech i Estapà. The mountain of Tibidabo derives its name from the Latin words, *'Haec omnia tibi dabo si cades adoraberis me'* ('All this shall I give you if you but adore me'), the words of the devil as quoted in St.Matthew's Gospel. A road to its summit was created in 1868, and among those who subsequently made the ascent was Juan Bosco, who dedicated the mountain to the Sacred Heart; the queen of Spain visited the mountain in 1888, on the occasion of the World Exhibition. However, the development of Tibidabo as a popular place of recreation for the people of Barcelona was due to the celebrated pill manufacturer Dr Andreu, who created in 1900 the *Sociedad Anónima del Tibidabo*, which not only promoted the garden suburb on the slopes of the mountain, but was also responsible both for the Blue Tram and the funicular. A public park was laid out in 1908 on the upper reaches of Tibidabo, and near the top of this there was later built an *amusement park, which was thoroughly overhauled in 1989. The very summit of the mountain is marked by the *Templo Expiatorio del Sagrado Cor, which was founded in 1902. This building of singular hideousness was designed by Enric Sagnier and intended as Barcelona's answer to the Sacré Coeur in Montmartre; its sole attraction is that you are able to climb almost to the top of its main spire, from where you can admire potentially extensive views that are usually marred by pollution. A more worthy addition to Barcelona's skyline crowns the summit of the neighbouring mountain of Collserola. This is the city's *Communications Tower, which was begun in 1989 and is expected to be completed in time for the Olympic Games. Designed by the British architect of the Pompidou Centre in Paris, Norman Foster, it is a structure faithful to Foster's belief in achieving the maximum of effect through the minimal of structural means; it comprises a mast-like central shaft of precast concrete supporting a skeletral framework of exceptional elegance.

Returning to the foot of the Avinguda del Tibidabo, you could continue a tour of Barcelona's lush and luxurious upper reaches by walking west along the Passeig de Sant Gervasi until you come to the Plaça de Bonanova, which is situated at the northern end of the Carrer de Muntaner (see p. 145). From here you could walk north up the Carrer de Sant Joan de la Salle, which eventually turns into the Carrer de Bellesguard. At the top of this street, which curves its way through a quiet residential quarter spread out on the slopes of the Collserola, is the *Convento del Redemptor, a curious Moderniste complex built by Bernardí Martorell Puig in 1926. Next to this, at Nos. 16–20 Bellesguard, is the **Casa Bellesguard**, which was built by Antoni Gaudí in 1900–02 over the scant remains of a summer residence commissioned in 1409 by Martí I, the last of the Catalan kings (the palace was known as *Bellesguard* after the Catalan word for 'beautiful view'). The medieval site inspired Gaudí to create a neo-Gothic castle-like structure which seems straight out of some expressionistic nightmare, the whole surmounted by a tall spire supporting a cross. The building, regarded by some as Gaudí's secular masterpiece, is also one of this architect's least-known works, the structure having always been in private ownership, and hidden until recently behind a large walled enclosure. The well-preserved interior, which is now divided into apartments, is still inaccessible to the public, but the present owners do at least allow visitors to walk around the large garden, thus allowing you an excellent view of the building's exterior.

Returning to the bottom of the street, and turning left into the Carrer de Vistahermosa, you will come shortly to the Carrer de la Infanta Isabel, where you will find at No. 4 the restaurant *La Balsa*, an almost Japanese-like glass, wood and brick structure, beautifully set amidst dense and luscious vegetation; this award-winning building was designed in 1978 by Lluís Clotet and Òscar Tusquets.

Back at the Plaça de la Bonanova and heading west along the Passeig de Bonanova, you will enter the luxurious residential district of **Sarrià**. Taking the fifth turning to the left, the Carrer Calatrava, you will reach at Nos 27–29 the *Museu Clarà, which is dedicated to the sculptor Josep Clarà, who was born in the nearby town of Olot, and died in Sarrià on 16 December 1878, working up to the very day of his death. The museum occupies the studio of his last years, which is situated in the small garden of the house which he shared with his sister Carmen, who donated both buildings to Barcelona Town Hall in 1969. Clarà, one of the leading sculptural associates of Noucentisme, spent an important period in Paris at the beginning of the century, falling there heavily under the influence first of Rodin and then of Maillol. His works, with their predominance of classical female nudes in white marble, have a very restful quality, which is perfectly complemented by the white simplicity of the museum. On display here are works from all periods of his career, including plaster-casts, watercolours and drawings, among which is an amusing series of sketches executed while on a visit with Ramon Casas to New York in 1924; the museum also features documentation relating to his life, a small collection of paintings that he amassed and works by friends and associates, for instance a death mask of the artist by Joan Rebull. Several of his works have been placed in the garden, where you will also find two blocks of Carrara marble which Clarà had been intending to carve at the time of his death; one of these is now inscribed with verses that the poet Joan Maragall dedicated to him in 1911.

At the western end of the Passeig de Bonanova you will come to the Plaça de Sarrià, from where you could begin climbing up the Carrer Mayor de Sarrià towards the wooded slopes of Vallvidriera. The northern continuation of this street is the verdant Avinguda de Vallvidriera, where you will pass at No. 44 *bis* the charming *Casa Dolcet, a Moderniste villa in brick and white plaster built by Rubió Bellver in 1906–07. Eventually you will reach another fine Moderniste structure, the *Funicular de Vallvidriera, a funicular station built by Bonaventura Conill and Arnau Calvet in 1905–06, and set above a modern railway station (Peu del Funicular) designed by Josep Llinàs in 1982; the latter station can be reached by train from the Sarrià Station. The old funicular will take you to the top of the wooded slopes of Vallvidriera, where you will find another and far more elaborate Moderniste station by Conill and Calvet. The woods of Vallvidriera were praised in the poetry of Maragall, and also provided a backcloth to the final home of another great Catalan poet, Jacint Verdaguer. This large Renaissance-style house of 18C origin where the poet died on 10 June 1902, is known as the Vil-la Joana, and is situated a ten-minute uphill walk from the Baixador de Vallvidriera railway station (one stop beyond Peu del funicular). It is now the *Casa-Museu Verdaguer, and, as well as numerous mementoes relating to the poet, features an outdoor gallery with wonderful views towards Montserrat, a place which inspired a number of his works.

C. The Park Güell, Parc de la Creueta del Coll and Horta

Of all the many sights in Greater Barcelona, the most popular is perhaps the **PARK GÜELL**, which can be reached by bus No. 24 or 25, or by walking from the metro station at the Plaça de Lesseps. The park, which was commissioned from Antoní Gaudí in 1900 by his great patron Eusebi Güell, was intended originally as a garden-city on the lines of English models such as Bedford Park (hence the reason why it is referred to by the English word Park rather than as *Parc* or *Parque*). The site chosen was an estate of 20 hectares attached to the slopes of the unpromisingly named Muntanya Pelada or Bare Mountain. The desolate nature of the surroundings, and the traditional poverty of the neighbourhood, help to explain why Güell's ambitious plans for the urban renewal of the area proved ultimately to be a failure, for in the end only two of the projected 60 houses were built, one of which being appropriated by Gaudí himself. Gaudí completed his work here in 1914, and in 1922 the abandoned garden-city was acquired by the Barcelona Town Hall for use as a municipal park. The Park Güell, despite failing its original purpose, has proved to be the most loved of all Gaudí's works, and has provided inspiration to countless visitors, including the young Salvador Dalí, who considered the place as one of the most powerful influences on his development as an artist.

The main entrance to the park, on the Carrer d'Olot, is marked by two fantastically-shaped and richly-polychromed pavilions of gingerbread appearance, one of which was built as the home of the guardian of the estate, the other as a communal building with lounges and medical facilities: the gate between the two pavilions is formed of spiky ironwork gates taken from Gaudí's Casa Vicens (see p. 146). A staircase laid out between walls of ceramics leads up to the **Sala Hipóstila**, a large covered space intended to house the market serving the estate. The space, though known as the 'Hall of the 100 Columns', is in fact held up by 84 Doric columns, the ones at the front leaning towards the centre. The front columns support an undulating entablature punctuated by dogs' heads, above which is the famous bench-balustrade surrounding the park's **CENTRAL SQUARE**, which is joined to the lower part of the park by flights of steps on either side of the Sala Hipóstila. The balustrade, which incorporates what is said to be the longest bench in the world, is a typical touch of Gaudí fantasy and symbolism, being shaped like a dragon who serves to protect the estate; it glistens with a magnificent ceramic mosaic coating executed by Gaudí in collaboration with his great assistant, Josep Juyol.

An extensive panorama of Barcelona can be had from the square, and there are few better places from which to admire the city than from the sinuous bench. On either side of the square are viaducts with leaning columns and an overall rustic appearance. The path to the east of the square will take you to the *Casa-Museu Gaudí, which occupies a house built by Francesc Berenguer in 1904, and acquired by Gaudí as a family home in 1906; among the items here are furniture designed by Gaudí for other buildings, and his own wardrobe and iron bed. The summmit of the park was originally to have been crowned by a chapel, but in its stead there is now a large cross, from where a further extensive panorama can be enjoyed.

On the slopes of the hill immediately to the north west of the Park Güell is one of Barcelona's more recent attractions, the **Parc de la Creueta del Coll** (which is reached by bus 28). Of all Barcelona's many recent squares and parks, this is in many ways the most attractive, not least because its major element is a large palm-lined and irregularly-shaped swimming-pool, one of Barcelona's most seductive open-air pools. The park, which occupies the crater of an abandoned quarry, was built in 1981–87 by Josep Martorell, Oriol Bohigas and David Mackay. The place is greatly enhanced by two monumental sculptures, one a vertical piece by Ellsworth Kelly, the other a huge concrete claw by Eduardo Chillida, the latter work being suspended from the cliff-slope by four cables; on the summit of the hill there will eventually be placed an immense female face by the 'pop artist' Roy Liechtenstein.

Two kilometres to the east of the Coll de la Creueta begins the lively district of Horta, the interest of which for tourists lies essentially in a small outlying area situated off the Passeig de Vall d'Hebró. The latter thorough-fare, which forms part of the network of dual carriageways surrounding Barcelona, can be reached from the metro station Horta by walking due north along the Carrer de Horta (a good 15 minutes' uphill walk), or else by taking bus 85, and alighting at the *Velòdrom d'Horta. The Velòdrom, a light and elegant stadium designed in 1983 by Esteve Bonell i Costa and Francesc Rius i Camps, is the centrepiece of another of Barcelona's Olympic areas, this one featuring not only newly-built sports facilities but also a large residential block which has been constructed with the initial intention of housing journalists during the Games. On the slopes of the hill to the north-east of the stadium hover two large round gasometers colloquially known as the 'Huevos de Porcioles', a reference to the testicles of the notorious Fascist Mayor of Barcelona, Porcioles, who was responsible for some of the more brazen building developments of the post Civil-War period. Scattered on the lawn on the western side of the stadium is a *visual poem by Joan Brossa, the 'poem' comprising a group of blocks representing letters and question marks. Immediately to the north of the stadium, hidden among trees, is the so-called **LABERINT D'HORTA**, a bosky late 18C park which in its own way is no less magical a place than the Park Güell, and a considerably less visited one.

The Laberint d'Horta was the creation of the learned and enlightened Joan Antoni Desvalls i d'Ardena, marquis of Llupià i Alfarràs (1740–1820). The marquis himself was responsible for designing and supervising the laying out of the park, though the complex nature of the steeply sloping site, and the need for elaborate water systems, forced him to enlist the help of the Italian engineer, Domenico Bagutti. Work on the park was begun in 1793 and completed in 1804; there are large plaques inside the park commemorating festivities organised here in honour of both Charles IV in 1802 and Alfonso XIII in 1929. At the entrance to the park stands the former country mansion of the Marquises of Llupià, which dates back to a castle built in the 14C for the Vallseca family, but owes its present appearance largely to neo-Moorish remodelling carried out in the mid 19C; at present undergoing much-needed restoration, the building, like the park itself, now belongs to the Barcelona municipality. On the steep wooded slopes behind the house extends a complex of cypress avenues, ponds, fountains, classical pavilions, statuary and enigmatic inscriptions. The park's creator, a true man of the Enlightenment, was greatly interested in philosophy, and the whole layout of the park can be interpreted as an initiation into the different forms of love. At the very centre of the park, preceded by a grotto containing statues of Echo and Narcissus, is the park's famous *laberint* or maze, in the middle of which is a representation of Eros. 'The Labyrinth is simple', an inscription outside assures you, 'you will have no need of the ring which Ariadne gave to Thisbeus'; however, tourists in a hurry might well have to resort to taking short-cuts through gaps in the tightly clipped cypress hedges. The progress of stumbling visitors through the Maze is observed by Venus, whose statue stands on a raised terrace behind, enclosed within a *tempietto*. Further up is a classical pavilion, beyond which is a shaded rectangular pool, featuring at its furthest end a statue of a nymph, whose pose of quiet repose signifies the peace at the end of Love's journey.

D.   Poble Nou and North-Eastern Barcelona

Poble Nou, which dates back to a 13C port, emerged in the 19C as the main industrial suburb of Barcelona. Crime, poverty and unemployment are rife in this district today, but the area has been subject recently to the type of radical urban schemes criticised by Vázquez Montalbán in his polemical work, *Barcelona, cap a on vas?*, (Barcelona, 1991); Barcelona, Where are You Going? Principal among these is the creation of the Vila Olímpica along the district's maritime façade (see p. 112). As with north-eastern Barcelona in general, Poble Nou has little of conventional tourist appeal, but deserves to be visited by anyone with a specialist interest in architecture, design and town-planning in Barcelona today.

Two blocks to the east of the Poble Nou metro station is the long Carrer Bac de Roda, which runs at its southern end through a decayed area of turn-of-the-century industrial warehouses. The seediness of the surroundings can at times be deceptive, for you will find within an extensive and superficially run-down industrial complex at No. 8 of the adjoining Carrer Pellaires, a group of fashionable design studios which includes that of one of Barcelona's leading personalities of today, Javier Mariscal. Born in Valencia in 1950, Mariscal moved to Barcelona in 1971 to study graphic design at the Escuela Elisava, and began making a name shortly afterwards as a comic illustrator, most notably in the undergound magazine *Rollo Enmascarado*, which he founded in 1973. Exhibitions held in the Sala Vinçon of his witty and curious designs and objects helped greatly to further his career, but his real breakthrough came in 1988, when his bear-like creation known as Cobi was chosen as the Olympic mascot for 1992.

One of Mariscal's favourite Barcelona sights is the bridge to be found at the northern end of the Carrer Bac de Roda, the **PONT DE FELIP II** (the nearest metro station is Navas). Built by Santiago Calatrava in 1984–87 to span the railway tracks which separate the southern from the northern sections of north-eastern Barcelona, this magnificent white structure in chrome, metal and concrete features balustrades that are tilted inwards at the same angle as the outer piers. The lightness and dynamism of the whole

Pont de Felip II built by Santiago Calatrava 1984–87

inspires an enormous sense of elation in those crossing the bridge, which must surely be one of the most beautiful of its kind in Europe. However, as with so many of Barcelona's more recent new features, the beauty of the bridge is at variance with its present surroundings, the landscape immediately below being a semi-wasteland populated by the odd gypsy and beggar. On the northern side of the bridge an attempt at urban improvement was made recently with the creation of the *Plaça del General Moragues, a bleak sloping square in brick, designed by O. Terrassó, and adorned with an enormous metal sculpture by Edward Kelly. A more successful recent urban space is the entertaining **Parc del Clot**, which can be reached from the square by walking west along the Carrer de Clot, or by taking the metro to the station of that name. This immensely lively park, animated in the late afternoons by musicians and other performers, was built by D. Freixes and V. Miranda on the site of a former railway works. Incorporated alongside the park's pools, lawns and grassy mounds are sections of the original brick and ironwork industrial complex, including chimney stacks, and a row of arches which resembles an acqueduct and supports a conduit of cascading water.

Heading east from the Pont de Felip II along the long and wide Carrer de Guipúscoa (take bus No. 43), you will reach the Rambla Prim. Near the intersection of the two thoroughfares is the *Plaça de la Palmera (the nearest metro station is La Pau), which was devised by the American conceptual artist Richard Serra. Bare and inhospitable, as with most of Barcelona's recent squares, the Plaça de la Palmera features a tall and solitary palm and chimney-stack, a black crane-like structure supporting football-stadium lights and a wall sculpture formed of two curved concrete blocks 52 metres long and three metres high. The southern end of the Rambla de Prim (accessible from the metro station Besós de Mar) is lined with dreary blocks of the 1960s but was attractively landscaped in 1987 by J. Sanjosé, who decorated its central lawns with undulating walls and green metal projections.

Another interesting modern promenade, on the north-eastern edge of the city, is the *Via Júlia, which was remodelled by B. de Sola and J.M. Julià with the intention of bringing new life to the declining area of Barris Nous. A long metal canopy and a monumental abstract work by Sergi Aguilar entitled The New Catalans adorn the northern end of the thoroughfare (served by the metro station Roquetes), while at the southern end (metro station Llucmajor) is the round Plaça de Llucmajor, which is dominated by a tall modern structure incorporating a Noucentiste bronze by Viladomat.

PYRENEES

FRANC

VALL D'ARAN

PICO DE ANETO
3404m

PIC DE
MONTCALM

CASAMANYA
2707m

ANDORRA

Vielha

SANT-MAURICI-
AIGÜESTORTES
NAT.PARK

Areu
3141m

Andorra
la Vella

Les Escaldes

Puigcer

MONTSENT
DE PALLARS
2883m

Boí

Sort

PUIG
291

El Pont
de Suert

Malpas

La Seu
d'Urgell

SERRA DEL CADÍ

SAN GERVÁS
1887m

La Pobla
de Segur

Guardiola
Bergueda

ARAGON

Tremp

Emb.d'Oliana

GALLINA
PELLADA
2307m

Prats
Lluca

COSCOLLET
1610m

Basella

Solsona

Navars

PON
1039m

Cardona

Moi

Torá de Riubregos

Montserrat

Balaguer

Agramunt

Calaf

Manresa
St F
de Codi

Tarrega

Cervera

Igualada

Terrassa

Lleida

Vallbona de
les Monges

Mon.St Cugat del Valles

Les Borges
Blanques

Sant Sadorni d'Anoia

St Joan
Despi

Fraga

Sarroca
de Segre

Montblanc

Vilafranca del
Penedes

Colonia
Güell

Segre

Mon.Poblet

Mon.
Santes
Creus

Casteldefels

Maials

La Granadella

PRADES
1201m

Valls

Alcover

El Vendrell

Sitges

Ebre

Flix

Falset

Reus

Vilanova
i la Geltrú

Ascó

Calafell

Móra d'Elbre

Salou

Tarragona

Gandesa

Vandellós

Platja
Miami

L'ESPINA
1182m

L'Ametlla de Mar

COSTA DAURADA

Golf de St. Jordi

Tortosa

L'Ampolla

La Cava

Amposta

St Carles de la Rápita

N

| 0 kilometres | 800 |
| 0 miles | 500 |

VALENCIA

Noguera Ribagorçana

Noguera Pallaresa

Llobregat

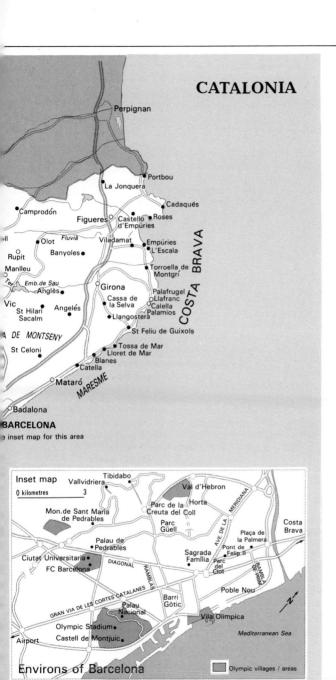

CATALONIA

Perpignan

Portbou
La Jonquera
Cadaqués
Camprodón
Figueres · Castello · Roses
d'Empúries
Olot · Fluvià · Viladamat · Empúries
ll · L'Escala
Rupit · Banyoles

Manlleu
Emb.de Sau
Anglès
Vic · Girona
St Hilari · Cassa de
Sacalm · la Selva · Palafrugel
Angelés · Llafranc
Calella
Llangostera · Palamios

DE MONTSENY · St Feliu de Guixols

St Celoni · Tossa de Mar
Lloret de Mar
Blanes
Catella · MARESME
Mataró

Badalona

BARCELONA
e inset map for this area

COSTA BRAVA

Inset map · Vallvidriera · Tibidabo · Val d'Hebron
0 kilometres 3 · Horta
Parc de la
Creuta del Coll
Mon.de Sant Maria · Parc
de Pedrables · Güell
Plaça de
la Palmera · Costa
Brava
Palau de
Pedrables · Sagrada · Pont de
Família · Felip II
Ciutat Universitaria · Parc
FC Barcelona · DIAGONAL · del
Clot
Poble Nou
GRAN VIA DE LES CORTES CATALANES
Barri
Gòtic
Palau
Nacional · Vila Olimpica
Olympic Stadium
Airport · Castell de Montjuic · Mediterranean Sea

Environs of Barcelona · ☐ Olympic villages / areas

4   EXCURSIONS FROM BARCELONA

Catalonia's combination of coastal and spectacular mountain scenery, and its wealth of monuments—particularly from the Romanesque, Gothic and Moderniste periods—allow for an exceptional range of excursions to be made from Barcelona. Most of Catalonia's places of major interest are within easy reach of the city by public transport, but the region should ideally be visited separately from its capital, and in the course of a leisurely journey by car. A detailed description of Catalonia's many riches is beyond the scope of the present guide, and the following paragraphs are intended essentially as suggestions for those planning day and half-day excursions from Barcelona. Excellent plans and pamphlets relating to many of the places listed below are provided by Barcelona's tourist offices (see Practical Information).

A.   South of Barcelona

An essential excursion for anyone interested in the works of Antoní Gaudí is to the **COLONIA GÜELL**, which is situated outside the small township of Santa Coloma de Cervelló, a 20-minute journey by train from Barcelona's Plaça d'Espanya. The colony was built in the 1890s for those working at Eusebi Güell's textile factory, which was transferred here from Barcelona in 1891. The residential area of the colony, with its curious brick buildings, central monument commemorating Güell himself, and its general character of decay, has a quiet haunting charm, but the main object of a visit here is to see Gaudí's unfinished church, which stands on a pine-shaded mound outside. The only part of the ambitious building to be completed was the crypt, an expressively shaped brick structure which rises above the ground like a monstrous crab; the sombre, grotto-like interior features stained-glass windows that open up like butterfly wings, stalls shaped like these insects, and a gloomy museum documenting Güell, Gaudí and the colony. On the way to the colony from Barcelona you could stop off at Sant Joan Despi (alight from the train at Cornellà and then take bus No. 52; another train service links Sant Joan Despi with the Central-Sants and Passeig de Gràcia stations). Next to the railway station of this small town is a villa of 1913–16 (the Torre de la Creu) by Gaudí's faithful collaborator Josep Maria Juyol; this dazzlingly-coloured and fantastically-shaped structure seems to combine Modernisme with the world of science fiction. In the centre of the same town is another villa by Juyol, the Casa Negra of 1915–30, a pastel-coloured structure which is perched over the tiny main square like an enormous butterfly; now serving as the Town Hall, it is at present undergoing drastic restoration.

The coastline of fine sandy beaches which stretches south from Barcelona to below Tarragona is known as the *Costa Dorada or 'Golden Coast', and is significantly cheaper than the Costa Brava to the north. The nearest of its resorts to Barcelona is Castelldefels (a half-hour journey by train from the Central-Sants or Passeig de Gràcia stations), but you would be better off staying on the train for another ten minutes until you reach **SITGES**. Though its beaches are uncomfortably crowded over summer weekends,

Sitges is virtually unique among Catalonia's resorts in not having been vulgarised by foreign tourism, and having retained instead an elegant turn-of-the-century character, as well as numerous monuments of much earlier date. Its sea-front is marked by a palm-lined promenade which is bordered to the north by a small rocky promontory on which stand both its cheerful baroque church and the warren of tiny streets and alleys comprising the old town.

A visit to Sitges is compulsory for anyone seriously interested in Modernisme, for it was here that the painter Santiago Rusiñol had his house and studio and organised the artistic gatherings known as the *Festes Modernistes*. Rusiñol's house and studio, occupying a palace of medieval origin spectacularly situated behind the church, have been perfectly conserved as the **Museu Cau Ferrat**, an atmospheric treasure-trove with dark-blue walls, wooden beam ceilings, and an over-abundance of ceramic decorations, turn-of-the-century mementoes and old master paintings, including a Virgin by El Greco which was paraded through the streets of Sitges during the first of the *Festes Modernistes*. No less interesting is the adjoining **Museu Maricel**, a former private residence which was remodeled by Rusiñol's friend and colleague Miquel Utrillo to house a most varied collection ranging from 14C Catalan altarpieces to murals by Josep Maria Sert. In the lower town of Sitges is the charming 18C residence constituting the *Museu Romàntic, the interior of which has been little altered since the beginning of the 19C.

The large town of **TARRAGONA** lies a further 54km down the coast from Sitges, and can be reached from Barcelona either by train from the Central-Sants or Passeig de Gràcia stations, or by the Bus Line 'Hispania Reus', which has its terminal at the junction of the Passeig de Sant Joan and the Carrer de Diputació. A far more important city than Barcelona in Roman times, Tarragona was made capital of *Hispania Citerior* by the Emperor Augustus; its wines were praised by Pliny, and Martial referred to its sun-baked shores and the fertility of its surroundings. Today a district capital and popular resort, Tarragona has been subject to extensive modern development, but still boasts remarkably extensive Roman remains which are heralded by a magnificent *Triumphal Arch of the 2C AD, situated 4km west of the city on the old Barcelona road (the Via Augusta). 6km further east from the arch is an imposing funerary monument of the same period (the Tower of the Scipios), while 4km north of the city on the Lleída road is a two-storeyed aqueduct over 120 metres long and dating back possibly to Trajan's reign. Within the city itself is a vast amphitheatre beautifully situated in lush parkland rolling directly down to the sea; above the park is an archaeological museum containing an impressive collection of mosaics, sarcophagi, statuary and other Greek and Roman finds. The museum stands at the entrance to the well-preserved medieval town of Tarragona, and is attached to the defensive walls which virtually encircle this part of the town. The dark and evocative warren of streets constituting the medieval quarter is dominated by the **Cathedral** in front of which a lively flea-market is held on Sunday mornings.

The cathedral, which was founded in 1171 and largely completed by the late 14C, has a west façade enlivened by a magnificent Gothic portal of 1289, covered with representations of prophets and apostles by Barthélemy 'le Normand'. The rest of the building, blending Gothic and Romanesque elements, features an especially gloomy interior centred on a fine Romanesque apse, and a splendid 13C–14C cloister with capitals adorned

PASSEIG ARQUEOLÓGICO

Sant Pau

Pal. Arzobispal

Seminario

Catedral

PASSEIG ARQUEOLÓGICO

C. COQUES

AV. DE CATALUNA

AVENIDA DE MARIA CRISTINA

LLANO DE CATEDRAL

Pta S. Antònio

MERCERIA

PASSEIG DE SANT ANTONI

GRANADA

ANTONIO

Pta. del Rosario

PL. DE FORO

VIA DEL IMPERIO

P. PALLOL

C. MAJOR

CAVALLERS

La Sangre

Ayuntamiento

PLAÇA DE LA FONT

NAU

P. DEL REI

Pta. de la Portella

Mus. Arqueologic

BARCELONA

museu Paleo-Cristiano

C. SAN FRANCISCO

C. DE LA LOND DE RIUS

RAMBLA VELLA

PESCADERIA

C. SAN AGUSTI

CALLE D'CIVADA

RAMBLA NOVA

PASSEIG DE LES PALMERES

Parc del Milagro

Roman Amphitheatre

TARRAGONA

0 yards	200
0 metres	200

N

with a myriad of curious carvings, including one of a cat's funeral conducted by rats.

The stretch of the town's ramparts to the west of the cathedral has been laid out with gardens and archaeological finds to form the so-called PASSEIG ARCHEOLOGIC which offers excellent views of the hinterland. Further west (at the end of the Avinguda Ramon y Cajal, the western continuation of the Rambla Nova) is a Paleo-Christian Museum situated next to a Romano-Christian necropolis of the 3C–6C and incorporating fragments of an early Christian basilica.

Within the province of Tarragona, a 28km drive from the city in the Sitges direction, is the coastal resort of **Calafell**, which is worth a visit for the breath-takingly spectacular discothèque known as the *Louis Vega*: occupying an area of over 3000 square miles, and with an outdoor rock-pool and illuminated waterfall, this was created in 1988 by the leading light of the Barcelona designer-bars, Alfredo Arribas.

Among the attractions of the Catalan interior south of Barcelona are the two Cistercian monasteries of **POBLET** and **SANTES CREUS**, both of which are situated in the province of Tarragona; these large and magnificent examples of the sober transitional style known as the Cistercian Gothic are greatly enhanced by their isolated position in green and wooded valleys. Just to the north of Poblet, but in the province of Lleida, is the Cistercian Nunnery of **Santa Maria de Valbonna**, another outstanding if smaller 12C foundation. None of these places is accessible by public transport, but by car they can easily be reached from Barcelona by driving along the A-2 motorway.

Nearer to Barcelona, and accessible by train from the Central-Sants station, is the wine-growing district of *Penedès, which is famous for its champagne-like wines known as Cavas. There is a *Wine Museum at the town of Vilafranca de Penedès, but more interesting are the informative tours of the Freixenet, Codorniu, Segura Viudas and Castellblanc *Bodegas*, all of which are situated at Sant Sadorní d'Anoia, 44km to the south of Barcelona.

B. West of Barcelona

One of the most popular exursions from Barcelona is to the MONASTERY **OF MONTSERRAT**, which lies 60km to the west of the city, and is set against an extraordinary background of eroded sandstone pinnacles that inspired Gaudí's plans for both the Sagrada Família and the church of the Colonia Güell. There is a direct bus service to the monastery from the Plaça d'Espanya, but a more enjoyable approach by public transport is by train from the station of that square. The train will leave you at Aeri Montserrat, from where the journey is completed by a dramatically swung cable-car offering vertiginous views. The Benedictine monastery, which was founded in the 11C, is more interesting for its magnificent views and historical and symbolical associations than for its architecture, most of the complex having been pompously transformed in the late 19C.

In the broad valley below Montserrat is the large industrial town of Terrassa (an hour's train journey from Barcelona from the Plaça de Catalunya station). This is a town of singular ugliness which none the less has managed miraculously to retain a remarkable complex of buildings dating back to the foundation of the town's bishopric in the 6C. This complex of Romanesque and pre-Romanesque buildings is set within a quiet verdant precinct which can be reached from the centre of the town by crossing a tall bridge spanning a lush, fertile enclave. To your left as you enter the precinct is the parish church of Sant Pere, a Romanesque remodelling of a 6C structure (of which the triple apse remains); next to this is a 6C baptistery, which features inside marble arcading, murals of Byzantine inspiration and a Romanesque sarcophagus serving as a font. The third of the buildings is the Church of Santa Maria, which was consecrated in 1122; fragments of Romanesque frescoes can be seen in its apse, but the building is remarkable above all for its altarpiece of Sts. Abdón and Sené, which was painted by Jaume Huguet in 1460. In the centre of the town is a charming small park containing a fantastical white structure of parabolic arches, the Masia Freixa, a former textile factory which was converted in 1907–10 into a family residence for the local textile manufacturer, Josep Freixa Argemí. The architect who undertook the conversion, Lluís Muncunill, was also responsible for the former Aymerich Factory of 1907–08, which is situated at No. 254 of the town's main street, the Rambla d'Egara. This large and curious Moderniste structure, one of the most important industrial buildings in Catalonia, now houses a fascinating and evocative industrial museum.

A visit to Terrassa by local train from Barcelona can be complemented by stopping off at Sant Cugat to see the **Monastery of Sant Cugat del Vallès**, which has a celebrated Romanesque cloister containing 145 carved capitals.

C. North of Barcelona

From Barcelona all the way to the French frontier, over 200km to the north, stretches the Costa Brava, which is served for much of its length (up to Torroella de Montgrí) by buses departing from the Plaça de Medinaceli. The transformation of the coast's tranquil fishing villages into loud and characterless resorts such as Lloret de Mar is vividly descibed in its early stages in Norman Lewis's masterly, *Voices of the Old Sea* (1978). The finer of the resorts are to be found to the north of Palamós, and include Llafranc and Calella, which can be reached by local bus from Palafrugell. The wildest part of the coast is the craggy peninsula on which is situated the now over-prettified fishing-port of **Cadaqués**, a place closely associated with the Surrealist painter Salvador Dalí. Cadaqués is linked by a regular bus service to the inland town of *Figueres, which in turn is accessible from Barcelona by train from the Central-Sants or Passeig de Gràcia stations. Figueres, which was the birth-place of Dalí, is best known for its eccentric and exceptionally popular *Dalí Museum, which was created by Dalí himself within the town's old municipal theatre, and contains the artist's embalmed corpse.

The train and inland route between Barcelona and Figueres passes through **GIRONA**, a large district capital containing one of Catalonia's finest medieval quarters. This quarter is to be found on the sloping eastern side of the

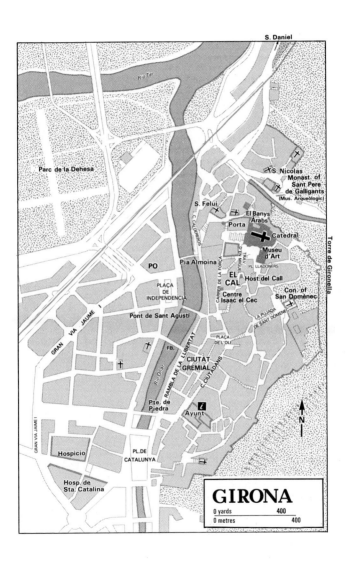

S. Daniel

Rio Ter

Parc de la Dehesa

S. Nicolas
Monast. of
Sant Pere
de Galligants
(Mus. Arqueòlogic)

S. Felui

El Banys
Àrabs
Porta
Catedral

Museu
d'Art

PO

Pia Almoina

PL. LLADONERS

EL
CAL

Host. del Call

Con. of
San Domènec

PLAÇA
DE
INDEPENDENCIA

Centre
Isaac el Cec

LA PUJADA
DE SANT DOMÈNEC

Pont de Sant Agustí

PLAÇA
DE L'OLI

GRAN VIA JAUME I

FB.

CIUTAT
GREMIAL

Pte. de
Piedra

Ayunt

GRAN VIA JAUME I

Hospicio

PL. DE
CATALUNYA

Hosp. de
Sta. Catalina

GIRONA

0 yards 400
0 metres 400

N

Torre de Gironella

C. CALDERERS

TRAV. D'EN MIGUEL

CARRER DE LA FORÇA

RAMBLA DE LA LLIBERTAT

R. Oñar

C. CIUTADANS

River Onyar, and is joined to the neo-classical Plaça de Independencia in the new town by a footbridge (the Pont de Sant Agustí) offering delightful views of a group of tall and brightly-coloured late medieval houses lining the river's eastern banks.

On turning right at the end of the bridge you will come almost immediately to the shaded riverside promenade known as the Rambla de la Llibertat. Behind this stretches the part of the old town sometimes referred to as the Ciutat Gremial after the medieval guilds that once were situated here. As with the Barcelona district of Sant Pere, this is an area combining corners of considerable medieval charm—such as the flight of steps leading up from the quaintly irregular Plaça de l'Oli towards the early Gothic convent of Sant Domènec—with a lingering commerical vitality. In contrast, the medieval area to the left of the Pont de Sant Agustí has the museum-like character of Barcelona's Barri Gotíc, with a stunning wealth of lovingly restored monuments, and a series of narrow pedestrian streets and alleys that seem almost too pretty and well-maintained to be those of a real town.

The second street to your left after crossing the bridge is the long and narrow CARRER DE LA FORÇA, which was once the main thoroughfare of one of Spain's most important Jewish ghettoes. The former synagogue might have gone but much of the claustrophobic character of the ghetto has survived, in particular in the dark and ivy-covered ascending alleys leading off from the Carrer de la Força. Along the first of these, the Carrer de Sant Llorenç, is the entrance to the *El Centre Isaac el Cec, a reconstruction of a Jewish patrician's house containing today a tourist office and an excellent small museum documenting the six centuries of the Jewish presence in Girona.

Turning left at the top of this alley on to the Travesia d'en Miquel you will come to the *Hostelleria del Call*, an intimate and preciously decorated restaurant serving some of the more exquisite and sophisticated of traditional Catalan dishes, such as goose cooked with pears.

The restaurant marks the northern edge of the former ghetto, after which you come out on to a square flanked to the north by the cathedral and to the west by the austere and massive block of the former Bishop's Palace. Since 1979, the 9C–16C palace has housed the **Museu d'Art**, the collections of which—ranging from Gothic alterpieces by the likes of Bernat Martorell and Lluís Borrassà to 19C Catalan masters such as Fortuny and Rusiñol— are beautifully and spaciously arranged in the well-restored medieval rooms. The adjacent **Cathedral**, meanwhile, is one of the great architectural jewels of Catalonia. Its baroque west façade, an unusually dramatic work for this region, features an elaborate frontispiece crowning a steep and monumentally tall flight of steps of 1607–90. The highly theatrical façade shields a single-aisled Gothic interior of unusual harmony and echoing proportions; this atmospherically-lit and elegantly austere interior was begun in the early 14C and brought to completion 100 years later by Antoni Canet and Guillem Bofill. To the left of the entrance is a door leading to the cathedral's excellent small museum (which is celebrated above all for its Romanesque tapestry depicting the Creation), and a Romanesque cloister adorned with among the most important series of Romanesque carvings in western Catalonia. A number of other important early medieval monuments are to be found just to the north of the cathedral, beginning with the curious public baths known wrongly as Els Banys Arabs; though inspired by Moorish and in turn Roman baths, this circular baptistery-like structure was built between the 12C and 13C, long after the Arab domination of the area.

Further north are the neighbouring Romanesque monuments of Sant Nicolau, and the **Monastery of Sant Pere de Galligants**, the latter containing a Museu Arqueòlogic, with local finds from the paleolithic period onwards.

Apart from numerous skiing resorts, dramatic scenery and isolated old villages, the Pyrenees offer an exceptionally large number of well-preserved Romanesque churches, most of which are characterised by tall arcaded belfries. A fine group of these churches can be seen in the Vall de Boí, which now forms part of one Spain's most recent National Parks, that of **Sant-Maurici-Aigüestortes** (which is served by the Barcelona–Viella bus). If using public transport, one of the few practicable day-trips to be made to the Pyrenees from Barcelona is to the towns of **Vic** and **Ripoll**, which are on the railway line from Barcelona to Toulouse. The cathedral at Vic, which was largely rebuilt in the neo-classical period, has a Romanesque crypt and cloister, and a nave decorated with powerful murals by Josep Maria Sert; Sert, a native of the town, will shortly be commemorated here by a museum. A visit should also be made to Vic's Municipal Museum, which was founded in the late 19C, and contains the earliest important collection of Catalan 12C–15C paintings, including works by Ferrer Bassa, Bernat Martorell and Jaume Huguet.

The architectural interest of Ripoll lies almost exclusively in its former monastery church of Santa Maria, a heavily restored Romanesque structure with extensive carvings in its cloister and an outstanding west portal richly carved with grotesques and bands of sculpture illustrating the scriptures.

A journey to Vic and Ripoll could be extended by stopping off at the small industrial town of Manlleu (the railway station immediately following that of Vic), where you can catch a bus to the Pyrenean village of **Rupit** (40km). The journey, through a dazzlingly verdant countryside offering ever more extensive views of distant snow-capped peaks, is remarkably beautiful, and Rupit itself has the reputation of being one of the prettiest mountain villages in Catalonia. It is indeed a showpiece of a village, its ruined castle and perfectly preserved balconied houses perched above a rushing stream which you can cross by way of a perilous-looking swinging footbridge with worn wooden slats. Inevitably, however, tourism has radically changed the character of this village, and its once poor inhabitants have now grown rich by turning their picturesque houses into shops selling 'typical' local specialties and pseudo-crafts objects. Sunday visits to Rupit should be avoided at all costs.

USEFUL CATALAN WORDS

GENERAL

ADÉU, goodbye
L'AGÈNCIA (f) DE VIATGE (m), travel agency
L'AIGUA (f), water
AMB, with
AMPLE, broad
L'ARBRE (m), tree
L'AUTOBÚS, bus
L'AUTOCAR, coach
L'AVINGUDA, avenue
LA BARCA, boat
BÉ, well
BEURE, drink
BON DIA, good day, good morning
EL BOSC, wood
LA BOTTIGA, shop
LA BÚSTIA, post box
EL CALL, Jewish ghetto
EL CARNISSER, butcher's
EL CARRER, street
LA CARRETERA, road
EL COGNOM, surname
EL COMPTE, bill
EL COR, choir
EL DINAR, lunch
EL DINER, money
LES DRASSENS, shipyards
L'ESGLÉSIA, church
ESTRET-A, narrow
LA FESTA, holiday
FRED-A, cold
LA GANA, hunger
EL GARATGE, garage
GRÀCIES (MERCÈS), thank you
L'HABITACIÓ, room
HOLA, hello
L'HORA, time
EL JARDÍ, garden
EL LLADRE, thief
LA LLIURE ESTERLINA, pound sterling
LA MALALTIA, illness
LA MALETA, suitcase
EL MAR, sea
LA MASIA, farmhouse
LA MATÁ, morning
EL MENJADOR, dining-room

EL METGE, doctor
MODERNISME, the Catalan term for what is referred to variously as Art Nouveau, Jugendstil, Sezessionstil and Stile Liberty
LA MUNTANYA, mountain
LA NIT, night
NOUCENTISME (m.), a term coined by Eugeni d'Ors (1882–1954) to describe the work of Catalan artists, architects and writers associated with the revival of classical forms and themes in the first quarter of this century
OBERT-A, open
ON, where
EL PASSEIG, promenade
LA PENSIÓ, boarding-house
PERQUÈ, because
LA PLAÇA, square
PLAURE, to please (SI US PLAU, please)
EL POBLE, village, town
LA RAMBLA, dry riverbed or boulevard
EL RIU, river
LA SARDANA, Catalan dance
LA SETMANA, week
EL SOBRE, envelope
SOLTER-A, single, unmarried
TANCAT, closed
LA TARDA, afternoon
LA TOALETA, toilet (SENYORS, gents; SENYORES, ladies)
EL TREN, train
LES VACANCES, holidays
EL VIATGE, journey

CHRISTIAN NAMES

CARLES, Charles
FERRAN, Ferdinand
JAUME, James
JOAN, John
PAU, Paul
PERE, Peter

DAYS OF WEEK

DILLUNS, Monday
DIMARTS, Tuesday

DIMECRES, Wednesday
DIJOUS, Thursday
DIVENDRES, Friday
DISSABTE, Saturday
DIUMENGE, Sunday

MONTHS OF THE YEAR

GENER, January
FEBRER, February
MARÇ, March
ABRIL, April
MAIG, May
JUNY, June
JULIOL, July
AGOST, August
SEPTEMBRE, September
OCTUBRE, October
NOVEMBRE, November
DESEMBRE, December

NUMERALS

UN (*m.*)/UNA(*f.*), one
DOS (*m.*)/DUES (*f.*), two
TRES, three
QUATRE, four
CINC, five
SIS, six
SET, seven
VUIT, eight
NOU, nine

DEU, ten
ONZE, eleven
DOTZE, twelve
TRETZE, thirteen
CATORZE, fourteen
QUINZE, fifteen
SETZE, sixteen
DISSET, seventeen
DIVUIT, eighteen
DINOU, nineteen
VINT, twenty
VINT-I-UN (I-UNA), twenty-one
TRENTA, thirty
TRENTA-UN (UNA), thirty-one
QUARANTA, fourty
CINQUANTA, fifty
SEIXANTA, sixty
SETANTA, seventy
VUITANTA, eighty
NORANTA, ninety
CENT, one hundred
CENT UNO (UNA), one hundred and one
DOS-CENTS (DUES-CENTES), two hundred
MIL, one thousand
DOS MIL (DUES MIL), two thousand
MIL CENT, one thousand one hundred
UN MILIÓ, a million

A CHRONOLOGY OF THE MEDIEVAL RULERS OF BARCELONA

Wilfred the Hairy (878–897)
Wilfredo Borrell (897–911)
Sunyer (897–947)
Borrell II (947–992)
Ramón Borrell (992–1018)
Berenguer Ramón I (1018–35)
Ramón Berenguer I the Old (1035–76)
Ramón Berenguer II (1076–82)
Berenguer Ramón (1076–96)
Ramón Berenguer III the Great (1096–1131)
Ramón Berenguer IV (1131–62)
Alfons I of Barcelona (1162–96)
Pere I the Catholic (1196–1213)
Jaume I the Conqueror (1213–76)
Pere II the Great (1276–85)
Alfons II (1285–91)
Jaume II the Just (1291–1327)
Alfons III (1327–36)
Pere III the Ceremonious (1336–87)
Joan I (1387–96)
Martín I the Humane (1396–1410)
Ferran I of Trastámara (1412–16)
Alfonso IV the Magnanimous (1416–1458)
Joan II (1458–78)
Ferran II the Catholic (1479–1516)

FURTHER READING

General

The most outstanding recent intoduction to Barcelona in English is Felipe Fernández-Armesto's stimulating, scholarly and delightfully perverse *Barcelona: a Thousand Years of the City's Past* (London, 1991); a thematic rather than a straightforwardly chronological account, this broadly-based work skilfully interweaves political, social and cultural history. Colm Tóibín's *Homage to Barcelona* (London, 1990) provides a more lightweight and hackneyed portrait of the city, but is highly readable. The less demanding traveller might also appreciate Alastair Boyd's rather precious *The Essence of Catalonia: Barcelona and its Region* (London, 1988).

Spanish readers should acquire a copy of Alexandre Cirici's *Barcelona paso a paso* (Barcelona, 1st ed., 1971), a classic of guidebook literature to be ranked with Lorenzetti's guide to Venice; this book, which exists also in a Catalan edition, is not to be confused with Christopher Turner's pedestrian work of the same title (*Barcelona Step by Step*, London, 1991). Less well known, but no less worthy of attention is José María Carandell's *Nueva Guía Secreta de Barcelona* (Barcelona, 1982), which is full of recondite information about the Old City, in particular relating to marginal life in the 1960s, 70s and early 80s. An excellent series of walks through the Old City is described in *Descubrir Ciutat Vella: 14 itinerarios urbanos* (Barcelona, 1990), a small but very informative booklet published by Barcelona's Town Hall. Carlos Soldevila's heavy tome entitled *Barcelona* (1st ed., Barcelona, 1951) is still available, but is of interest principally for its superlative black and white photographs. A general work on Barcelona which combines beautiful literary evocation with penetrating analysis and insight is Manuel Vázquez Montalbán's *Barcelonas* (Barcelona, 1990; also available in a Catalan edition). Anyone interested in an alternative and cynical account of the Barcelona of 1992 should read this same prolific author's published dialogue with the radical lawyer Eduardo Moreno; entitled *Barcelona, cap a on vas?* (Barcelona, 1991; in Catalan only), this polemical work compares the urban policies of the socialist major of Barcelona, Joan Maragall, with those of his Francoist predecessor Porcioles. Montalbán's entertaining novels featuring the gourmet detective Pepe Carvalho should also be read for the portrait they give of modern Barcelona; one of the finest of these, *Southern Seas* has been published by Pluto Books in an English paperback edition (London, 1986).

Another Catalan writer of today whose works have dealt extensively with Barcelona is the novelist Eduardo Mendoza. His exceptionally lively and enjoyable novel *City of Marvels* (1st English ed., 1989) provides a fantastical but solidly researched portrait of Barcelona between the World Exhibition of 1888 and the International Exhibition of 1929 (much of the research for this book was later re-used for his excellent work of non-fiction, *Barcelona Modernista* [Barcelona, 1989], which he wrote with his sister Cristina). Mendoza's slighter and more recent novel *Sin Noticias de Gurb* (Barcelona, 1990) is a witty satirical look at the Barcelona of the near future. A less accessible Barcelona novelist, and one as yet untranslated into English, is Juan Marsé, whose novels often feature the impoverished Barcelona district of his childhood, most notably, *Si te dices que caí* (Barcelona, 1973); theme. The theme of Barcelona's immigrant community is beautifully treated in Marsé's *Ultimas tardes con Teresa* (Barcelona,

1966). Juan Goytisolo's *Juan the Landless* trilogy (*Marks of Identity, Count Julian and Juan the Landless*; translated into English in Serpent's Tail paperbacks, 1989–91) make for similarly difficult reading, but include fascinating cameos of Barcelona life; recollections of Goytisolo's childhood, adolescence, and sexually adventurous Barcelona youth are to be found in the first volume of his memoirs, *Forbidden Territory* (Ist English edition, London, 1989). André Genet's *A Thief's Journal* (1st English ed., London, 1964) includes a celebrated account of lowlife in the city's Barri Xinés, while Raul Nuñez's amusing if artistically undistinguished *Lonely Hearts Club* (1st English edition, London, 1990) gives a more up-to-date account of the seedier side to the city. Another recent novel to feature Barcelona as a setting is Colm Tóibín's *The South* (London, 1990), which might be enjoyed by some for its evocations of the city's streets and hidden corners.

Art and Architecture

Few other cities are so well served as Barcelona for architectural guides and surveys. The fundamental work is the *Catàleg del patrimoni arquitec-tònic historico-artistic de Barcelona* (Ajuntament de Barcelona, 1987), which includes photographs and location maps of most buildings of archi-tectural interest within the city centre; a new edition is currently being prepared to deal more thoroughly with the architecture of the suburbs and to take into account the buildings of the last few years. Less expensive and marginally less heavy and unwieldy is the *Arquitectura de Barcelona* (Col-legi d' Arquitectes de Catalunya, 1990), which features a broad selection of the most interesting of the city's buildings, complete with ground plans, elevations, photographs and lengthy, subjective descrip-tions; the text is in Catalan, Spanish and English, but is often barely comprehensible in any language. The earlier, more popular edition of this guide (*Guía de Arquitectura de Barcelona*; Barcelona, 1987) is far smaller in size and rather more practical for carrying around the city. A book for consultation only is J. Fabre *et al, Monuments de Barcelona* (Barcelona, 1984), a catalogue of the city's public statuary which includes much inter-esting information regarding not only the works themselves but also the subjects of the statues.

Numerous architectural and other guides to Barcelona are published by the Barcelona firm of Gustavo Gili. The finest of all of these is perhaps R. Lacuesta's and A. González's *Arquitectura modernista en Catalunya* (Bar-celona, 1990), a detailed but practically-sized guide to the numerous art nouveau monuments in Barcelona and its surroundings. Designers, and those with an interest in the design aspects of modern Barcelona, will find some useful adresses, if little else, in the *Barcelona Design Guide (Gustavo Gili, 1990)*, which has texts in Spanish and English. The city's most recent architectural developments and projects are published in Bohigas, Oriol, et al., Barcelona, City and Architecture, 1980–92 (Barcelona, 1991).

Among the general works on Catalan art and architecture, the best introduction in English to the early medieval paintings is Charles L. Kuhn's *Romanesque Mural Painting of Catalonia* (Cambridge, 1930); further infor-mation on the extraordinary Romanesque murals to be found in Barcelona's Museu d' Art Antigua can be gleaned from the chapter on Catalonia in C.R. Dodwell's *Painting in Europe, 880–1200* (Harmondsworth, 1971). Gothic and early Renaissance painting in Catalonia are covered respectively in volumes VII and XII of C.R. Post's *A History of Spanish Painting* (Princeton, 1938 and 1958). A readable account of the architecture of this period is

Alexandre Cirici's *L'art gotic català: l'arqutectura als segles XV i XVI* (Barcelona, 1979). For late Renaissance and baroque art in Cataonia, see Arnau Puig's *Història de l'art Català del Rinaixement al Barroc* (Barcelona, 1970). The great majority of the publications on Catalan art and architecture are devoted to the years between the World and International Exhibitions, and include the exemplary exhibition catalogue, *Homage to Barcelona: The City and its Art, 1888–1936* (London, Hayward Gallery, 1986), which features a detailed bibliography. For a charming introduction to the Barcelona art world of the turn-of-the-century you should read Josep Pla's *Santiago Rusiñol i el seu temps* (Barcelona 1961; 1st Spanish ed., Barcelona 1989); an enjoyable account of this period written by one of its protagonists is Miquel Utrillo's *Història anecdòtica del Cau Ferrat* (Sitges, 1989). The literature on Gaudí is particularly extensive, and very variable; a good short introduction with a select bibliography is David Mower's *Gaudí* (London, 1977); to the series of *Guías de arquitectura* published by Gustavo Gili has recently been added Xavier Güell's *Gaudí* (Barcelona, 1991), a useful book for on-the-spot investigation of the buildings. Monographs on the other leading *Moderniste* architects include María Lluisa Borràs' *Domènech i Montaner: architecto del modernismo* (Barcelona, 1971); Ignací Solà-Morales *Jujol* (Barcelona, 1990); and Enric Jardí i Casany's *Puig i Cadafalch, arquitecte, polític i historíador de l'art* (Barcelona, 1975). Jardí i Casany was also the author of *El noucentismo Catalan*, a thorough and very accessible study of the subject. John Richardson's masterly *A life of Picasso, vol. 1: 1881–1906* (London, 1991), the first of a projected four-volume biography of the artist, offers a much-needed reassessment of Picasso's earliest years,as well as a wealth of new information on the Barcelona of Picasso's youth; the traveller to Barcelona could supplement this with José María Carandell's excellent pamphlet, *Guía de la Barcelona de Picasso* (Barcelona, 1982). The best general biography of Picasso remains the enjoyable if highly uncritical *Picasso* by Roland Penrose (1st ed. 1958), who was also the author of a short and lively monolograph on Miró in the Thames and Hudson *World of Art* series (London, 1970). Ian Gibson, the biographer of García Lorca, has recently begun work on what will be the most enthusiastic biography of Salvador Dalí, but until that is completed you would be best off reading the artist's entertaining autobiographical musings, *Diary of a Genius* (London, 1960) and *My Secret Life*, by Salvador Dalí (New York, 1948). Similarly for Tàpies, you should turn to Tàpies' own *Memoria Personal* (Barcelona 1977; 1st Spanish ed. Barcelona, 1984). Finally, anyone interested in the Barcelona design world of today should try and read Guy Julier's jargon-filled and misleadingly titled *Modern Spanish Design* (London, 1991), a book which is almost exclusively devoted to Catalonia.

Food, Wine and Bar-life

The standard work on Catalan food in English is Colman Andrews' exhaustive and scholarly *Catalan Food* (London, 1989); also good is the section on Catalonia in Patience Gray's culinary classic, *Honey from a Weed* (London, 1986). Among the more prolific writers on the subject in Spanish are Nèstor Luján (see, for instance his *La Cocina Moderna en Catalunya* (Madrid, 1985) and Vázquez Montalban, the latter being the author of *La Cocina Catalana* (Barcelona, 1979) and *Las Recetas de Pepe Carvalho (Barcelona, 1989)*. For wines you should read the section on Catalonia in Jan Read's *The Wines of Spain* (London, 1982). The most recent guide to Barcelona's bars is Àngel Juez and Oriol Comas, *Noche de Bares* (Barcelona, 1990), which has an infuriatingly jokey text in Spanish and English; more useful, though now difficult to obtain, is *Barcelona Bar* (Barcelona, 1987), a work published by Barcelona's Town Hall.

INDEX

Topographical names appear in CAPITALS, and names of people in roman. Places outside Barcelona are sub-indexed under ENVIRONS.

ADMINISTRATIVE PAVILION 135
Aguilar, Sergi 153
al-Mansur 11, 61, 82
Albeniz 132
ALFONS XIII PAVILION 115
Alfonso XIII 134, 150
Amadó i Cercós, Maria Roser 128
Amargós i Samaranch 109
Amat, Fernando 130
Amat, Jacinto 130
Amat i Junyet, Manuel 46
Amigó, Bonaventura 126
Amigó, Joaquim Bassegoda 126
Andersen, Hans Christian 19, 49
ANELLA OLÍMPICA 119
Arbei, Pere 101
ARENES, LES 114
Arnau, Eusebi 60, 127, 129, 132, 137, 138, 139
Arribas, Alfredo 99, 116, 139, 145, 159
Arriola, Andreu 114
Artal, Joaquín Miguel 67
Artell, Roser Segímon i 130
Atché, Rafael 97, 108, 110
Aulèstia, Salvador 98
Aulenti, Gae 118
AVINGUDA D'ICÀRIA 113
AVINGUDA DE GAUDÍ 134
AVINGUDA DE L'ESTADI 119
AVINGUDA DE LA CATEDRAL 64
AVINGUDA DE LA REINA MARIA CRISTINA 115
AVINGUDA DE MIRAMAR 122
AVINGUDA DE VILANOVA 111
AVINGUDA DEL PARAL-LEL 95
AVINGUDA DELS MONTANYANS 117
AVINGUDA DIAGONAL 131
AVINGUDA PORTAL DE L'ÀNGEL 78
Azua, Fèlix d' 115, 125

Bach, Jaume 146
Balaguer, Víctor 94
Ballarín, Manuel 79, 127
Balthus 122
BANC VITALICI D'ESPANYA 126
BANCO ESPAÑOL DE CREDITO 125
Barceló, Miquel 131
Bargués, Arnau 62, 69, 70

BARRI GÒTIC 55
BARRI XINÈS 53, 92
BARRIO ANDALUZ 116
BARRIO BAJO 142
Barsa, Tomàs 67
Bassa, Ferrer 118, 163
Beatles, The 114
Beltran 130
Berenguer, Canon Vila 61
Berenguer i Mestres, Francesc 133, 145, 150
Bermejo, Bartolomé 62, 63, 119
Beuys, Joseph 90
Blanca of Anjou 59
Blay, Miquel 81, 106, 114
Blay, Pere 77
Bocabella, Josep M. 133
Bofill, Guillem 162
Bofill, Ricardo 111, 114, 145
Bohigas, Oriol 112, 150
Bona, Eusebi 142
Bonafè, Macià 62
Bonell i Costa, Esteve 150
Bonet, Jordi 133
Bonet i Bertran, Pep 115, 129
Bonifaci, Lluís 91
Borbán, Lorenzo García 144
Borgoña, Juan de 62
Borrassà, Lluís 118, 162
Boscà, Joan Almugaver 76
Bosch, Andreu 91
Botero, Fernando 109
Botticelli, Sandro 142
Bover, Joesp 101
Brossa, Joan 150
Bru, Anye 119
Bru, Lluís 81
Bruant, Aristide 79
Bru i Salelles, Lluís 127
Brull, Joan 106
Bugutti, Domenico 150
Buïgas, Carles 112, 115, 116
Buïgas i Monravà, Gaietà 97
Buixareu, Josep 102
Bulla, José López 48
Busquets i Sindreu, Xavier 64

CAIXA DE PENSIONS PER A LA VELLESA I D'ESTALVIS 80

Calatrava, Santiago 151
Calder, Alexander 90, 122
Calvet, Arnau 148
Campeny, Damia 101, 102
Campmany, Ricard de 54
Canals, Ricard 80, 107
Canamàs 58
Canet, Antoni 162
Canonge, Fructuòs 49
Canyelles 101
CAPELLA, DE SANT LLÀTZER 92
Carandell, José María 93, 102
Carbonell, Antoni 59
Carbonell, Guillem 59
Carbonell, Pere 97
Carcassó 97
Caro, Anthony 90
Carreño, Juan 119
CARRER AMPLE 74
CARRER BASSES DE SANT PERE 82
CARRER CORREU VELL 75
CARRER D'ARAGÓ 128
CARRER D'AVINYÓ 74
CARRER D'EN GIGNÀS 74
CARRER DE ALSINA 73
CARRER DE ARIBAU 136
CARRER DE BAILÈN 132
CARRER DE CARDERS 83
CARRER DE CASANOVA 138
CARRER DE CASP 135
CARRER DE COMTAL 80
CARRER DE CONSELL DE CENT 126
CARRER DE FERLANDINA 89
CARRER DE FERRAN 73
CARRER DE HOSPITAL 91
CARRER DE JOAQUIM COSTA 89
CARRER DE LA BOQUERÍA 72
CARRER DE LA CANUDA 43
CARRER DE LA CERA 93
CARRER DE LA LLIBRETERIA 57
CARRER DE LA PORTAFERRISSA 45
CARRER DE LA PRINCESA 83
CARRER DE LA RIERETA 93
CARRER DE LES CAPUTXES 87
CARRER DE LES JONQUERES 80
CARRER DE LLANÇÀ 115
CARRER DE LLEDÓ 76
CARRER DE LLEIDA 123
CARRER DE MALLORCA 129
CARRER DE MARINA 135
CARRER DE MARLET 71
CARRER DE MONTCADA 83
CARRER DE MONTSIÓ 78
CARRER DE PARÍS 138
CARRER DE PETRITXOL 72
CARRER DE PROVENÇA 131
CARRER DE RAURIC 73

CARRER DE RIVADENEYRA 78
CARRER DE SANT DOMÈNEC
  DEL CALL 71
CARRER DE SANT PACIÀ 93
CARRER DE SANT PAU 93
CARRER DE SANT PERE MÉS ALT 81
CARRER DE SANT PERE MÉS BAIX 82
CARRER DE SANT PERE MITJÀ 82
CARRER DE SANTA ANNA 78
CARRER DE SICÍLIA 132
CARRER DE VALÈNCIA 132
CARRER DEL ARC DEL TEATRE 52
CARRER DEL BISBE 65
CARRER DEL CALL 71
CARRER DEL CARME 45, 90
CARRER DEL COMERC 87
CARRER DEL PARADÍS 60
CARRER DEL PI 72
CARRER DEL REC 87
CARRER DEL REGOMIR 75
CARRER DEL ROSELLÓ 131, 138
CARRER DEL SOTS-TINENT
  NAVARRO 57
CARRER DEL TIGRE 89
CARRER DEL VEGUER 57
CARRER DEL XUCLÁ 45
CARRER DELS BANYS NOUS 72
CARRER DELS COMTES 60
CARRER DELS ESCUDELLERS 53
CARRER DELS TALLERS 88
CARRER GIRALT I PELLICER 83
CARRER HOSTAL D'EN SOL 75
CARRER MONJUÏC DEL BISBE 65
CARRER MONTALEGRE 90
CARRER NOU DE LA RAMBLA 50, 95
CARRER SANT FELIP NERI 66
CARRER SANT JAUME GIRALT 83
CARRER SANT RAMON DEL CALL 71
CARRER SOMBRERERS 86
CARRER TORRES I AMAT 89
Carreras, Joan 127
Carvalho, Pepe 31
CASA AMATLLER 127
CASA BATLLÓ 128
CASA BELLESGUARD 147
CASA BONET 127
CASA BRUNO QUADROS 47
CASA CALVET 136
CASA CASAS 130
CASA CLARIANA PADELLÀS 57
CASA COMALAT 132
CASA COMPANYS 138
CASA DE CONVALESCÈNCIA 90
CASA DE LA CIUTAT 69
CASA DE LA PAPALLONA 115
CASA DE LA PIA ALMONINA 64
CASA DE LACTÀNCIA 137, 138

CASA DE LES PUNXES 132
CASA DEL BARÓ DE CASTELLET 84
CASA DEL GREMI DELS
    CALDERERS 65
CASA DEL GREMI DELS
    SABATERS 66
CASA DELS GUALBES 75
CASA DOLCET 148
CASA FUSTER 131
CASA GOLFERICHS 136
CASA GREMIAL VELERS 81
CASA LLEÓ MORERA 127
CASA LLOPIS BOFILL 132
CASA MACAYA 132
CASA MARCH DE REUS 54
CASA MARTÍ 78
CASA MILÀ 129
CASA MONTANER 129
CASA MULLERAS 127
CASA PASCUAL I PONS 126
CASA PLANELLS 132
CASA SAYRACH 139
CASA SERRA 139
CASA TERRADES 132
CASA THOMAS 129
CASA VICENS 146
CASA-MUSEU GAUDÍ 150
CASA-MUSEU VERDAGUER 149
CASAL DE SANT JORDI 136
Casals, Pau 132
Casas, Ramon 20, 46, 79, 93, 106, 130,
    148
CASES D'EN XIFRÉ 102
CASES DELS CANONGES 66
CASES ROCAMORA 126
CASTELL DE MONTJUÏC 122
Catà i Catà, Enric 117, 125
CATALANA DE GAS I
    ELECTRICITAT 78
CATEDRAL 60
CATHEDRAL MUSEUM 63
CEMETERI VELL DE BARCELONA
    113
CENTRE OF THEATRE STUDIES 51
CERCLE DE SANT LUC 72
Cerdà, Ildefons 18, 124
Cerdà, Josep 126
Cermeño, Juan M. 122
Cermeño, Pedro M. 112
Cervantes 71
CHAPEL OF ST. MICHAEL 143
Charles III 90
Charles IV 150
Charles V 74
Chillida, Eduardo 58, 122, 150
Chopin 42
CINE COLISEUM 136

Cirici, Alexandre 129
Cirici, Cristià 116, 129
CIUDAD UNIVERSITARIA 144
Clarà, Josep 70, 148, 107
Clavé, Josep Torres i 82, 89
Clotet, Lluís 129, 148
Cobi 108, 151
Coderch de Sentmenat, José
    Antonio 144, 145, 146
COLEGI DE CIRURGIA 90
Colet, Dr Melicor 139
COLLEGE OF SANT ANGELO 49
COLONIA GÜELL 156
Columbus, Christopher 58
Comillas, Marquis of 51
Companys, Lluís 67, 121, 122
Conill, Bonaventura 148
CONSELL DE CENT 71
CONVENT OF SANTA MÒNICA 55
CONVENTO DEL REDEMPTOR 147
Correa i Ruiz, Federico 144
Cortïs, Pepe 131
Costa, Esteve Bonell i 150
Count Wilfred II 10

Dacian 62
Dalí, Salvador 50, 107, 108, 149, 160
Dalmau, Josep 45
Dalmau, Lluís 119
Darder, Antoni 125
Dario, Rubén 79
Desvalls i d'Ardena, Joan Antoni 150
Días, Carlos 90
DIOCESAN MUSEUM 64
Domènech i Estapà, Josep 78, 111, 129,
    147
Domènech i Montaner, Lluís 64, 81, 93,
    99, 104, 107, 110, 128, 129, 131, 134,
    135
Domènech, Puigcercós, Ignasi 32
Domènech i Roura, Pere 121, 125, 134
DRASSANES 97
DUANA VELLA 102
Dubuffet 90
Duchamp 122
Duran i Reynals, Raimon 143

Echevarría, André Calzada 115
EDIFICI DE LA UNIVERSITAT 136
EDIFICI DE LLOTJA 101
EDITORIAL MONTANER I SIMON 128
Einstein 102
EIXAMPLE 124
Eiximenis, Francesc 31
EL BORN 87
El Greco 119, 157
ELS QUATRE GATS 79

ENVIRONS:
CADAQUÉS 160
CALAFELL 159
CALELLA 160
COSTA DORADA 156
DALÍ MUSEUM 160
FIGUERES 160
GIRONA 160
LLAFRANC 160
MONASTERY OF MONSERRAT 159
MONASTERY OF SANT CUGAT
DEL VALLÈS 160
MONASTERY OF SANT PERE DE
GALLIGANTS 162
POBLET 159
RUPIT 163
SANT-MAURICI-AIGÜESTORTES
163
SANTA MARIA DE VALBONNA 159
SANTES CREUS 159
SITGES 156
TARRAGONA 157
TERRASSA 159
VALL DE BOÍ 163
VIC 163
WINE MUSEUM, VILAFRANCA DE
PENEDÈS 159
Ernst, Max 122
Escaler, Lambert 47
ESCUELAS DE LA SAGRADA
FAMÍLIA 134
ESGLÉSIA DE BETLEM 45
Espinagosa, Juan 82
ESTACIÓ BARCELONA CENTRAL-
SANTS 24, 138
ESTACIÓ DE FRANÇA 24, 102
ESTACIÓ DEL NORD 111

FABRA OBSERVATORY 147
Fabre, Jaume 61
Fàbregas, Joan 101
Fages i Ferrer, Antoni 96
Falguerra i Sivilla, Antoni de 137, 138
Falqués i Urpí, Pere 48, 104, 110, 111,
134, 137, 138
Fària i Monteys, Pere Garcia 98
Ferdinand II the Catholic (Ferran II) 58
Ferdinand VII 103
Ferran, Agulló 32
Ferrer, Francesc 20
Ferrer, Pere 67
Fiter, Antoni Serra 127
Fiveller, Joan 76
Flaugier, Josep 45, 89
Fleming, Sir Alexander 90
Florensa i Ferrer, Adolf 99, 115
Flotats, Joan 108

Foix, Terenci 88
Folch i Torres, Joaquim 117
Folguera, Francesc 116
FONT DEL GENI CATALÁ 102
FONT MÀICA 115
Fontana 90
Fontserè i Mestres, Josep 87, 103, 108,
108 , 109
Ford, Richard 61
Forestier, Jean C.N. 104, 113
Fortuny, Marià 105, 162
FOSSAR DE LA PEDRERA 121
FOSSAR DE LES MORERES 87
Foster, Norman 147
Fragonard 142
Francis, Sam 122
Freixa Argemí, Josep 160
Freixes, D. 152
Friedrich, Johann 62
FUNDACIÓ MIRÓ 121
FUNICULAR VALLVIDIERA 148
Fuxà, Manuel 101, 108, 110

Gaig, Josep 75
GALERIA DE CATALANS
ILLUSTRES 77
Galí i Camprubí, Beth 114, 121
Galí, Francesc 101, 105, 117
Galtes, Charles 61
Gamot, Josep 97, 108
Ganchegui, Luis Paña 138
Gardner, Ava 102
Gargallo, Pablo 81
Gargallo, Pau 107, 121
GATCPAC 89, 145
Gaudí, Antoni 49, 50, 51, 72, 107, 108,
109, 128, 130, 132, 133, 134, 135, 142,
146, 147, 149, 150, 156, 159
Gautier, Théophile 42
Genet 93
GERMAN PAVILION 116
Gil i Serra, Pau 134
Gimeno, Francesc 107
Ginesi, Antoni 113
Giráldez Dávila, Guillermo 144
Girona, Manuel 61, 79
Goday i Casals, Josep 100
GOTHIC HALL 101
Goytisolo, Juan 92, 98
GRÀCIA 107, 145
GRAN VIA DE LES CORTS
CATALANES 135, 136
Granados, Enric 132, 139
Granell i Barrera, Jeroni 126, 127
Graner Prat, Josep 115
Grassi, Francesc Folguera i 136
Grau, Jaume Torres i 78, 100

Gual, Jaume Sabartés i 84
Guàrdia i Vial, Francesc 129
Güell, Count Eusebi 47, 50, 51, 142, 149, 156
Güell i Ferrer, Joan 51
Guimerà, Àngel 43, 73
Gurb, Bishop Arnau de 65
Gurri, Salvador 101

Hassardi, Rabbi Samuel 71
HIDROELÈCTRICA DE CATA-LUNYA 111
Homar, Gaspar 129
HOSPITAL DE LA SANTA CREU I DE SANT PAU 134
HOTEL ESPAÑA 93
Huguet, Jaume 58, 59, 60, 63, 160, 163

INEFC 120
Iñigo, Pedro López 144
INSTITUT DE CULTURA I BIBLIO-TECA POPULAR PER A LA DON 82
Isabel Cristina of Brunswick 74
Isabel of Portugal 74
Isabella I the Catholic 58
Isozaki, Arata 121

Jackson, Michael 44
Jaume I 42, 69
Jaume II 12, 59, 143
Jaume II 61
Joan II 14, 59
Joan, Pere 67, 68, 76
Jujol, Alfons 132
Jujol, Josep Maria 114, 115, 128, 130, 132, 149, 156
Juli, Josep 45, 91
Julià, J.M. 153
Julier, Guy 138
Juyol, Alfons 127

Kelly, Edward 152
Kelly, Ellsworth 150
Klee, Paul 90

LA MERCÈ, CHURCH OF 74
LA RAMBLA 42
Labarta 101
LABERINT D'HORTA 150
Le Corbusier (Jeanneret) 143
Léger 122
Lewis, Norman 160
Liechtenstein, Roy 150
Llimona, Joan 110
Llimona, Josep 65, 72, 104, 106, 111, 115, 135
Llinàs, Josep 123, 148

Llobet, Pere 69, 101
Lloret i Homs, Joaquim 145
Lluís, Dalmau 13
Llupià, Josep Francesc Ferrer de 43
Lochner, Michael 61, 62
Luna, Bigas 131
Lynch, David 139

Macaulay, Rose 61
Macià, Francesc 67
Mackay, David 112, 150
Madonna 146
Madorell i Rius, Miquel 136
Magallán, José Luis Sanz 144,
MANZANA DE LA DISCORDIA 126
Maragall, Joan 73, 83
Maragall, Pasqual 112
Maragliano, Mario 127
Marés, Frederic 60, 70, 92, 104
Mariscal, Javier 47, 54, 99, 108, 116, 131, 147, 151
MARKET OF THE BORN 87
Marti I 44, 58
Martorell, Bernat 112, 162, 163
Martorell, Josep 150
Martorell i Montells, Joan 132, 133, 143
Martorell i Peña 109
Martorell Puig, Bernardí 147
Mas, Bartolomeu 72
Mas i d'Ordal, Josep 45
Mas i Vila, Josep 69
Massanés, José 102
Mateu, Miquel 90
Mateu, Pau 67, 68
Meifrèn 106
Méndez, Nicomedes 54, 67
Mendoza, Eduardo 104, 124
Mercat de la Llibertat 145
MERCAT DE SANTA CATERINA 83
MERCAT DELS FLORES 123
Merz 90
Mestres, Josep Oriol 61, 73, 77
Milà i Camps, Pere 129, 130
Milà i Sagnier, Alfonso 144, 147
Millares 122
Mir, Joaquim 80, 107
MIRADOR DEL REI MARTÍ 59
Miralda, Antoni 97
Miralles, Francesc 106
Miranda, V. 152
Miró, Joan 45, 47, 50, 70, 72, 73, 121, 122
Mitjans i Miró, Francesc 144
Molina, Francesc Daniel 46, 74, 99, 102
MOLL DE LA FUSTA 99
MONASTERY OF SANT AGUSTÍ 91
Monpart, Isidro 67
Monserdà, Enric 132

Montcada i de Pinós, Elisenda de 143
Montgroí, Torroella de 107
MONUMENT A COLOM 95
MONUMENT AL DOCTOR ROBERT 135
Moore, Henry 122
Mora, Gabriel 146
Moratín, Leandro 72
Morton, H.V. 46
Motherwell 122
Muncunill, Lluís 160
MUSEU ARQUEOLÒGIC 123
MUSEU CAU FERRAT 157
MUSEU CLARÀ 148
MUSEU D'ART DE CATALUNYA 117
MUSEU D'ARTE CONTEMPORANI 89
MUSEU D'ART MODERN 104
MUSEU D'ARTS, INDÚSTRIES I TRADICIONS 117
MUSEU D'HISTORIA DE LA CIUTAT 58
MUSEU DE CERA 54
MUSEU DE CERÀMICA 142
MUSEU DE GEOLOGIA 109
MUSEU DE LA CIÈNCIA 146
MUSEU DE LA MÚSICA 132
MUSEU DE ZOOLOGIÁ 110
MUSEU DEL CALÇAT ANTIC 66
MUSEU DEL EXERCIT 122
MUSEU ETNOLÒGIC 123
MUSEU FREDERIC MARÉS 60
MUSEU I CENTRE D'ESTUDIS DE L'ESPORT DR MELCIOR COLET 139
MUSEU MARICEL 157
MUSEU MARITÍM 98
MUSEU PEDAGÓGIC DE CIENCIAS NATURALS 49
MUSEU PICASSO 84, 85
MUSEU ROMÀNTIC 157
MUSEU SENTIMENTAL 60
MUSEU TAURI 135
MUSEU TÈXTIL I DE LA INDUMENT-ÀRIA 85

Nagel, Andrés 138
Navarro, Vicenç 65
Nebot i, Francesc de P. 125, 136, 142
Nicholson, Jack 51
Nicolau, Simon 58
Nobas, Rossend 97
Nogués, Xavier 116
Nola, Robert de 31
Nolas, Rossend 108
Nonell, Isidre 80, 107
NOU MONESTIR BENEDICTÍ 143
Nunces, José María 89
Nuñez y Navarro 137

Nuñez, Raul 47

Obiols, Josep 101
Oldenburg, Cla es 90
Oliver 101
Ollegarius 62
OLOT 106
OLYMPIC STADIUM 121
Ordeig, Gabriel 132
Ordóñez, Bartolomé 62
Ors y Rovira, Eugeni d' 46, 80, 107
Orwell, George 44, 125, 133
Oscoz, Pedro Cendoya 117
Oviedo, Juan de 60

Padró, Tomàs 102
Pagès, Francesc 108
PALAU BERENGUER D'AGUILAR 84
PALAU CENTELLES 73
PALAU DE COMUNUCACIONS I TRANSPORTS 115
PALAU DE JUSTICIA 111
PALAU DE LA COMTESSA DE PALAMÓS 77
PALAU DE LA GENERALITAT 66
PALAU DE LA MÚSICA CATALANA 81
PALAU DE LA VIRREINA (THE VICEREINE'S PALACE) 46
PALAU DE LOS MARQUESES DE LLIÓ 85
PALAU DEL LLOCTINENT 59
PALAU DEL TREBALL 115
PALAU EPISCOPAL 65
PALAU GÜELL 50
PALAU MOJA 45
PALAU NACIONAL 117
PALAU QUADRAS 132
PALAU REIAL DE PEDRALBES 142
PALAU REIAL MAJOR 59
PALAU SESSA LARRARD 75
Pallás, Paulino 48
PARC DE L'ESPANYA INDUSTRIAL 138
PARC DE LA CIUTADELLA 103
PARC DE LA CREUETA DEL COLL 150
PARC DEL CLOT 152
PARC ZOOLÒGIC 108
PARK GÜELL 149
Pasco i Mensas, Josep 130
Pasqual, Lluís 146
PASSATGE DE LA CONCEPCIÓ 131
PASSATGE PERMANYER 126
PASSEIG D'ISABEL II 101
PASSEIG DE GRÀCIA 125
PASSEIG DE PICASSO 87
PASSEIG DE SANT JOAN 132

PASSEIG DE SANTA MADRONA 123
Pastor, Francesc 97
PATI D'EN LLIMONA 75
PATI MANNING 90
Pau, Claris 110
Pavarotti, Luciano 121
PAVELLÓ D'ALEMANYA 116
PEDRALBES 142
Pellicer, Cirici 127
Pellicer, Josep-Lluís 110
PENDÈS 159
Penrose, Sir Roland 122
Peppers, B. 111
Pere II 59, 66, 97
Pere III 12, 59, 66, 97, 101, 118
Pey, Josep 127
Philip V 16, 44, 67, 103
Picasso, Pablo 52, 73, 80, 84, 101, 102, 106, 107
Pichot, Ramon 80
Pijoan, Josep 117
Piñón Pallarés, Helio 138
PLA DEL PALAU 102
Pla, Josep 33, 84
PLAÇA D'ANTONI LÓPEZ 100
PLAÇA D'ARMES 104
PLAÇA D'ESPANYA 113, 114
PLAÇA DE CARLES IBÁÑEZ 123
PLAÇA DE CASTELLA 89
PLAÇA DE CATALUNYA 124
PLAÇA DE RAMÓN BERENGER 57
PLAÇA DE SANT AGUSTÍ 91
PLAÇA DE SANT AGUSTÍ VELL 83
PLAÇA DE SANT FELIP NERI 65
PLAÇA DE SANT JAUME 68
PLAÇA DE SANT JUST 76
PLAÇA DE TOROS
  MONUMENTAL 135
PLAÇA DE L'ÀNGEL 55
PLAÇA DE L'UNIVERS 115
PLAÇA DE LA BOQUERÍA 47
PLAÇA DE LA PALMERA 152
PLAÇA DE LA SEU 64
PLAÇA DEL PEDRÓ 92
PLAÇA DEL PI 72
PLAÇA DEL REI 58
PLAÇa DEL TEATRE 52
PLAÇA DUC DE MEDINACELI 99
PLAÇA PAÏSOS CATALANS 138
PLAÇA PORTAL DE LA PAU 95
PLAÇA RAQUEL MELLER 95
PLAÇA REIAL 49
PLAÇA SANTA MARIA 87
POBLE ESPANYOL 116
POBLE NOU 151
PONT DE FELIP II 151
Ponz, Antonio 60

PORCIOLES 150
Puig i Cadafalch, Josep 19, 78, 80, 92, 107, 113, 114, 115, 117, 127, 128, 132, 138, 139
Puigdomènech, Albert 112
Puigserver, Fabià 146
Pujol, Jordi 67

QUADRAT D'OR 125
Quintana, Màrius 114
Quintana i Vidal, F. 134

Rovira i Rabassa, Antoni 130
Rafa 136
RAMBLA DE CANALETES 43
RAMBLA DE CATALUNYA 125
RAMBLA DE LA FLORS 46
RAMBLA DE LOS CAPUTXINS 47
RAMBLA DELS ESTUDIS 44
Ramón Berenguer I 11, 63
Ramón Berenguer III 11
Ramón Berenguer IV 12
Ramón Berenguer the Old 61
Ramos, Ferran 116
Raurich, Nicolau 107
Rauschenberg, Robert 122
RAVAL, THE 88
Rebull, Joan 148
Reig, Bernat 91
Retz, Alexandre de 91, 103
Reventós, Ramon 116
Reynés, Josep 110, 111
Ribera, Romà 106, 119
Rigalt, Antoni 81, 129
Rigalt, Granell 47
Rigalt, Joan 127
Rigalt, Lluís 99
RIPOLL 163
Riquer, Alexandre de 110
Rius i Camps, Francesc 150
Rivas i Margarit, Josep 75
Rivera, Primo de 20, 68
Rius i Taulet, Francesc de P. 97, 103, 110
Robert, Dr Bartolomeu 135
Roca, Bernat 77
Roca, Miquel Garriga i 47
Rodriguez, Ventura 90
Rogent, Elias 136
Rohe, Mies van der 116
Roig i Soler, 106, 108
Romeu, Pere 79
RONDA DE SANT PAU 95
Rovira i Trias, Antoni 103, 124
Rubió i Bellvé, Joan 136, 138, 146, 148
Rubió i Tudurí, Nicolau M. 114, 115, 142, 143

Rusiñol, Santiago 79, 80, 83, 106, 130, 157, 162

Safont, Joan 77
Safont, Marc 67, 68, 84
Sagarra, Josep Maria de 52
Sagnier i Villavechia, Enric 80, 98, 111, 126, 127
SALA HIPÓSTILA 149
Sala, Andreu 45
Salariche, Jaume 18
SALESIAN MONASTERY 132
Salvador, Santiago 48, 67
Samsó, Eduardo 131, 145
Sand, George 42
Sanjosé, J. 153
SANT CRISTÒFOL, CHAPEL OF 75
SANT FELIÚ, CHAPEL OF 77
SANT JAUME, CHURCH OF 73
SANT JORDI SPORTS PAVILION 121
SANT JUST, CHURCH OF 76
SANT MIQUEL DEL PORT 112
SANT PAU DEL CAMP 94
SANT PERE DE LES PUELLES 82
SANT PERE NOLASC 89
SANT SADORNÍ D'ANOIA 159
Santa Anna 78
Santa Eulàlia 55, 62
SANTA MARIA DEL PI 72
Santacruz, Francesc 45
Santiago, Salvador 54
Santigosa i Vestraten, Anicet 99
Satie, Eric 106
Saura 122
Schneider, Marie 51
Scott, Ridley 145
Segímon i Artell, Roser 130
Seguí, Salvador 21
Serra, Jaume 118
Serra, Joan 118
Serra, Narcís 112
Serra, Pere 118
Serra, Richard 152
Sert, Josep Maria 70, 82, 105, 121, 157, 163
Sert i López, Josep Lluis 89, 126, 143, 145
Simon, Montaner i 128
Snowflake 108
Sola, B. de 153
Solà-Morales, Ignasi de 48, 116
Solà-Morales, Manuel de 99
Solanas, Antoni 114
Soler i Faneca, Joan 54, 75, 101
Soler, Tomàs 101
Soqué, Antoní Maria Galissa 71, 132
Soteras i Mauri, Josep 144

Springsteen, Bruce 44
St. Dominic of Guzmán 71
Starck, Philippe 131
STATUE OF SANTA EULÀLIA 92
Steegemnn, Enric 118
STUDIO PER 129
Subias i Fages, Xavier 144
Subirachs, Josep Maria 75, 134
Subirana i Subirana, Joan B. 89
Sugrañes, Domènech 133
Sunyer, Joaquim 107

Tamburini 106
TÀPIES FOUNDATION 128
Tàpies, Antoni 43, 87, 146
Tarradellas, Josep 67
Taruella, Sandra 131
Tasso, Torquat 110, 111
Tato, Sen 116
TEATRE DE LICEU 47
TEATRE LLIURE 146
TEATRE TÍVOLI 136
TEMPLE DE LA SAGRADA FAMÍLIA 132
TEMPLO EXPIATORIA DEL SAGRADO COR 147
Thyssen-Bornemisza, Baron 143
TIBIDABO 147
Tóibín, Colm 65
Toledano, Miguel 92
TORRE DE JAUME I 112
TORRE DE SANT SEBASTIÀ 112
Torres-Garcia, J. 68
Townsend, Joseph 18
Tusquets, Oscar 81, 90, 129, 148

UNIVERSITAT INDUSTRIAL DE BARCELONA 138
Utrillo, Maurice 79
Utrillo, Miquel 73, 79, 80, 106, 116, 157

Valadon, Suzanne 79
Valeri i Pupurull, Salvador 132
Vallmitjana, Venanci 108
Valls i Galí, Antoni 126
Valls i Vergés, Manuel 144
Vals, Vilarèi 90
Vázquez Montalbán, Manuel 31, 32, 48, 94, 151
Velasco, Francisco Fernándo de 16
VELÒDROM D'HORTA 150
Vendrell, Emili 93
Verboom, Jorge Próspero de 103, 104, 111
Verdaguer, Jacint 45, 149
Veyreda, Joaquim 106
VIA LAIETANA 80

Viaplana i Vea, Albert 138
VICTÒRIA EUGÈNIA PAVILION 115
VILA OLÍMPICA 112
Vila, Francesc 102
Viladomat, Antoni 95, 110, 119, 153
Viladomat, Josep 21
Vila i Domènech, 47
Vilanova, Antoni 97, 111
Vilaseca, Josep 104, 109
Villa, Pedro 62
Villalbí, Gual 20

Villar, Francesc de P. de 133

Wagner, Richard 48
Wilfred the Hairy 10
Wolhguemuth, Alexander 97

Xifré i Casas, Josep 102
Xirgu, Margarita 83

Young, Arthur 18

Zurburan 119

Metro

Baixador de Vallvidriera
Peu del Funicular
Reina Elisenda
Sarrià
Les Tres Torres
La Bonanova
Zona Universitària
Palau Reial
Maria Cristina
Les Corts
Plaça del Centre
Plaça de Sants
Can Vidalet
Pubilla Cases
Collblanc
Badal
Hostafrancs
Mercat Nou
Sta Eulàlia
Torrassa
Florida
Can Serra
Rambla Just Oliveras
Avinguda Carrilet
Bellvitge
Feixa Llarga

Av. del Tibidabo
El Putget
Pàdua
Pl Molina
Muntaner
Sant Gervasi
Gràcia

Montbau
Vall d'Hebron
Penitents
Vallcarca
Lesseps
Fontana
Diagonal
Passeig de Gràcia
Provença
Hospital Clinic
Entença
Barcelona Sants Estació
Espanya
Rocafort
Poble Sec

Horta
Vilapicina
Virrei Amat
Maragall
Guinardó
Congrés
Alfons X
Hospital de Sant Pau
Joanic
Camp de l'Arda
Sagrada Familia
Verdaguer
Girona
Arc de Triomf
Marina
Urquinaona
Jaume I
Ciutadella
Catalunya
Universitat
Liceu
Drassanes
Paral lel
Urgell

Roquetes
Llucmajor
Trinitat Vella
Torras i Bages
Sant Andreu
Fabra i Puig
Sagrera
Navas
Clot
Glòries

Sta. Coloma
Baró de Viver
Pep Ventura
Gorg
Sant Roc
Joan XXIII
Verneda
La Pau
Besòs
Besòs-Mar
Selva de Mar
Poblenou
Llacuna
Bogatell
Barceloneta

Palau Nacional

Line 1
Line 2
Line 3
Line 4
Line 5
FF.CC.Generalstat
Connecting Station

Printed and bound in Great Britain by
Butler & Tanner Ltd, Frome and London